W9-AVC-410

SAFETY HARBOR
PUBLIC LIBRARY
SAFETY HARBOR, FLORIDA
Presented by
CHRISSIE SHULL
ELMORE LIBRARY
FUND

GUIDE TO BUSINESS PLANNING

OTHER ECONOMIST BOOKS

Guide to Analysing Companies
Guide to Business Modelling
Guide to Economic Indicators
Guide to the European Union
Guide to Financial Management
Guide to Financial Markets
Guide to Investment Strategy
Guide to Management Ideas and Gurus
Guide to Organisation Design
Guide to Project Management
Numbers Guide
Style Guide

Book of Obituaries
Brands and Branding
Business Consulting
Business Strategy
China's Stockmarket
The City
Dealing with Financial Risk
Economics
Emerging Markets
The Future of Technology
Headhunters and How to Use Them
Mapping the Markets
Successful Strategy Execution

Essential Economics
Essential Investment
Essential Negotiation
Essentials for Board Directors

For more information on these books:
www.bloomberg.com/economistbooks

GUIDE TO BUSINESS PLANNING

Graham Friend
and
Stefan Zehle

Bloomberg Press
New York

THE ECONOMIST IN ASSOCIATION WITH PROFILE BOOKS LTD

This edition published in the United States and Canada by Bloomberg Press
Published in the U.K. by Profile Books Ltd, 2009

Printed in Canada

1 3 5 7 9 10 8 6 4 2

Library of Congress Cataloging-in-Publication Data

Friend, Graham.
Guide to business planning / Graham Friend and Stefan Zehle. -- 2nd ed.
p. cm.
Includes bibliographical references and index.
Summary: "A comprehensive guide to every aspect of preparing and using a business plan--newly updated and revised. New businesses and existing businesses fare better with well-thought-out plans. It is essential to have a good business plan to raise capital--either for a new venture to get additional capital or within most corporations for new initiatives or for accelerated growth" --Provided by publisher.
ISBN 978-1-57660-328-4 (alk. paper)
1. Business planning. I. Zehle, Stefan. II. Title.

HD30.28.F747 2009
658.4'012--dc22

2009003707

Contents

1 Introduction

Successfully launching a new business or initiative requires careful planning and the results of a business planning process are usually captured in a business plan. Any investor or those in an existing business responsible for approving new initiatives will invariably want to see a business plan before making any financial commitment. The business plan, besides being a prerequisite for gaining access to finance, also provides the blueprint for successfully creating and running a new venture. Even in fast-moving markets where the plan itself may quickly become outdated the insight gained from the planning process that created it remains invaluable. This book describes a business planning process that will generate crucial insights for the entrepreneur or existing business as well as supporting the preparation of a compelling business plan and the creation of a successful business.

A business plan describes the business's vision and objectives as well as the strategy and tactics that will be employed to achieve them. A plan may also provide the basis for operational budgets, targets, procedures and management controls. No two businesses are identical and no two business plans are ever exactly the same. This guide examines the different reasons for preparing a business plan. It identifies who the potential audiences for a business plan are; how they read it; and what things different members of the audience will be looking for. The task of writing a business plan is a lot easier if you have a template that can be tailored to the specific needs of your business. Chapter 2 provides one. Also explained is how to design and present a business plan to maximise the likelihood of its gaining approval or funding.

Although the presentation of the final business plan is important, ultimately the substance of the plan is most crucial. The strategies and tactics described in the plan should be the outputs from a logical and appropriately comprehensive business planning process. The main emphasis of this guide is on the various stages of that process. This book provides a practical step-by-step business planning process and a reference for the tools and techniques necessary to complete it. It begins with an overview of a typical business plan and the remaining chapters correspond to the stages of the business planning process described in Chart 1.1 on the next page.

The process should begin by evaluating the environment in which the business operates before analysing the specific industry and the suppliers, competitors and customers within it. The insight from this analysis and an understanding of the strengths and weaknesses of the business or new venture, combined with a set of expectations about the future, can be coupled with creative and innovative thinking to develop a range of strategic options for evaluation. The evaluation stage includes developing forecasts (notably for market demand), financial projections and, in some cases, a range of valuations, as well as calculating various measures of performance with which to validate and benchmark the forecasts. The business planning process should test alternative ideas and assumptions, as one of the main reasons for planning is to help the business prepare for an uncertain future. Following stages include an examination of the funding issues and risk analysis, and lastly presenting and gaining approval for the business plan, and then implementing it. Because of the rapidly changing world in which businesses must operate, this guide places

Chart 1.1 **The business planning process**

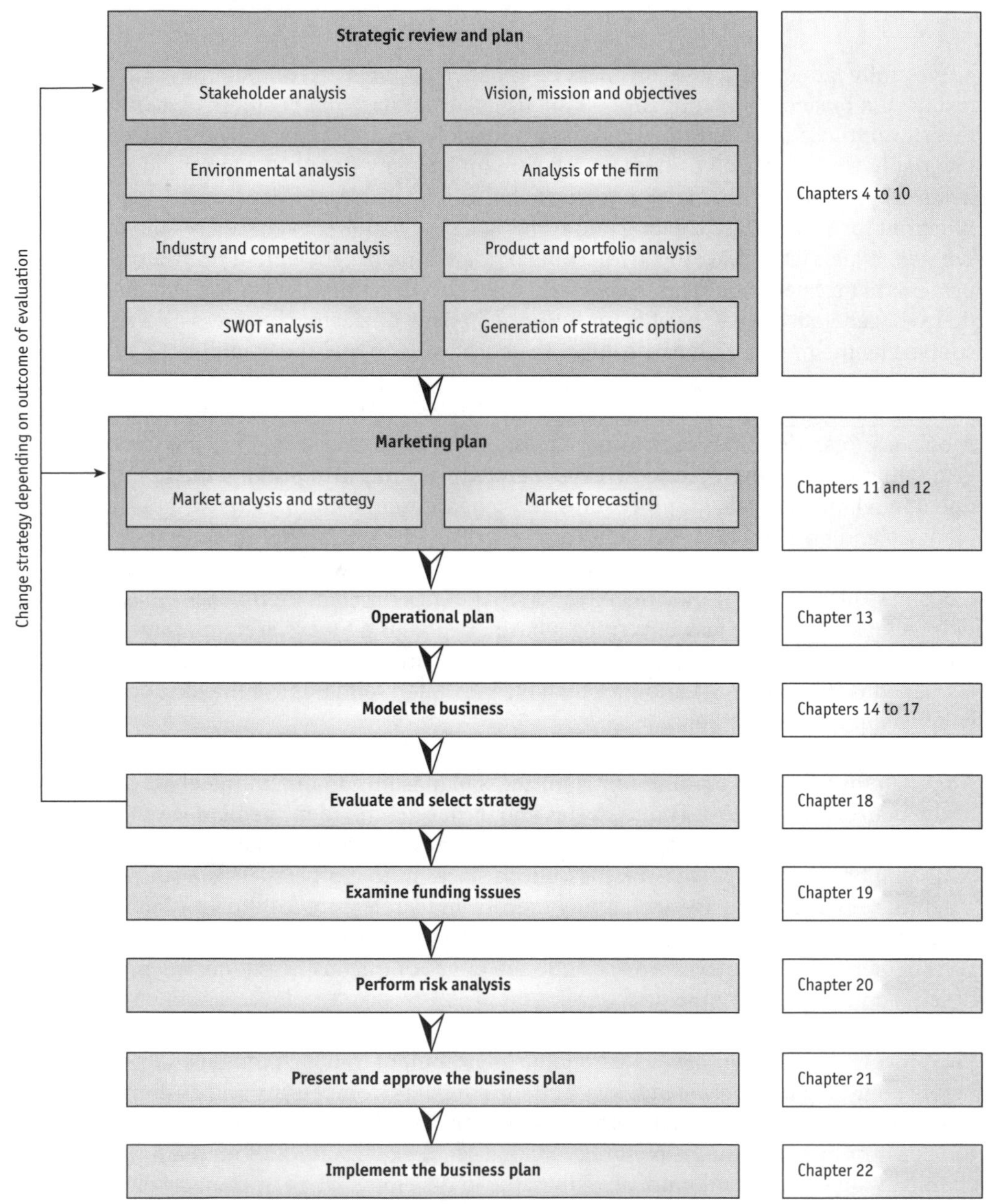

considerable emphasis on business planning in the face of uncertainty and makes use of techniques such as scenario planning.

All business plans require some form of financial analysis and forecasts for the business or project. Most financial projections are prepared in a spreadsheet package such as Microsoft's Excel. Chapter 14 describes the generic Excel spreadsheet business model that accompanies this book and that can be used within your own business. The model also forms the basis for the detailed worked examples that are used to explain the basic principles of accounting and the preparation of financial statements in Chapters 15 and 16. This book is not, however, about business modelling, which is dealt with in *The Economist Guide to Business Modelling*.

THE BUSINESS PLANNING MODEL

A business planning model built in Microsoft's Excel is available for the readers of this book. To download the model visit www.guidetobusinessplanning.com and follow the simple download instructions. There are two versions available. The blank version (Blank Model) is designed to help the reader understand and apply the accounting techniques discussed in Chapters 15–17. For experienced business modellers, this version can be customised to meet the specific needs of their business. There is also a completed version (Complete Model), which represents the end result of working through the examples in the book. A full set of outputs from the completed model can be found in the Appendix.

USING THE BOOK

Although this book provides a step-by-step guide to business planning, it can also be dipped into by those wanting to apply the techniques to address a specific business appraisal or analytical challenge. Chart 1.2 on the next page provides a quick reference to all the business planning techniques used in the book, including the typical applications for each technique and where they can be found.

PREPARING YOUR BUSINESS PLAN

When considering the forecasting and accounting needs for your own business, you are strongly recommended to gain professional assistance from trained accounting personnel if the accounting and modelling issues extend beyond those covered in this book. The banks from whom you hope to raise finance may be able to provide assistance with the creation of your financial projections or alternatively you can seek the help of a professional accounting firm or management consultancy. You may also be able to obtain help from government organisations established to support new business ventures. The specific details of setting up a new company or partnership are beyond the scope of this book, but Chapter 13 provides a useful checklist of the issues that should be considered when creating a new company. The first thing that you should think about, however, is whether you are emotionally prepared for the inevitable stress that running your own business entails. We hope that this book will at least alleviate some of the pressures of preparing your first business plan.

Chart 1.2 **Quick reference guide to business planning techniques**

Technique	*Application*
Benchmarking	Obtaining financial and operational data from competitors against which a business can measure its own performance. Helps to set targets and focus improvements on areas where this is most needed. Chapter 7, page 63
Brand perception map	Shows how a brand appeals to a differentiated set of customer needs. If customer segmentation is needs based, the product should score highly against the targeted needs. Relevant for developing the marketing strategy. Chapter 11, page 105
Business/industry attractiveness screen	A matrix commonly known as the GE Business/Industry Attractiveness Screen. It is used to evaluate the position of a business or business unit. Chapter 8, page 81
Core competencies	The functions or practices that are central to a business. The activity (or activities) that the business believes it does best. If a business's core activity is closely aligned with its core competencies it is better placed to achieve competitive advantage. Chapter 6, page 44
Curve fitting	A form of extrapolation used for market forecasting. It is based on the observation that technological and market developments usually follow an s-shaped pattern. Chapter 12, page 122
Diffusion of innovation	A model that describes how a new product or service is adopted by a population, most commonly known as the Bass model. Used for market forecasting. Chapter 12, page 125
Directional policy matrix	A technique derived from the growth-share matrix, but using a much wider range of factors to analyse a portfolio of products in terms of business sector prospects and business position. Chapter 8, page 74
Discounted cash flow	One of the most fundamental techniques for evaluating a business opportunity. It examines the amount, timing and risk associated with the cash flows of the business. An essential technique for evaluating strategic options. Chapter 18, page 210
Economies of scale	Economies of scale may occur when production volumes increase. Important in the context of cost leadership strategies and forecasting. Chapter 8, page 65
Experience curve	The relationship between cumulative production volume and unit costs. Unit costs can decline in a predictable manner as the cumulative quantity produced over time increases. Useful for strategic planning and forecasting. Chapter 8, page 65, and Chapter 12, page 126
Financial forecasting	All business plans require financial projections for the business's profit and loss, balance sheet and, most crucially, its cash flow. Financial forecasting often involves preparing a spreadsheet model. Chapter 14, page 144

Generic strategies	Porter's three generic strategies, cost leadership, differentiation and focus. The focus strategy has two variants: cost focus and differentiation focus. Used to generate strategic options. Chapter 10, page 90
Growth-share matrix	Used to analyse a portfolio of products using market growth and market share. It has strategic implications, particularly for resource allocation in a multiple product business. Chapter 8, page 69
Industry life cycle	A concept that describes the different stages of an industry's maturity. Chapter 7, page 56
Key differentiators and unique selling points	Unique attributes that differentiate a business from its rivals. A business should leverage the key differentiators in order to achieve competitive advantage. Chapter 6, page 42
Key success factor ranking	A method of analysing competitors against your own business, applicable to the analysis of the firm as part of strategic planning. Chapter 7, page 62
Market research	Collecting and analysing data from prospective customers to establish the likely demand for a new product or service or to understand better customers' preferences for existing products. Chapter 12, page 111
Market segmentation	A market segment is defined as a sufficiently large group of buyers with a differentiated set of needs and preferences that can be targeted with a differentiated marketing mix. To be of value, the benefits of segmentation must outweigh the costs. Useful for developing the marketing strategy and for forecasting. Chapter 11, page 100, and Chapter 12, page 112
Marketing mix	A tool to position products in the target market. The marketing mix is defined by the four Ps: product, price, promotion, place. All elements of the marketing mix together constitute the "offer". Relevant for developing the marketing plan. Chapter 11, page 103
PEST analysis	An extremely useful technique for examining the environment in which the business operates. PEST is an acronym for the Political, Economic, Social and Technological influences on the business. Chapter 5, page 32
Porter's five forces model	Provides an analytical framework for the analysis of the structural factors that shape competition within an industry and from which a number of generic competitive strategies can be derived. Chapter 7, page 58

Portfolio analysis	Uses techniques such as the growth-share matrix to analyse a portfolio of products or strategic business units to make decisions about their strategic direction and resource allocation. Chapter 8, page 65
Price elasticity of demand	Measures how sensitive changes in demand for a product are to changes in the unit price of the product. Used in market forecasting. Chapter 12, page 127
Product life cycle	A concept that describes the different stages of a product from introduction through growth to maturity and decline. Has applications in market forecasting as well as in strategic and tactical planning. Chapter 8, page 66, and Chapter 12, page 124
Product positioning map	A technique to map the position of a firm's products and those of its rivals to the needs of the customer. Relevant for marketing strategy and planning. Chapter 11, page 103
Project management	Techniques for managing efficiently the process of business planning. For a lone entrepreneur, issues of co-ordination do not arise and there is less need for detailed project management. In larger organisations, where the business planning process involves a large number of people across a range of different departments, effective project management of the process becomes essential. Chapter 3, page 23
Ratio analysis	Certain financial ratios can be calculated from the projected financial statements that allow the liquidity, profitability and efficiency of the business to be evaluated. Ratio analysis can be applied to evaluate strategic options as well as for validating the realism of financial forecasts. Chapter 17, page 188
Regression analysis	A statistical technique that examines the relationship between dependent variables, such as sales, and independent variables, such as price and commission. This methodology can be used for market forecasting as well as tactical decision-making. Chapter 12, page 119
Resource audit	Identification of operational, human, organisational and financial resources coupled with an analysis of efficiency and effectiveness of their utilisation. A business that makes optimum use of its resources may gain competitive advantage. Chapter 6, page 49
Risk analysis	Faced with an uncertain future, a business must examine the risks that it might face and the tactics that can be used to mitigate them. Chapter 20, page 238
Scenario planning	A powerful technique for developing different views of the possible future environments facing the business. It is often used in conjunction with PEST analysis and is useful for forecasting in uncertain markets. Chapter 5, page 36

Strategic business unit (SBU)	A division or department of a corporation that is sufficiently self-contained and could operate independently from the whole business. In larger organisations, strategic planning can be carried out at the level of the SBU. The concept is applicable to portfolio strategies. Chapter 4, page 25
SWOT analysis	A simple and effective technique that analyses a business's Strengths, Weaknesses, Opportunities and Threats. Chapter 9, page 85
Time series analysis	A statistical analysis technique that examines how observed sequences of observations evolve and develop over time. Often used in market forecasting. Chapter 12, page 114
Value add analysis	Identifies how much value is created at different stages of the value chain. This enables a firm to focus improvements or strategic change on areas where more value can be added. Chapter 6, page 46
Value chain analysis	Explores the configuration and linkage of different activities that form a chain from original raw materials through processing, manufacturing, packaging, distribution, retailing and customer care to the end customer. It is used to optimise the allocation of resources. Chapter 6, page 46
Value system	Extends the value chain beyond the boundaries of the business and recognises that a business is dependent on relationships with suppliers and customers. It can be used to make decisions about backward or forward integration to help position a business at the most valuable parts of the value system. Chapter 6, page 49
Vision, mission and objectives	Vision explains what the business intends to do. Mission explains how this vision is to be turned into reality. Objectives provide a yardstick against which success can be measured. Chapter 4, page 27
VRIO analysis	A technique for analysing whether a resource is Valuable, Rare and Imitable and whether the Organisation is taking advantage of the resource. Chapter 6, page 43

2 The business plan

Business decisions should always be made on the strength of the underlying business idea, but it is much easier to come to a decision if the idea is communicated simply and clearly in a well-written business plan. The discipline required to articulate the business's strategy, tactics and operations in a written document ensures rigorous analysis and greater clarity of thought. If the strategy of the business cannot be clearly and convincingly described on paper, the chances of its working in practice are slim.

No two businesses are ever identical and no two business plans are ever alike, but good business plans always contain a number of common themes. They "tell a story" and explain how the business will achieve its objectives in a coherent, consistent and cohesive manner. The "story" will be focused on the needs of the customer. The plan will identify the market, its growth prospects, the target customers and the main competitors. It must be based upon a credible set of assumptions and should identify the assumptions to which the success of the business is most sensitive. It should also identify the risks facing the business, the potential downsides and the actions that will be taken to mitigate the risks. As the blueprint for the business, it should describe what makes the business different from its competitors: its source of competitive advantage and how it will be sustained in the longer term. It should describe the experience and track record of the management team, and, within larger organisations, the plan should have the support of those in the different functions who will be involved in implementing it. Most importantly, it should identify the funding being sought from potential investors, how the funding will be used and the investors' expected return.

A good business plan checklist:

- tells a coherent, consistent and cohesive, customer focused story;
- clearly defines the market, its prospects, the customers, suppliers and competitors;
- contains credible business planning assumptions and forecasts;
- describes how the business will achieve sustainable competitive advantage;
- identifies the assumptions to which the business is most sensitive, the potential risks and any mitigating actions;
- is supported by those that must implement it;
- contains a description of the individuals involved in managing the business;
- identifies the funding requirement for the business, the use of the funds and investors' expected returns.

What are they for?

Before starting to write a business plan it is important to appreciate the reason for preparing one. The focus and level of detail will vary depending on the decision the business plan has been designed to support.

Securing finance

Most business plans are prepared in order to secure some form of funding. In the case of new business ideas, banks, venture capitalists, private equity and other providers of capital place great emphasis on the business plan, as this is often all they have to rely upon. The business plan will generally focus on the growth prospects for the market and the sources of sustainable competitive advantage for the business. The emphasis will be more on strategic and tactical considerations, as well as the financial projections and investor returns, rather than on operational detail.

Operational management and budgeting

The business plan can also provide the basis for the creation of business processes, job descriptions and operational budgets. It can also provide the basis for monitoring and analysing performance. In this instance, the business plan will say little about strategic and tactical considerations and will focus on technical details, process descriptions and product specifications.

Other uses

To get approval or finance for a project and to help manage it are the common reasons for producing a business plan. However, the process of preparing one can be used as a mechanism for reconciling conflicting views and building consensus, as well as communicating the vision, mission and goals of larger companies.

Business plans may also be prepared as part of a tender process for the right to operate assets or services that are allocated by a government body. The tender process is sometimes referred to as a "beauty parade" as the companies must prepare a business plan that displays their technical, operational and business skills in the best light. A beauty parade might be used for the allocation of radio spectrum, or the right to administer a national lottery or operate rail services.

Who are they for?

In the same way that no two businesses are alike, no two readers will be looking for exactly the same issues or messages in the business plan. Indeed, the different needs of different audiences can be such that it may be necessary to create more than one version of the same plan.

Bankers and others providing debt financing

When lenders review a business plan they are concerned with three main issues:

- If the loan is only one element of the financing necessary to fund the business plan fully, are the other sources of finance in place and secure?
- Will sufficient cash be generated by the business to meet interest payments on the loan and to repay the principal?
- Are there physical assets, or other forms of collateral, within the business against which a loan can be secured so that, were the business to fail, the lender would be able to get all or some of its money back?

Bankers will look closely at the financial forecasts contained within the business and the underlying assumptions on which those forecasts rely. They will wish to satisfy themselves that they are credible. As part of their financial analysis of the business plan they will look closely at the balance sheet to assess its strength and the liquidity of the business. They will examine the gearing, the ratio of debt to equity within the business, to ensure that the business does not become too heavily geared towards debt, which will increase the possibility of default on the loan. They may also examine ratios such as interest cover which is described in more detail in Chapter 17. If the loan agreement contains financial covenants, certain levels of performance the business must meet, then the financial forecast must unclude the measures associated with any covenants and demonstrate sufficient headroom so that the lenders can be confident the covenants will not be breached.

Providers of equity funding

There are many organisations and individuals who might provide equity funding to support a business plan. Family and friends are often the first port of call for smaller business ventures. The providers of more substantial levels of equity or share capital for new business ventures include venture capitalists and private equity houses, who have a shorter investment time horizon compared with, say, institutional investors. Pension funds and other institutional investors may already be investors in an existing business and will be among the first to be approached when additional capital is required. Another source of equity funding may be a business considering some form of merger or partnership, which it may achieve through an equity injection into the business. The appropriate sources of funding for different business plans are discussed in detail in Chapter 19. As providers of equity finance or share capital are last in the line of creditors to be paid when a firm goes bust, their concerns are different from those of bankers:

- What are the funds to be used for?
- Is the business proposition a strong one and is there an identifiable source of sustainable competitive advantage that will allow the business to outperform the market in the long term?
- What is the expected return on equity (ROE – see Chapter 17)?
- How experienced and capable is the management team?
- Is the business plan fully funded and what are the risks that more equity capital will be needed, leading to a dilution of the equity stakes of those who invest first?
- What are the growth prospects for the business and the potential for capital appreciation and/or a strong dividend stream?
- What returns have been achieved on any previous equity injections into the business?
- How will the providers of equity be able to exit from the business and realise the gain on their investment?

The providers of equity will look closely at the credibility of the financial statements and the level of gearing (the ratio of debt to equity within the balance sheet). The more highly geared the business, the greater is the level of financial risk faced by the equity providers. These themes are explored in more detail in Chapter 20.

The management team of a large, existing business

It is usual for business units in large organisations to prepare business plans in order to gain approval (and resources) for new business initiatives from senior management and the board. The issues that they will wish to see addressed vary from organisation to organisation and according to the strategic, tactical or financial challenges facing the business at the time. However, it is possible to say that they will wish to be presented with a business plan that is consistent with their stated objectives, strategic imperatives and financial constraints. The following list gives an indication of the questions they are likely to ask:

- Is the plan consistent and supportive of the business's overall strategy?
- What is the likely impact on the overall financial performance of the business in terms of revenue growth, profitability and gearing?
- Will adopting the business plan require the raising of additional financing?
- Does the business plan reinforce the position of the business's brand?
- Is the business plan feasible and within the scope of the organisation's capabilities?
- How will the press and the financial markets react to the adoption of the business plan?
- Will the adoption of this business plan have an impact on other areas of the business?
- What alternative opportunities could be pursued?

The list of potential questions is endless and those responsible for writing the business plan need to anticipate and address the issues that will be of most concern to those who make the final decision on whether to go ahead with the project or not.

A BUSINESS PLAN TEMPLATE

The style, length and content of a business plan will depend on the business decision or activities the plan is designed to support and the audience for whom the plan is to be prepared. There are no hard and fast rules as to length, but a business plan should be as short as possible while meeting all the needs of those who will read it. During the heyday of the dotcom boom, business plans were occasionally presented as "elevator pitches": those with a business idea had as long as an elevator journey to convey the main thrust of their business plan. These days, as in pre-dotcom days, business plans are expected to be more substantial. A business plan for a small and straightforward business may range from 20 to 40 pages, whereas a "beauty-parade" document may run to over 500 pages once all the technical appendices have been included. In large organisations the format for business plans may be predefined, and in the case of tenders or beauty parades a structure may be provided as part of the "Request for tender" document.

On the next page is a template for a generic business plan. The headings used have been expanded to provide more insight into the contents of each section. In the final business plan more succinct section headings would be used. It is unlikely that all the sections contained within the template will be relevant, but it may be necessary to include additional sections or subsections to reflect the peculiarities of a specific business.

A business plan template

Executive summary
Vision, mission, objectives
Current state of the business
Products and services
Strategy and sources of sustainable competitive advantage
Customer acceptance
Summary financial forecasts
Money required, timing and deal on offer

Basic business information
Title
Contents
Contact information
Document control
Professional advisers
Definitions
Legal structure and corporate data

Current business situation
Definition of the current business and its market
Corporate history, major events and past financial performance
Current business and market position
Core competencies
Current business organisation and outline business infrastructure

Strategic analysis
Political, economic, social and technological analysis and impacts
Key differentiators and unique selling points
VRIO analysis
Core competencies
Configuration of resources
Value add analysis
Value chain analysis
Value system
Resource audit
Operations resources
Human resources
Organisational resources
Financial resources
Industry life cycle
Industry structure
Competitor analysis
SWOT analysis

Strategic plan
Vision, mission and objectives
Sources of sustainable competitive advantage
Competitive position
Market positioning
Brand strategy
Portfolio strategy
Business design

Marketing plan
Market segments, size and growth
Description of customers and customer needs
Target market segment
Product positioning and value proposition
Marketing mix
Description of products and services
Pricing and discounting
Advertising and promotional plans
Channel and distribution strategy
Guarantees and warranties
After-sales service and customer care
Comparison with competition
Performance and economics
Marketing forecasts

Operations/production
Physical location
Make or buy considerations
The production process
Facilities, equipment and machinery
Scalability of operations
Engineering and design support
Quality control plans
Staffing requirements
Sources of supply of key materials

Research and development
Objectives
Organisation
Plans
Resources

Management and organisation
Organisation chart
Top management
Management's ability to deliver the plan
Corporate governance and shareholder control
Staffing
Recruitment
Training
Labour relations
Office space and amenities
Employment and related costs

Forecasts and financial data
Summary of performance ratios
Sales forecast
Assumptions underpinning financial forecasts
Profit and loss account (income statement)
Balance sheet
Cash flow statement
Evaluation criteria and valuation
Discounted cash flow
Internal rate of return
Payback
Breakeven
Return on investment
Benchmarks
Sensitivity analysis

Financing
Summary of operations prior to financing
Current shareholder loans outstanding
Funds required and timing
Use of proceeds
The deal on offer
Anticipated gearing and interest cover
Expected returns
Exit routes for investors

Risk analysis
Risk overview
Limiting factors
Critical success factors
Alternative scenarios and strategic responses
Specific risks and risk-reduction strategies

Business controls
Information technology
Financial
Sales and marketing
Operations
Other controls

Appendices
Glossary of terms
Details of market research
Consultants' reports
Product specifications
Marketing collateral
Orders in hand
Organisation charts
Curricula vitae
Detailed financial forecasts
Technical data
Details of patents, copyright

In tailoring the template to meet the specific needs of the project or business being presented, the following questions should be asked:

- What is the ultimate objective of preparing the business plan?
- How will the business plan be used and by whom?
- To what level of detail should the plan be prepared: will the plan be used to examine high-level strategic issues or for actually running the business?
- What is the scope of the business plan: does it relate to the entire business, a division or geographic region or just a product or service?
- For what time period should the business plan be prepared?
- Should the financial projections within the plan be prepared on a monthly, quarterly or annual basis or some combination, for example monthly for the first two years and quarterly thereafter?

LAYOUT AND STYLE

In large organisations, the layout of the document may be prescribed by the company's approval process; in others, although ultimately the contents of the plan are critical, the document should be attractive, impressive and as easy to read as possible.

General appearance

The plan should have a hard front and back cover to prevent the pages from becoming damaged. The cover should be simple and pleasing to the eye, featuring the business logo (if one exists), the name of the business, the date and some basic contact details. In the case of large business plans, dividers can be used to make the contents of the document more accessible.

The document should be securely bound; comb or ring binders work well and ensure that the document can be read easily when placed flat on a table. The plan should be printed on good-quality paper using a good-quality printer. Plain white paper is usually best, especially if colour diagrams are to be included. Each page should follow a standard layout with clear, easy-to-follow headings and subsection headings. Each new section should begin on a fresh page. Diagrams should be used where they help to convey an important message or a complex subject more clearly.

Page layout

The layout of the page should be consistent with size of paper being used. The standard office document size in the UK is A4 (297mm x 210mm). In the United States the standard is 280mm x 216mm. For a business plan aimed at both sides of the Atlantic, make the design and layout work to 280mm x 216mm.

The page should be laid out to avoid presenting the reader with too much dense text; allowing adequate space between lines and paragraphs will help make the page less intimidating. The choice of font is a matter of personal preference or may be dictated in a larger business by the "house style". The chosen font should be clear and easy to read such as Times New Roman or Arial. The size of the font is important: nothing smaller than 10 points should be used for the main body of the text; 12 points is probably the ideal. If the pages are to be printed only on one side, there should be a larger margin on the left-hand side to allow for binding because once the document has been bound the text should appear to be centrally positioned on the bound page. If the document is to be printed double sided, larger margins will be required on the left-hand side of the facing page and the right-hand side of the underside to ensure that the text is consistently aligned.

A simple and clear structure for headings and subheadings should be used throughout the document. If there are more than four levels of headings and subheadings, the document rapidly becomes unwieldy and difficult to follow: three levels or fewer are ideal. Each heading should be numbered and the numbers should be based on the current section, as this will make editing the section easier. The use of capital letters in headings – including headings for charts and diagrams, which may be prepared using a different software package – should also be consistent. Where figures, charts and graphs are used, all axes should be clearly labelled and all units of measurement should be consistently and clearly stated. If appropriate, the sources for any data should also be included.

Headers and footers can be used to convey additional pieces of information, which are valuable for the purposes of editing, reviewing and version control. Information that is useful to place in a header or footer includes:

- Document title
- Date
- Page number
- File name
- A confidentiality message
- Copyright

Writing style

A clear and concise writing style is crucial. Readers will not appreciate the brilliance and lucidity of an idea if it is described in a clumsy and convoluted manner. Sentences and paragraphs should be kept short and precise. The opening sentence or paragraph should make the writer's point. The writer should think carefully about the point he wishes to make and then should make it as simply and succinctly as possible. The main body of text should then provide evidence or arguments to support the writer's position before finally repeating, expanding or refining the statement. The same structure should be applied to the document as a whole and throughout each section of the document. *The Economist Style Guide* contains many useful tips.

Page set-up

On the opposite page is an example of a business plan page. It was prepared in Microsoft Word and utilises a number of useful formatting functions.

Mobile Business – Business Plan 2008

3 Current business situation

3.1 Definition of the business and market
Mobile Business operates a mobile telecommunications network in Ruritania and provides mobile voice and data services to both business and consumer customers. The mobile telecommunications market in Ruritania consists of three companies: Mobile Business, Wireless Business and Cellular Business.

3.2 Historic performance
Mobile Business was launched on January 1st 1999 and grew rapidly in terms of both customer growth and revenues. In March 2003, Mobile Business became the second largest operator in Ruritania in terms of customer numbers.

Revenue has grown by 23% per annum on a compound basis since launch and the business became profitable at the operating level after two years of operation. In the last fiscal year the business generated revenues of €600m and operating profits of €180m.

3.3 Current market position
The mobile market in Ruritania is close to saturation with penetration of mobile devices at 82%. Mobile Business has a market share of 38% and a reputation for delivering high quality service and strong customer care. Mobile Business has a dominant position in the corporate and small to medium enterprise segments and the highest revenues per customer in the market.

3.4 Core competencies
Mobile Business's core competencies are network design, construction, maintenance and operation as well as customer care and billing.

THE PROCESS OF WRITING THE BUSINESS PLAN

When and how to write

Everyone has his or her own preferred routine for writing. Some prefer to wait until all the analysis has been completed before writing the business plan; others prefer to write each section as soon as they have collected the material necessary to complete it. The authors of this book prefer to write a business plan in parallel with the business planning activities. The discipline of translating the results of analysis into clear and concise prose can identify flaws in the business logic. Flaws in the business logic can invalidate subsequent analysis and conclusions. Attempting to identify any flaws early on, through the process of writing, can make the process of business planning more efficient and avoid inappropriate or invalid analysis.

Before embarking on the business planning process, it is often useful to attempt to write a first draft of the executive summary without any prior preparation or analysis. This will provide a reference point for all future business planning activity and ensure that activity remains focused on meeting the business planning objectives. The executive summary also provides a useful reference point before commencing writing any new sections and helps provide continuity and consistency of content and style. When business planning in the face of uncertainty or when preparing a business plan under considerable time pressure, the executive summary can also provide a hypothesis for the proposed strategy or tactics. The business planning activities that follow will aim to prove the hypothesis. Whatever the circumstances, the executive summary will evolve and develop as the business planning process provides new insights into the market and how the business should be established and run.

Managing information

It is useful to create a file with sections either physically using a ring binder, or electronically using a folder structure. Each folder should be labelled with the appropriate heading from the business plan template; subfolders can also be created for the subheadings. As the business planning process gets under way, the results of any work can be placed in the relevant folders. When the process is complete, the files in each folder can be arranged in a suitable order. With a predefined structure and if materials are logically ordered, it is much more likely that the plan will be well thought through and coherent, and writing it will certainly be much simpler.

Who should write

For new ventures that involve only one or two key people, the choice of author is usually obvious. In larger companies, there should be one person with overall responsibility for the business plan who will ensure that the document is internally consistent in both content and style. However, individual sections should, wherever possible, be written by those responsible for implementation or the analysis supporting the section's conclusions.

Project management

Small projects involving one or two key individuals do not usually require extensive project management and co-ordination. But complex plans, which run to hundreds of pages and may involve many authors, require careful project management. A project manager should allocate specific tasks to each author and agree deadlines for when certain sections will be delivered. In some cases there will be inter-dependencies between sections. These should be identified and incorporated into the project plan, which should then be used to monitor the progress of the preparation of the document. In preparing the project plan, the project manager should allow plenty of time for amalgamating the various sections from the different authors and standardising the style, removing repetition and ensuring consistency. It is easy to underestimate the time required to perform this crucial task.

Document version control

Project management and document version control go hand in hand. A file-naming convention should be agreed and adhered to. Each version of the document should be clearly labelled and a control schedule should be included at the front to record amendments, changes and updates. Old versions of the document should be maintained as back-ups. The following structure provides a useful starting point for a file-naming convention:

Project title – Section title – Author initials – Date – Version

An example of a typical file name is:

US Expansion – Executive summary – GF – 20 Sep 08 – V2.2

Getting started

The basic business information

The basic business information can usually be prepared and written quickly and will be a valuable reference for future contributors to the document. It should include the following:

- Title
- Contents
- Contact information
- Document control
- Professional advisers
- Definitions
- Legal structure and corporate data

Prepare a title for the document and a contents page. Establishing the contents page at the outset will provide a structure for the document and is a useful tool for checking completeness.

The contact details of the individual responsible for the business plan should be easily accessible. A page should be devoted to document and version control so that any reader can be confident that they are reading the latest version and can also see where the most recent changes have been made. Where professional advisers such as bankers, accountants, lawyers or management consultants have been involved, their contact details should also be provided. In business plans with a large amount of technical information, a glossary will often be necessary as an appendix. However, it is often useful and less frustrating for the reader if some key definitions can be provided early in the document. Definitions should be provided in the basic business information section and terms should be used consistently throughout the document. When a term is used for the first time in the main text it should be defined again.

The section of legal structure and corporate data should include the following pieces of information:

- The full name of the business
- The corporate status of the business
- Its capital structure
- The address of the registered office
- The registration number
- The head office address

The executive summary

The executive summary is the most important section of the business plan since it may be the only section that is read; and because it is usually the first section to be read it must engage readers and excite them about the potential of the business idea. It should not be an introduction to the business plan; it should be a 2–3 page encapsulation of the defining characteristics of the business proposition and the request being made to the reader in terms of approvals or funding. The executive summary should be the most carefully written of all the sections. Any errors in it will undermine the reader's confidence in the accuracy and credibility of the whole plan.

The executive summary should contain the following information:

- Current state of the business
- Products and services and the customers
- Sources of sustainable competitive advantage
- Shareholder objectives and business strategy
- Summary financial forecasts
- Decision or funding being sought, the use of funds raised and expected returns

The historic elements

The history of the business is another useful section to write before starting the business planning process. Capturing the evolutionary path of the business to its current state provides a valuable context for the business planning activities and is useful to those who are not familiar with the business. The history should include the following:

- Date founded
- Founders
- Changes in name
- Scope
- Environmental (political, economic, social-cultural and technological) changes
- Dates and explanations of any major acquisitions or divestitures
- Major obstacles faced
- Periods of growth and slow-down

Once the outline of the business plan has been prepared and a first draft of the executive summary written, the process of generating the content to complete the remainder of the business plan can begin.

3 The business planning process

The world in which businesses operate has become increasingly uncertain, so some of the assumptions upon which a business plan is based are likely to have become invalid before the plan has even been circulated. Irrespective of how uncertain the future may be, those being asked to finance or approve a project will almost always wish to see some form of business plan. They will want reassurance that the managers have thought through how their market may evolve and how their strategies and tactics could alter, depending on the future environment they encounter.

Not all future events are entirely independent of the actions of the business. By planning and identifying future risks and opportunities the business can act immediately to help create the most favourable future outcome. Stephen Covey, in his book *The Seven Habits of Highly Effective People*,[1] describes the time management matrix shown in Chart 3.1.

Chart 3.1 **Time management matrix**

	URGENT	NOT URGENT
Important	**Quadrant I** Crises Pressing problems Deadline driven projects	**Quadrant II** Relationship building Identifying opportunities Business planning
Not important	**Quadrant III** Some reports Some meetings Popular activities	**Quadrant IV** Tidying the desk Some mail Pleasant activities

Source: Covey, S., *The Seven Habits of Highly Effective People*

The matrix divides activities up into those that are urgent and those that are not urgent. It also examines activities that are important and those that are not important. Many businesses with poor planning processes find that they are dominated by Quadrant I activities because they are continually having to react to events for which they are ill prepared. Businesses permanently operating in this quadrant are unlikely to achieve even short-term goals.

To minimise Quadrant I activities and to increase the ability to achieve their objectives, businesses must plan. Business planning sits firmly in Quadrant II, an activity that is important but not urgent. Initially, however, the only way to create time for business planning is by eliminating activities in Quadrants III and IV. As a result of effective planning, the number of Quadrant I activities will eventually diminish.

The nature of the business planning process

The business planning process should be continuous and iterative. How regularly the business plan is reviewed and updated will depend on the degree of change facing the business. In fast-moving industries, business planning activities must be swift, as must decision-making, and regular updates to the business plan will be required. Some may even go as far as creating a modular business plan document so that update sheets can be inserted and removed as the market evolves and tactics change. Scenario planning techniques, which are discussed in Chapter 5, can be used to identify what may happen in the future and what the warning signs are that suggest a potential scenario is evolving. The environment should be continually monitored and, when the signals are received that the market is shifting, the tactics, strategies and operations should be reviewed.

OVERVIEW OF THE BUSINESS PLANNING PROCESS

The business planning process must be flexible as well as continuous with feedback at every stage. Chart 3.2 reproduces the outline of the business planning process introduced earlier. This process can be tailored to meet the specific planning needs of the organisation, business or project. The timing of the process within existing businesses should be such that it co-ordinates well with other activities such as budgeting which will depend on the outcome of the more strategic business planning process.

Strategic review and plan

The process begins with a strategic review that is designed to examine the current state of the business and also identifies the axes around which the future might evolve. A business's vision, mission and objectives can be an input or an output of the business planning process. This is discussed in detail in Chapter 4.

The strategic review examines the business's customers, suppliers and competitors as well as the industry dynamics that govern how these groups interact. The review also includes the wider environment in which the business operates and might take in the political, economic, social and technological changes that affect the business. Lastly, the review examines the business itself and the analysis may include the financial capabilities of the firm, its operating infrastructure, patents and knowledge and the skills of its staff.

Marketing plan

Having examined the current state of the business and its environment, the planning process examines the future. Scenario planning techniques can be used to forecast a variety of future market environments in which the business may have to operate and for which alternative marketing strategies and tactics can be developed within the marketing plan. The distinction between strategy and tactics is not always particularly clear. Strategic planning addresses the issue of what the business should do. Tactics are sometimes portrayed as addressing the question: "How should the business do it?"

Operational plan

By this stage of the process the business should be clear about its vision and mission as well as some of its objectives. A number of strategic options will have been arrived at, designed to achieve these goals, and the strategies will be supported by a set of tactics. The tactics can then be broken down into operational plans, which spell out how the tactics are to be executed. When the business planning process has reached the operational planning stage a financial model should be developed.

Chart 3.2 **The business planning process**

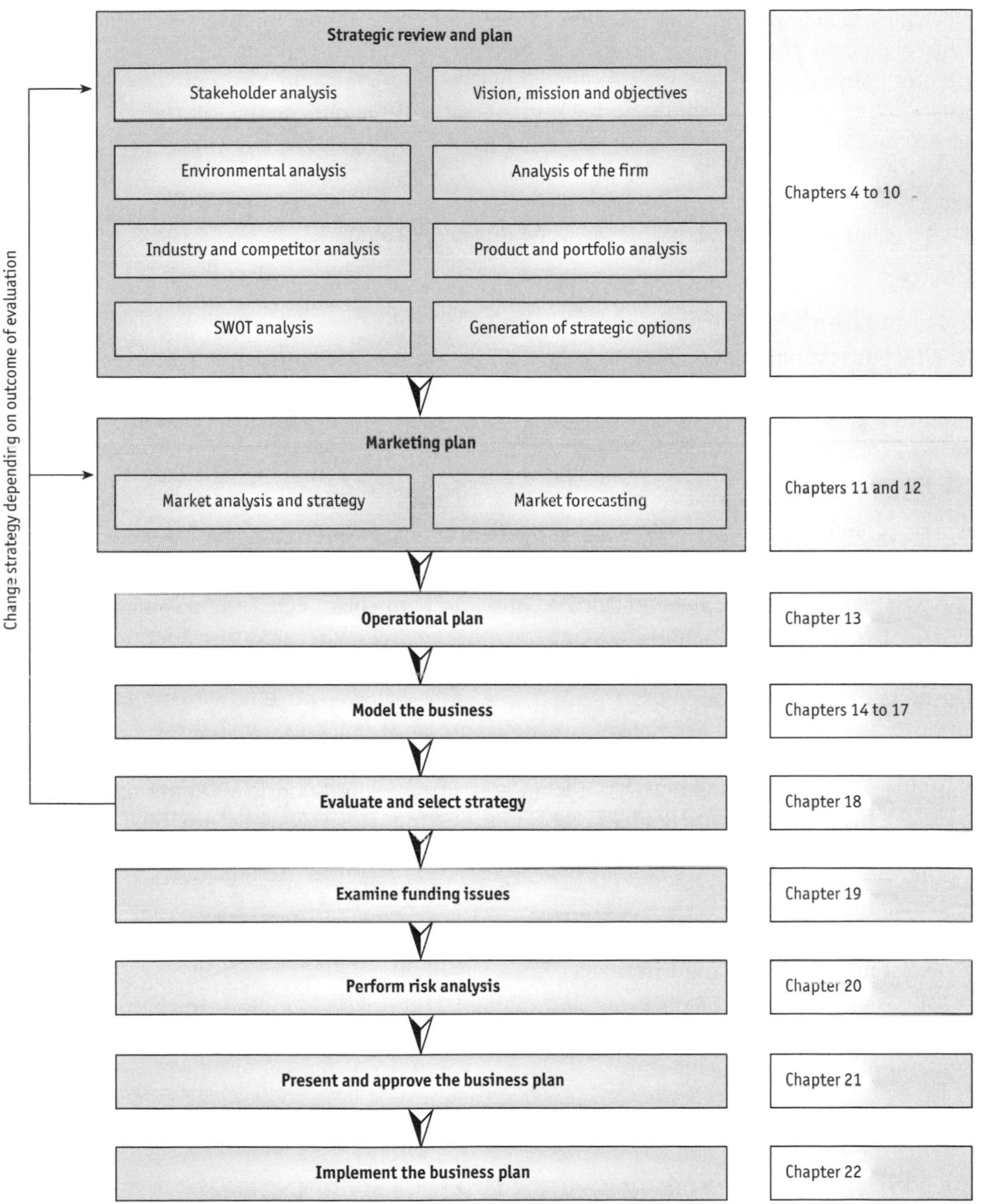

Model the business

A financial or business model provides a rigorous framework for examining the business's strategies, tactics and operational plans to see if they will enable the business to achieve its financial goals. The strategic choices will be assessed qualitatively throughout the business planning process, but a business model allows them to be evaluated quantitatively. Typical quantitative measures include the net present value of the project, the internal rate of return and the payback period (discussed in detail in Chapter 18). The business modelling exercise provides insight into the financial strength of the strategic plan and supporting tactics; and through an iterative process the strategy and tactics evolve until the optimal strategic solution is found that delivers the business's financial goals.

Examine funding issues

The business model can then be used to identify the funding requirement and for how long that funding must be available. The funding requirement and the assumptions that lie behind it will be thoroughly scrutinised by those providing the finances or who have responsibility for approving the plan.

Perform risk analysis

Investors will also want to have a good understanding of the risks involved in the proposal. Risk analysis can be performed at both the qualitative and the quantitative level. Qualitative risk analysis involves asking the question "what if?" and then identifying the actions that can be taken to mitigate any potential risks. On the quantitative side, the business model can be used to identify the variables (such as price) to which the important outputs (such as sales) of the model are most sensitive. Once these variables have been identified, sensitivity analysis can be performed by changing the input levels of variables individually and together. Techniques such as Monte Carlo simulations can also be used. Risk analysis usually takes place once the financing strategy of the business has been agreed so that any risks to bank covenants, such as interest cover or gearing ratios, can be examined.

Present and approve the business plan

It is now time to write the plan and ensure that it is consistent, credible and compelling. Once written it must be presented to those who will agree to finance the project or who will approve its implementation.

PARTICIPANTS IN THE BUSINESS PLANNING PROCESS

In new and small businesses the owner or manager may have full responsibility for undertaking the business planning process, but in larger organisations many people may be involved. In this case, it is not essential that those who do the work on a particular section of the business plan also write it, but it often helps to ensure that the plan, as written, properly reflects the conclusion and insights gained from the analysis. However, it is more important that those who will ultimately be responsible for implementing and delivering the business plan should be responsible or, at the very least, closely involved in preparing it. The implementers of the plan must feel "ownership" of it, as even a well researched and robust business plan will fail if it does not have the support of those who are responsible for its execution. Other people whom it is useful to involve in the planning process are those who will decide whether to approve it or not. Involving the decision-makers ensures that their particular concerns are taken into account and gives them time to "buy in" before they are required to approve it formally.

There should be one person with overall responsibility for the business plan, even if others write sections of it. Whoever has overall responsibility should focus on the broader, bigger issues and ensure that a consistent style and a consistent set of messages are presented across all sections. Sections of the business plan and tasks within the business planning process can often be broken down easily along functional lines, and the heads of functional areas such as sales and marketing can be given responsibility for their sections. As the business plan represents a blueprint for the business, all the major disciplines within the organisation should be involved, or at least consulted, on the contents.

In the case of large business planning exercises involving many people, it is useful to have a dedicated project manager reporting to the person with overall responsibility to ensure that the activities of all those involved are co-ordinated and to make sure that the plan is prepared on time.

It is also important to have on the team a skilled business modeller who takes responsibility for developing the business model and who is often closely involved with funding issues and risk analysis. This role is usually best suited to individuals with financial training and with strong spreadsheet skills.

MANAGING THE BUSINESS PLANNING PROCESS

Large-scale business planning projects should begin with a meeting of all those involved to explain how things are to proceed. A review meeting of the team is valuable after the completion of the strategic review to discuss everyone's findings and to identify areas of desirable or essential additional research. It is best to have the next review point after the evaluation of strategic options and when a decision is required on the strategy that will be selected for the business plan. The remainder of the process can involve additional review points depending on the complexity and sensitivity of financing issues and the degree of risk associated with the project.

Reference

1 Covey, S.R., *The Seven Habits of Highly Successful People*, Sagebrush Education Resources, 2001.

4 Strategic planning

OBJECTIVES

The objective of strategic planning is to achieve a sustainable competitive advantage that will deliver healthy profits. The strategic plan analyses the optimum fit between a business's resources and opportunities and takes into account how a business may, or will, need to adapt to thrive in a changing competitive environment. Strategic planning focuses on the medium- to longer-term future of a business, generally a time horizon of three to five years, or occasionally up to ten years.

Gary Hamel and C.K. Prahalad, two business strategists, advocate that strategy involves setting goals that stretch the business, but the strategic planning element of a business plan should focus on the tangible and concrete rather than the aspirational.

For a new business, the strategy is the foundation on which the business plan is built. For a business being developed within an existing business, the strategy behind the new business must fit with the overall strategy of the existing business.

The marketing strategy will be either implicit in the strategic plan or an explicit subsection of it. Chapter 11 focuses on marketing analysis and strategy.

APPROACHES TO STRATEGIC PLANNING

All businesses have a strategy, be it implicit or explicit. At its simplest, the strategic plan is a description of what the business is doing and the rationale behind it. In larger businesses, strategic planning has become a formalised process with a department dedicated to that process. In other cases, strategy is part of the marketing function, that is, strategic planning is synonymous with strategic market planning.

Some authors distinguish between "prescriptive" and "emergent" approaches to strategic planning. The prescriptive approach emphasises the sequential nature of the planning process as shown in Chart 4.1 on page 26. This implies that analysis and strategy selection are distinct from implementation.

The emergent approach is more experimental – a strategy is constantly adjusted in the light of operational reality. This implies a more short-term tactical approach to planning. In practice, the difference between the two approaches may simply be the frequency of reviews. Although it would be wrong to follow blindly a prescribed course once it has been set, a "flavour of the month" supposedly emergent approach to strategy makes organisational life extremely difficult.

A business plan should involve a prescriptive approach because it relates to a point in time at which the business plan is made.

PLANNING AT STRATEGIC BUSINESS UNIT LEVEL

Strategic planning is often associated with larger businesses, but start-up businesses and existing small businesses seeking funding must have some form of strategic plan that underpins the business plan. In small businesses, such as a builder or retailer, the owner or owner-manager generally carries out strategic planning.

In larger organisations, strategic planning can be carried out at the corporate level and at the strategic business unit (SBU) level. At the corporate level, it is overseen by senior management, for example the board. An SBU is a division or department of a corporation that is sufficiently self-contained to be able to operate independently from the whole business.

A business that is organised on the basis of products often has managers responsible for particular products or groups of products. The product managers carry out their own strategic planning within the overall corporate framework. Larger businesses generally adopt a divisional structure and a division can be treated as an SBU.

The concept of the SBU has important implications for resource allocation. Resources are limited and should be allocated where they achieve the greatest return on investment. Within corporations, SBUs may have to submit strategic plans and business plans as part of the corporate capital allocation process. For example, Whitbread, which operates several companies in the UK leisure market (hotels, eating out, and health and fitness), carries out a formal annual planning process, which includes a strategic plan. The planning process is formalised in the form of a booklet, which the SBUs have to complete.

THE STRATEGIC REVIEW AND PLANNING PROCESS

Chart 4.1 on the next page provides a framework for the strategic review and planning process. The steps involved are dealt with in detail in later chapters.

The strategic planning process should kick off with a stakeholder analysis. Following this, the vision, mission and objectives for the business can be established. These concepts are discussed below.

Central to the strategic planning process is how to make the most of a business's resources (internal factors) given the environment (external factors). The analysis of internal and external factors allows management to set (or review) objectives and strategy and generate alternative strategic options. Qualitative screening of options and numerical analysis using spreadsheet or other business models are required to select the most appropriate strategy from these options. Once a strategy has been selected it must be implemented. This will involve resource planning and allocation, and in the case of an existing business may require organisational changes.

Given the medium- to long-term nature of strategic planning, a business is unlikely to review its strategy more than once a year. Thus a strategic review should normally be an annual process. At the very least, managers should ascertain whether the strategic

Chart 4.1 **The strategic review and strategic planning process**

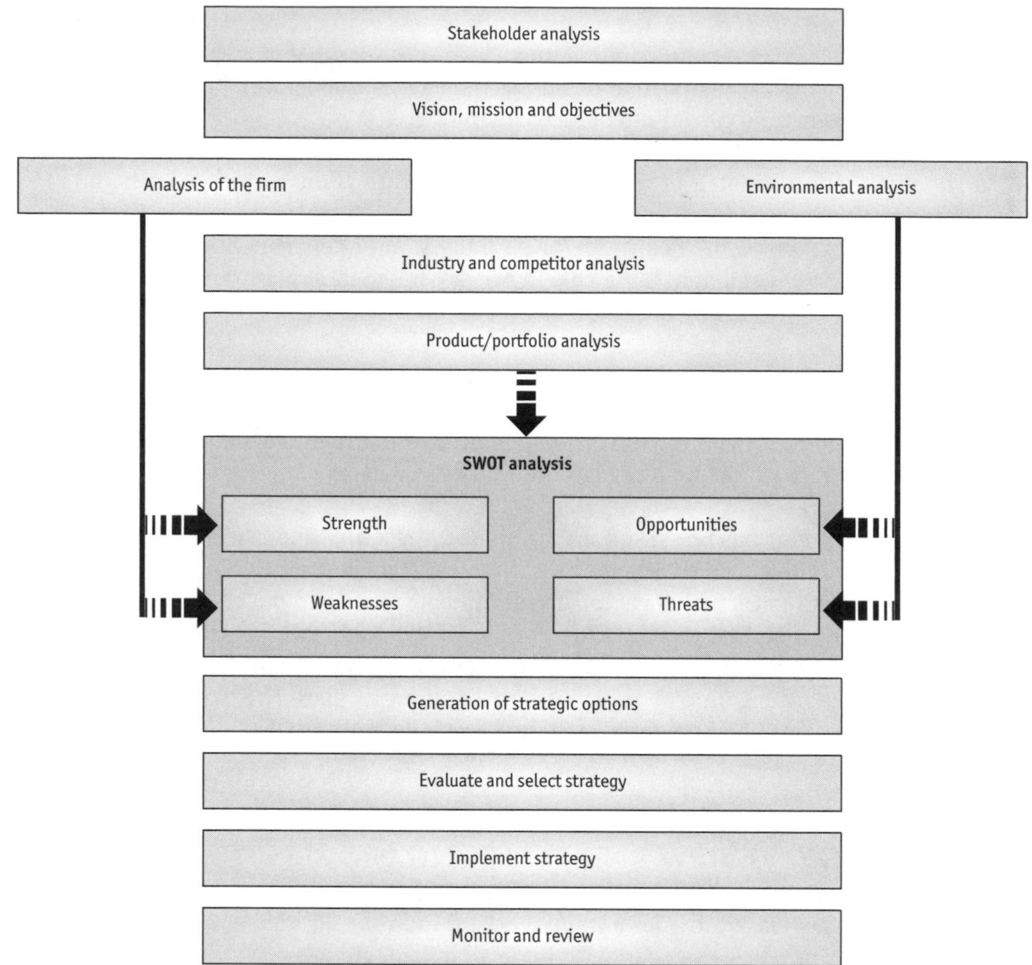

objectives have been reached. If the objectives have not been reached, a strategic review should be triggered. This should lead to a new round of business planning, for example realigning budgetary and long-term forecasts. Cataclysmic events, such as the collapse of the dotcom bubble, may trigger an urgent review. In such cases, a strategic review can lead to a fundamental reappraisal of the vision, mission and objectives.

STAKEHOLDER ANALYSIS

Stakeholders are those who can affect (or be affected by) the business. They include shareholders, lenders, customers, suppliers and even society at large.

A stakeholder analysis does not have to be a lengthy process, but it should identify the primary and possibly conflicting expectations of different stakeholders and their power and influence. Chart 4.2 provides an example of this. Stakeholders are likely to have conflicting interests, so an order of priority of whose interests matter most must be established and conflicts then resolved through negotiation.

Chart 4.2 **Stakeholder analysis**

Stakeholder	*Expectation and objectives*	*Power and influence*	*Commonality and conflict*
Shareholders	Share price growth, dividends	Appoint board	Conflict: bargaining with staff
Lenders	Interest and principal to be repaid, maintain credit ratings, risk averse	Can enforce loan covenants	Similar to shareholders, but not in financial crisis
Directors and managers	Success on CV, salary, share options, job satisfaction	Make most decisions, have detailed information	Some alignment with shareholders if rewards are linked to profits or share price
Staff and unions	Salary, job security, job satisfaction	Customer experience, strike, staff turnover	Conflict: bargaining with shareholders
Suppliers	Long-term orders, payment	Pricing, quality	Conflict: generally seek high prices
Customers	Reliable supply of goods and/or services	Revenue is derived from customers	Seek low prices
Community	Environment, local impact, local jobs	Indirect, local planning, opinion leaders	Often same as staff
Government	Operate legally, tax receipts, jobs	Regulation, subsidies, taxation, planning	Diverse, balancing

VISION, MISSION AND OBJECTIVES

New businesses generally start with an entrepreneurial idea, or vision, and must then explain how the vision is to be turned into reality. Businesses should also provide clear objectives against which success can be measured. Existing businesses have established visions, missions and objectives, be they implicit or explicit. A strategic review may lead to a reassessment of these; indeed, its main purpose may be to review the vision in order to improve the performance of a company.

The statements of vision, mission and objectives (see Chart 4.3) should be concise, easy to understand and enduring. They should not be bland or meaningless or full of phrases that reflect the latest fad. Normally, the vision statement is one sentence or paragraph, and the mission and objectives statements consist of no more than five bullet points each.

Chart 4.3 **Vision, mission and objectives**

Vision	Sets out the purpose (what business the organisation is in) and direction of the business (where it is trying to go).
Mission	Outlines how the vision is to be translated into reality; that is, what should be done to achieve it.
Objectives	Set specific quantified targets against which the success of the strategy and the business plan can be measured.

The vision, mission and objectives statements provide a summary of what a business is about and should be included in the executive summary of the business plan. They also provide a theme that should be reflected throughout the business plan, helping to ensure that it is consistent and coherent.

The vision statement

The vision statement defines what business the organisation is in and gives the broad direction in which the organisation is heading. For example, a caterer may state its vision as "to become the leading provider of organic lunches to office workers in Boomtown".

The mission statement

The mission statement explains how the vision is to be achieved. It tells investors, managers, staff and customers what the business is about to do. For example, the caterer may decide to achieve its objective by creating a distribution system that ensures rapid order fulfilment, using only the freshest products and high-quality ingredients, and promoting the company by "taking the city block by block".

Objectives

The business should have a set of objectives against which the success of the strategy can be measured. Objectives should be SMART:

- Specific
- Measurable
- Achievable within the stated time frame
- Relevant in the context of the vision
- Time bound

The caterer, for example, could set the following objectives:

- Source 95% of ingredients from certified organic producers within six months.
- Within one year provide 800 meals per day, increasing to 1,200 in two years and 1,500 in three years.
- The average value per sale should be at least $8.
- Achieve an operating margin of x% in year one, increasing to y% in year two.
- Customers and staff should develop a feeling of empathy with the business.

Clear quantitative objectives will please financial backers and bankers. They also provide implementation milestones that allow you to assess whether the business plan is on track, and if not, to take remedial action.

Financial and non-financial objectives

Most of the above objectives are financial, and financial objectives are extremely important. In some cases, companies agree to specific covenants with bondholders or other lenders, for example to reach a particular interest cover ratio (expressed as a multiple of earnings before interest, taxes, depreciation and amortisation or EBITDA) within a defined time frame. In extreme cases, not achieving these targets can wipe out 100% of shareholder value.

Objectives do not have to be exclusively financial. The last of the caterer's objectives is not financial and at first appears to be impossible to measure. However, surrogate measures could be used, such as staff turnover and repeat sales, or a staff and customer survey could be carried out.

Focusing purely on financial objectives introduces a degree of myopia into business decision-making. The limitation of managing purely by financial measures is explicitly recognised by techniques such as the "balanced scorecard", which was developed by Robert Kaplan and David Norton. They describe it as follows:[1]

> *The balanced scorecard retains traditional financial measures. But financial measures tell the story of past events, an adequate story for industrial age companies for which investments in long-term capabilities and customer relationships were not critical for success. These financial measures are inadequate, however, for guiding and evaluating the journey that information age companies must make to create future value through investment in customers, suppliers, employees, processes, technology, and innovation.*

EXIT STRATEGY

The strategic plan focuses on the business itself. However, when a business plan is prepared for the purpose of attracting investors, consideration must be given as to how they can recoup their investment. Venture capitalists, for example, will always look for an exit strategy that realises the maximum value of their investment and returns cash, which can then be invested in new ventures. The value of a business can be realised through:

- a trade sale – selling to a competitor or other firm which may have a strategic interest in the business;
- a public sale through an initial public offering (IPO) – the company will be listed on a suitable stock exchange.

The potential exit strategy should be outlined and its credibility demonstrated in terms of the financial projections. Normally, the best prices will be obtained once a business has reached a degree of stability; that is, it has achieved breakeven or is cash flow positive at operating level, or even overall cash flow positive. In some circumstances an earlier sale may be possible. For example, a small biotechnology company may sell out to a larger company immediately after a breakthrough technology has been patented. Depending on investor appetite, early IPOs may be possible. The dotcom bubble was characterised by the listing of internet-based businesses that had hardly any revenue and were years away from profitability.

JUDGING A STRATEGIC PLAN

Strategic planning is sometimes criticised because it appears to be removed from reality and irrelevant to the day-to-day running of a business. However, good strategic planning is not an academic process but a tool for successful management. Strategic plans must be articulated in words and numbers; measurement is key. It is not necessary to produce huge volumes of prose as a lot can be achieved with bullet points and checklists.

Without the benefit of hindsight it is not possible to say whether a strategy will succeed. However, if it lacks certain attributes it will be less likely to succeed. Broadly, any strategy should:

- be feasible considering internal and external constraints;
- lead to a long-term competitive advantage;
- add value for stakeholders;
- be sustainable in the long term;
- be adaptable to cope with a changing environment.

Reference

1 Kaplan, R.S. and Norton, D.P., *The Balanced Scorecard: Translating Strategy into Action*, Harvard Business School Press, 1996.

5 Analysing the environment

Businesses are subject to many forces over which they have limited control: government economic policy, attitudinal changes among consumers and the development of new technology, to name a few. Environmental analysis examines such forces to predict the environment in which a business may have to operate. Environmental factors may be "macro", such as the level of inflation, interest rates and exchange rates, or "micro", such as local business taxes, flooding or the creation of a new road or rail link. For the business plan, the skill lies in determining which factors currently have an impact on the business or may do so in the future, and understanding what and how large the impact is likely to be. It requires an ability to think beyond your current frame of reference in order to identify the future influences on the business.

SPEED OF ENVIRONMENTAL CHANGE

The speed of environmental change should be taken into account in a business plan. There are three levels of environmental change: stable, dynamic and turbulent. In stable markets, a well-defined strategic plan can be developed from the outset; but in highly turbulent markets, strategic decisions are more likely to evolve as events unfold and uncertainty reduces.

Stable

There is little or no change in the environment. Any change that does take place is slow, readily identifiable and predictable. The relationships between suppliers, customers, distributors and manufacturers are well established and unlikely to change. Such stability can be found in mature markets such as food processing and road haulage.

Dynamic

There is change in the environment but the pace of change is moderate. Some of the changes are predictable, others are not. There may be some new entrants as well as some businesses exiting. Levels of merger and acquisition activity will be low, but businesses will have to adapt in order to remain competitive. Dynamic markets often arise once a highly regulated market is liberalised.

Turbulent

Turbulent markets are characterised by a great deal of unpredictable, rapid change. There are many new market entrants and experimentation with different business models. The relationships between suppliers, manufacturers, distributors and customers are continually changing. Markets are often characterised by high levels of technological development. These markets are often associated with the initial and growth phases of the product life cycle described in Chapter 8.

PEST ANALYSIS

Defining PEST analysis

A PEST analysis of Political, Economic, Social and Technological factors will reveal many of the external environmental influences on a business's performance. Some practitioners have extended the acronym to PESTEL to include environmental and legal considerations.

Sources of information

Much of the information useful for PEST analysis may already have been gathered in carrying out, say, competitor analysis and strategic and tactical planning activities. More up-to-date information can be obtained from high-quality newspapers and journals. Government bodies, industry bodies and research organisations produce detailed forecasts, country reports and industry reports. Stockbroking firms also produce research that contains valuable information on the trends and factors influencing the markets. For small businesses, a great deal of useful information can be found on the internet.

Applying PEST analysis

Those setting up a new business must be realistic about their knowledge and awareness of the environment the business will be operating in and how it might change, and they should avoid brushing aside the factors they are uncertain about. In larger organisations, it is often useful to bring together a number of different people with different knowledge and expertise in a PEST analysis workshop.

In advance of the workshop everyone should be given a background briefing pack covering the objectives of the workshop and any existing material that examines environmental trends. The workshop should begin by agreeing and clearly defining the objectives. These may be to maximise profits, grow revenues, increase shareholder value or capture a greater proportion of market share. The participants should then "brainstorm" all the environmental factors that could affect the business's ability to achieve its objectives, either now or in the future. The participants should be challenged to think widely and laterally around the problem. Factors that today are benign may be highly influential in a number of years' time. When brainstorming, the workshop facilitator should enforce some simple rules:

- The participants, in turn, should be asked to write an environmental factor on a piece of paper that can then be placed on an appropriate sheet of flip chart paper, each representing one of the PEST categories.
- If a participant cannot think of a factor, the facilitator should move quickly on to the next person.
- The process can go more than once round the participants, but when a few people have passed consecutively the facilitator should ask for any more contributions before swiftly bringing the session to a close.
- There should be no discussion of or judgments on any contributions during the brainstorming process; all contributions are assumed to be equally valid.
- Note that it may be better to run four shorter sessions, each considering one of the four PEST categories.

The following sections list typical environmental factors, but every business is different so the list should act only as a starting point.

Political

Local, national and supranational political issues to consider include:

- Direct and indirect taxes, such as income tax and VAT, influence consumer spending and market demand.
- Corporate taxation has an impact on the profitability of businesses.
- Public spending by central and local government has a direct impact on the level of demand within the economy.
- Regional and industrial policy can affect businesses at a micro level, and the availability of regional grants or other forms of assistance may be a deciding factor on where to locate a business.
- Monetary policy and the level of interest rates will affect demand and a business's ability to service its debts. Exchange rate policy can have a critical effect on importers and exporters.
- Changes in international trade can create new export markets. For example, China becoming a member of the World Trade Organisation, in theory at least, makes China's huge market much more open to exporters.
- Competition law lays down rules on what a business can and cannot do and may be a crucial factor in the case of a merger or acquisition.
- Regulation and deregulation can have a dramatic impact on the business environment and individual business sectors.
- Local practices such as onerous bureaucracy or corruption can complicate business in certain markets.
- Education and training will have a long-term impact on a business's ability to recruit suitably qualified staff and to compete effectively at international level.

Economic

Local, national and global economic factors to consider include:

- Business cycle. Developed economies often follow a pattern known as the business cycle where periods of faster growth are followed by years of slower growth or even recession. Some sectors, such as advertising, leisure and restaurants, are more susceptible to the impact of the business cycle than others, such as the manufacturers of foodstuffs where demand is less cyclical.
- Employment levels. These are closely related to the economy's position within the business cycle but also to the state of the local economy. High levels of unemployment in a region will reduce demand there but will also mean that labour is easier and cheaper to hire.
- Inflation. This can affect a business in many ways; for example, if the rate of increase in the price of raw materials is greater than the rate of inflation for the business's products, then the business will experience a fall in profitability over time.
- Interest rates and exchange rates, as mentioned under political factors, can critically affect a business's profitability, although certain risks can be hedged.

- House prices and stockmarket prices. The growth or fall of house prices and the movement in stockmarket levels affect consumer confidence and hence consumer spending.
- Economic development. The stage of economic development – underdeveloped, developing or developed – will influence the nature of the products and services that can effectively be marketed within a country and the level of infrastructure that exists to support the performance of business activities. The increasing wealth of countries such as China and India is leading to an increase in demand for products and services which were previously beyond the reach of many households.
- Availability of credit. The credit crunch that began in 2007 dramatically reduced the availability of credit or debt finance for businesses and where credit was available a reassessment of the pricing of risk meant that the finance that was made available was much more costly. The result was that new businesses and projects found it hard to secure finance and had to deliver higher levels of financial return to compensate for the increased cost of borrowing.
- Oil and commodity prices. The dramatic increase in the price of oil during the early 1970s and also in 2007 and 2008 as well as substantial increases in prices for commodities such as tin and copper have placed downward pressure on profits in many parts of the economy.

Social

Shifts in a country's demography and social and cultural values usually occur over many years. However, with improvements in communication and increased employee mobility between countries, the speed of social and demographic change can be expected to increase. The population and its values represent the starting point for a discussion of market demand. The impact of social and cultural change is best examined in relation to a specific product or service, but some macro-level observations are provided for both developed and developing economies:

- Population growth. The rate of growth of the population will have a direct impact on the size of the potential addressable market for a product or service. Population growth is typically higher in developing than in developed countries, although in some countries with high AIDS infection rates population levels are actually in decline.
- Age structure. In the developed, western world, economies are experiencing a significant increase in the average age of their populations. In less developed economies, populations are generally much younger, as birth rates are high and the longevity of the population is lower. Differences in the age structure of the population have implications for the overall level of saving compared with consumer spending and the relative sizes of the working and dependent sections of the population. As the population ages the demand for products and services also shifts.
- Rural to urban migration. Migration in the population can take place at many levels, including internationally. In developed European markets, labour mobility has increased following the creation of a single market. Developing economies often experience a migration of the population from rural to urban areas. The increased

concentration of potential consumers in an urban location has implications for a business's sales and distribution strategy.

- Social and cultural shifts. Attitudes towards risk-taking and entrepreneurship differ by country and will affect the number of new start-ups and potential competitors. Attitudes towards work and leisure will affect the demand for certain products as well as the supply side of the economy in terms of available labour. The role of women in the economy influences demand and supply.

Technological

Changes in technology can have a rapid and dramatic impact on an economy. Issues to consider include:

- Level of expenditure on research and development by competitors. This will provide an indication of whether any changes in technology-driven production processes or new products should be anticipated.
- New markets. Does the introduction of new technology create a new market for a particular technology-based product or service?
- Production methods. How might technology be utilised to improve production methods within the business, and how might competitors utilise technology to gain competitive advantage?
- Rate of adoption of new technology. It is often a considerable time before new technology gains mass-market appeal. The business plan must examine how long it will take the new product to penetrate the market.

On the next page is a summary of PEST analysis for mobile broadband access, a telecommunications technology that enables fast data speed delivered over a wireless network.

Mobile and fixed broadband data access

The availability of broadband access for homes and businesses and the range of digital services that it can support is a critical element of many business's strategic plans, especially those in the television, media, music, video, advertising and gaming sectors. Broadband access refers to a high-speed data connection from the home or office to the suppliers of digital services such as e-mail, interactive games, internet access and music and video downloads. Broadband technologies include cable and digital subscriber lines (DSL) and most households have now replaced their slow dial-up services provided over traditional telephone lines with fast broadband connections. High-speed data connections have, until recently, been limited to a fixed location such as the home or office or within the coverage of a WiFi network such as a hotel lobby or airport. However, advancements in mobile networks have meant that high-speed data connections are increasingly available on a much wider geographic basis. As broadband access is now both fixed and mobile many companies are exploring the implications for converged services which can be deployed across any network be it fixed or mobile. In order to develop their strategic plans, businesses must establish a vision of what the future converged customer might look like. In the remainder of this chapter we use PEST analysis and scenario planning to develop this vision, concentrating on the impact of convergence on the typical retail customer rather than business customer. Figure 5.1 contains the results of PEST analysis.

Chart 5.1 **PEST analysis**

POLITICAL	ECONOMIC
• Privacy laws relating to personal information such as location-based information enabled by mobile technologies • Availability, conditions and price of additional radio spectrum for wireless service providers • Competition law in relation to mergers between network providers • Competition law in relation to mergers between networks and content suppliers • Regulation of access to the "local loop"	• Consolidation or exit within the mobile telecoms sector • Consolidation within the broadband market • Access charges to the "local loop" from the owners of "last mile of copper" to the home • Rate of economic growth and changes in consumer spending • Interest rates • Availability of credit • Inflation • Exchange rates • Costs of laptop computers
SOCIAL AND DEMOGRAPHIC	**TECHNOLOGICAL**
• Penetration of laptop computers • Continuing popularity of social networking sites • Available leisure time • Home working / teleworking • Demand for television and video delivered on the move • Attitudes towards the use of mobile devices in public places • Acceptance of advertising supported services on mobile • Rate of adoption of new technologies and services • Demand for gaming services on small-screen devices • Acceptance and growth of e-commerce on mobile phones • The perceived value of a single customer bill for fixed and mobile services	• Increased data speeds on fixed DSL and cable networks • Developments in data speeds over mobile networks • Developments and roll-out of alternative mobile data technologies such as WiFi and WiMAX • The costs of meeting the capacity demands on mobile networks • Increased battery life to support more sophisticated mobile devices • Security and virus concerns for mobile devices • Software application developments and an increasing range of applications developed for both fixed and mobile devices

SCENARIO PLANNING

PEST analysis is a useful starting point for thinking about the future environment in which a business may have to operate. When PEST analysis is combined with scenario planning the results make a valuable contribution to the business planning process. In stable markets, predicting the future is straightforward; it is likely to be similar to the past. However, for dynamic and especially for turbulent markets, the future may be unrecognisable from the past so a forecast based on an extrapolation of past events could be misleading. Scenario planning represents a solution to this problem, providing a structured approach to thinking about uncertainty. Scenarios describe different environments in which a business may have to operate and highlight trends and interactions that may characterise their development.

A characteristic of a good business plan is that it should "tell a story". Scenario planning helps develop the story behind the plan and also provides the framework and narrative for a market forecast. Developing a number of scenarios also increases the understanding of the forces shaping the industry and how it might evolve.

The stages of scenario planning

The four stages of scenario planning are as follows:

1. Identify factors of high uncertainty and high impact.
2. Describe alternative behaviour patterns for those factors.
3. Select the three or four most informative scenarios.
4. Write the scenario descriptions.

Identify factors of high uncertainty and high impact

Scenarios are developed around the factors that have the highest degree of future uncertainty and the greatest impact on a business's objectives. The list of environmental factors generated through PEST analysis can be allocated across the four quadrants of an impact/uncertainty matrix (see the example in Chart 5.2). Uncertainty relates to how easy it is to predict the future behaviour of a factor. Impact relates to how significantly a factor influences business performance. Factors that are currently certain and benign may become highly volatile and influential in the future.

Chart 5.2 **The impact/uncertainty matrix**

		Business impact	
		LOW	HIGH
Uncertainty	HIGH	◩ Demand for gaming services on small-screen devices ◩ Security and virus concerns for mobile devices ◩ Acceptance of advertising supported services on mobile devices ◩ Continuing popularity of social networking sites ◩ Inflation ◩ Exchange rates ◩ Interest rates ◩ Increased battery life to support more sophisticated mobile devices	◩ Penetration of laptop computers among consumers ◩ Software application development and an increased range of applications developed for both fixed and mobile devices ◩ Developments and roll-out of alternative mobile data technologies such as WiFi and WiMAX ◩ Availability, conditions and price of additional radio spectrum for wireless service providers ◩ Demand for television and video delivered on the move ◩ Rate of adoption of new technologies and services
	LOW	◩ Homeworking/teleworking ◩ Attitudes towards the use of mobile devices in public places ◩ Available leisure time ◩ Availability of credit ◩ Rate of economic growth and changes in consumer spending ◩ Regulation of access to the "local loop" ◩ Increased data speeds on fixed DSL and cable networks ◩ Competition law in relation to mergers between network providers ◩ Competition law in relation to mergers between network providers and content suppliers ◩ The perceived value of a single customer bill for fixed and mobile services	◩ Access charges to operators for access to the "local loop" ◩ Costs of laptop computers ◩ Developments in data speeds over mobile networks ◩ Costs of meeting capacity constraints on mobile networks ◩ Privacy laws relating to personal information such as location-based information enabled by mobile technologies ◩ Consolidation or exit within the mobile telecoms sector ◩ Consolidation or exit within the broadband market ◩ Acceptance and growth in e-commerce on mobile phones

Describe alternative behaviour patterns

The upper-right quadrant of the matrix contains all the environmental factors that have the greatest potential impact on the business and the highest level of future uncertainty. Ideally, two and no more than three different development paths for each of the factors in the quadrant should now be described; the paths should be as contrasting as possible while remaining realistic. Chart 5.3 shows some examples for domestic consumers.

Chart 5.3 **Potential development paths**

Environmental factor	*Path 1*	*Path 2*	*Path 3*
Penetration of laptop computers among consumers	Laptops replace desktop PCs in the home but remain a shared family purchase	Everyone has a laptop in the same way that everyone has a mobile phone	
Software application development	Few compelling applications are developed for converged networks	A plethora of small software developers create a vast range of compelling applications	
Roll-out of alternative mobile data technologies	WiFi and WiMAX networks remain limited to key public places such as airports and hotels	WiMAX and WiFi are extended to provide wide area coverage in major cities	WiMAX networks are rolled out in all cities and towns
Availability, conditions and price of additional radio spectrum	Spectrum is available on a technology neutral basis and at low prices	Spectrum is available on a technology neutral basis and prices are high	
Demand for television and video delivered on the move	Customers do not like watching television and video clips on small screens	Demand for small video clips such as YouTube is high on mobile devices but longer programmes are not popular	Customers consume demand on mobile devices in the same way they consume it on the PC and television
Rate of adoption of new technologies and services	New technologies are adopted in line with historic take-up rates	The speed with which new technologies are adopted accelerates	

Select the three or four most informative scenarios

Combining different development paths can generate the basis for many potential scenarios. The goal is to identify no more than three or four of the most interesting which will form the basis of the market demand forecast and strategy formulation. During the initial scenario development phase, the scenarios are derived from combinations of just two inputs at a time and their respective development paths. An example two-by-two scenario matrix is presented in Chart 5.4 on the next page.

Chart 5.4 **Initial scenario matrix**

Software application development	Penetration of laptop computers: PATH 1	Penetration of laptop computers: PATH 2
PATH 1	Laptops replace desktop PCs in the home but remain a shared family purchase Few compelling applications are developed for converged networks	Everyone has a laptop in the same way that everyone has a mobile phone Few compelling applications are developed for converged networks
PATH 2	Laptops replace desktop PCs in the home but remain a shared family purchase A plethora of small software developers create a vast range of compelling applications	Everyone has a laptop in the same way that everyone has a mobile phone A plethora of small software developers create a vast range of compelling applications

Only scenarios that are realistic, contrasting and relevant to the business planning problem should be selected. The scenario from the bottom-right quadrant of Chart 5.4 has been selected as the example for the remainder of this chapter.

Write the scenario descriptions

Use evocative names. Each of the selected scenarios should be given an evocative name. The name should be a vivid description that captures the essence of the scenario. Descriptions that say something about the assumptions and the business context are much more valuable as a communications tool than the traditional "base case" and the inevitable "low" and "high" variations. The name chosen for the example scenario is "Convergence is king".

Describe the essence of the scenario. A description of how the scenarios will evolve over time should be prepared. Below is a scenario description for convergence is king. Once the basis of the scenario has been determined, additional factors from the upper-right quadrant should be included. After that, additional factors from the other two quadrants can be incorporated. The interactions and development paths of the newly introduced factors should be consistent with the overall theme of the scenario. As the impact and uncertainty of the inputs diminish, less detailed descriptions are required for the development of the remaining factors.

The initial scenario description for convergence is king is presented in the box on the next page.

Convergence is king

The cost of laptop computers continues to fall as an increasing number of manufacturers in China and other developing economies raise production levels and compete for market share. The lower cost, coupled with the strategies of some telecoms companies to subsidise the selling price of laptops in return for customers signing long-term contracts, results in increasing laptop penetration. Within a few years anyone who has a mobile phone is also likely to have a personal laptop computer. Laptop users are able to connect their laptop to a wide range of broadband services using both fixed and wireless solutions as mobile networks compete with newly launched WiMAX networks for the growing laptop connectivity market. The increased number of alternative wireless networks was enabled through the release of significant amounts of additional radio spectrum at prices considerably below historic levels. Increasing technological development has reduced the value placed on spectrum as a scare resource. Following the success of open platforms for software developers a wide range of compelling and reasonably priced applications are available. Many of the applications make use of gaming as well as video and music content. Customers rapidly embraced the idea of watching video clips, for example from YouTube, not only on their laptop or television but increasingly their mobile phone. The speed of take-up of the new services surprised many in the industry and the acceleration in the adoption of new technologies was largely attributed to the ever-increasing popularity of social networking sites where applications and content and quickly shared. Customers are becoming increasingly indifferent as to whether they access content and applications over their laptop, television or mobile phone – to the customer, they appear the same. Convergence has become a reality.

ENVIRONMENTAL ANALYSIS AND BUSINESS PLANNING

Environmental analysis is a crucial step in the business planning process. PEST analysis identifies the elements within the environment that may affect a business's performance and that should be considered in the planning process. These elements are often beyond the control of the entrepreneur and may be subject to high levels of uncertainty. In this case, PEST analysis can be effectively combined with scenario planning techniques to generate a vivid description of the anticipated future environment in which the business may have to operate. The assumptions about the market inherent within the scenario description provide the context for many of the remaining stages of the business planning process.

6 Analysing the firm

OBJECTIVES

The objective of analysing a business, or firm, is to identify its resources and explore how these resources are used to contribute to its competitive advantage. Businesses that allocate and deploy their resources in the most efficient manner are likely to achieve a greater return on capital employed than those that do not. There are three aspects to the analysis of the business:

- The resources themselves. These can be a competitive advantage, as rivals may not have access to the same resources and may not be able to duplicate or substitute the resources employed by a particular business. This is the central tenet of the resource-based view of competitive advantage and is analysed using tools such as VRIO analysis (see below). The analysis of the firm should answer the question: "What do we have that competitors do not have and cannot replicate?"
- The configuration of resources. These can also be a source of competitive advantage. If a business configures its resources optimally, it will have a competitive advantage over its rivals. This view is central to the value chain and value system concept of competitive advantage.
- The resource audit. This covers operational (tangible and intangible), human (capabilities) and financial resources. The objective of the resource audit is to identify resources and ascertain how efficiently resources are utilised and how effectively they are deployed.

Chart 6.1 shows the components of the analysis of the firm and the principal analytical concepts and tools employed. Some of these concepts may seem more applicable to larger corporations, but most can also be applied to small businesses.

Chart 6.1 **Analysis of the firm**

Component	*Analytical concepts and tools employed*
Resource based view	Key differentiators and unique selling points
	VRIO analysis
	Core competencies
Configuration of resources	Value add analysis
	Value chain
	Value system
Resource audit	Identification of resources
◩ Operations resources	Resource utilisation
◩ Human resources	Effectiveness of deployment
◩ Organisational resources	
◩ Financial resources	

RESOURCE-BASED VIEW OF THE FIRM

The objective of strategic planning is to achieve, sustain and enhance the competitive advantage. Within an industry some businesses are more successful than others because they have resources that are inherently different from those of their competitors, who furthermore cannot easily acquire these resources. Businesses should therefore try to acquire or develop such unique resources in order to attain competitive advantage (see Chart 6.2).

The following techniques can be used to identify unique resources and ascertain whether these resources will result in a competitive advantage. You can use them jointly or select the one best suited to your purpose. Many of the concepts used are similar, and the difference between one method and another is in the approach to analysis rather than anything fundamental.

Chart 6.2 **Resource-based model of sustainable competitive advantage**

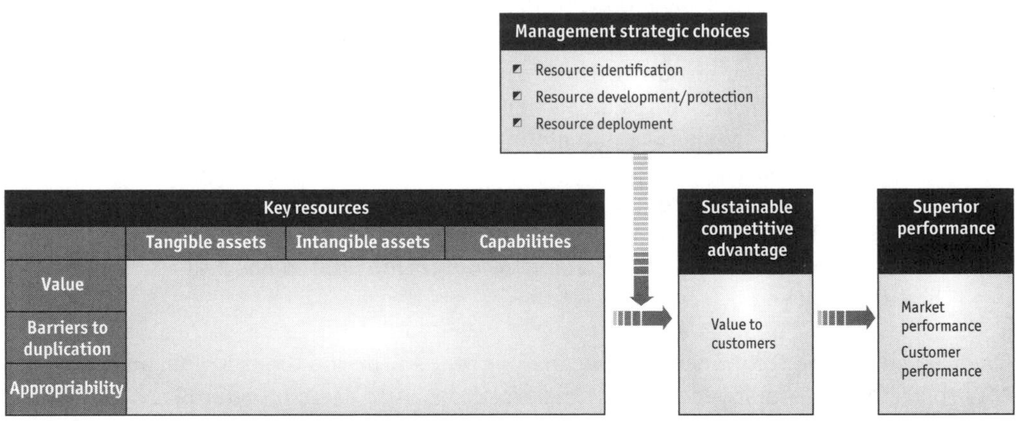

Source: Fahy, J. and Smithee, A., "Strategic Marketing and the Resource Based View of the Firm", *Academy of Marketing Science Review*, Vol. 1999, No. 10, 1999

Key differentiators and unique selling points

Each business is likely to have some unique attributes that differentiate it from its rivals. Although the concept of a unique selling point (USP) is more related to marketing tactics, it can be associated with a fundamental difference that cannot be easily replicated by competitors.

To achieve competitive advantage, a business should leverage its key differentiators. A key differentiator does not have to be a financial asset. For example, a name such as Air France gives the airline an advantage when competing in the air-transport market to and from France but not when competing for traffic between Amsterdam and London. This is an important consideration in the context of the consolidation of the European airline industry. Another example is a company with rights to a brand or patent which it might be able to exploit.

Do not forget that a differentiator can also be a problem. For example, a company with a near monopoly position, such as an electricity supplier, may be heavily regulated and have little freedom to set prices. It may be forced to separate its business into a part that deals with power generation and distribution and a part that deals with retailing. Many telecoms operators and pharmaceutical companies find themselves in a similar position because they have a dominant market share or unique access to patents for medicines, such as drugs to combat AIDS.

Start by making a list of your key differentiators. The next section describes a structured framework for analysing these and deciding whether they can be a basis for competitive advantage.

VRIO analysis

To conduct a resource-based analysis of a business, Jay Barney proposed a structured approach based on analysing whether a resource is Valuable, Rare and Imitable, and whether the Organisation is taking advantage of the resource.[1]

- **Valuable.** A resource is valuable if it can be used, for example, to increase market share, achieve a cost advantage or charge a premium price. This question has to be answered first because a resource that is not valuable or is irrelevant cannot be a source of competitive advantage.
- **Rare.** Rarity is important because if competitors possess the same resources, there is no inherent advantage in the resource. Of course, different businesses can configure the same resources differently to achieve competitive advantage, but this is not the focus of the resource-based view of the firm. If a valuable resource is not available to all competitors it is "rare" and therefore a potential source of competitive advantage.
- **Imitable.** It must be difficult or expensive for competitors to imitate or acquire the resource. This can apply to patents and copyright, but also to other forms of resources, such as brand perception. Although it is possible to change a brand and the perception of it, rebranding is expensive. If a resource is easy to imitate it confers only a temporary competitive advantage, not a sustainable one.
- **Organisation.** A business must be capable of taking advantage of the resource. If a resource is valuable, rare and difficult to imitate, a business must be able to exploit it, otherwise it is of little use. This may require reorganising the business.

The VRIO analysis framework shown in Chart 6.3 on the next page links the VRIO resource analysis with the competitive advantage, the likely economic impact on the business and what this means in terms of the SWOT (strengths, weaknesses, opportunities and threats) analysis (see Chapter 9).

Chart 6.3 **VRIO analysis framework**

Resource characteristics				Strategic implications		
Valuable	Rare	Costly to imitate	Organisation exploits it	Competitive implication	Impact on economic performance	SWOT category
No	–	–	No	Competitive disadvantage	Below normal	Weakness
Yes	No	–		Competitive parity	Normal	Weakness or strength
Yes	Yes	No		Temporary competitive advantage	Above normal	Strength and core competence
Yes	Yes	Yes	Yes	Sustainable competitive advantage	Above normal	Strength and long-term core competence

Source: Based on Barney, J.B., *Gaining and Sustaining a Competitive Advantage*, Addison-Wesley, 1996

Core competencies

The concept of core competencies has two facets and they often overlap. First, one business may be better than another in running some aspects of the business; in other words, one business is more competent in key areas. These are organisational core competencies. Second, in order to fulfil their primary purpose, businesses generally carry out a range of core activities as well as support or peripheral activities.

Core competencies are identified in several ways:

- They are identified as a strength in the SWOT analysis.
- The human resource audit identifies particular know-how within the business.
- Value add analysis identifies the activities where most of the value add activities take place.

Organisational core competencies

Core competencies are

> *a set of differential technological skills, complementary assets, and organisational routines and capacities that provide the basis for a business's competitive capacities in a particular business.*[2]

Once core competencies have been identified, managers can deploy resources to strengthen and develop them. The four dimensions of core competence are qualifications, norms and values, organisational competence and managerial competence (see Chart 6.4).

Chart 6.4 **The four dimensions of core competence**

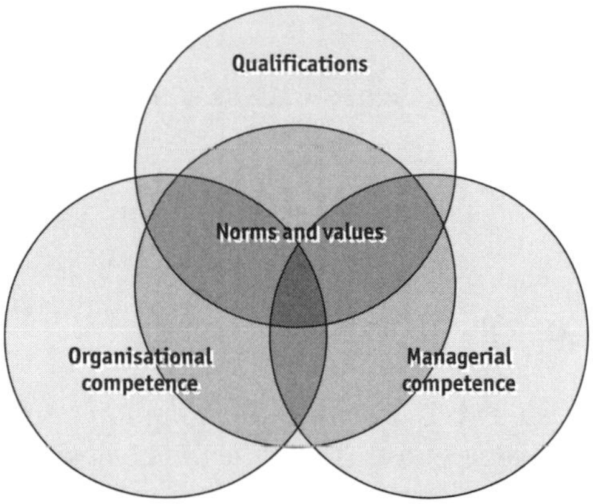

Source: Leonard-Barton, D., "Core Capabilities and Core Rigidities: A Paradox in Managing New Product Development", *Strategic Management Journal*, Vol. 13, 1992

An activity or human resource may be a core competence because it confers a unique competitive advantage. For example, a food retailer may have a unique ability to pick sites for its stores. Managing a property portfolio does not need to be a core activity for a food retailer, but in this case the retailer derives a significant advantage from it because once a particular site has been acquired, it is not available to a competitor. Therefore store site selection and acquisition is a core competence.

As businesses become more knowledge based, the importance of core competencies increases. Some businesses, such as consulting firms, are almost exclusively defined by the competencies of the individuals in the organisation and how they relate to each other.

Core activities

Focusing on core activities has been a management mantra for some time. In recent years, many companies have outsourced non-core activities. For example, many companies that previously ran their own staff canteen or employed cleaning staff now engage contractors to provide these services, and others have outsourced their IT department. This concept of core competencies is associated with "organisational focus" and "the lean organisation", the idea being that resources should be concentrated on where they achieve the greatest effect. However, this strategy also increases risk, notably because of the increased dependency on suppliers or contractors.

In the context of a business plan, ask whether some of the planned activities are really core, particularly if investment is required to perform them. Funding is always scarce. By focusing on core activities, available funds can be concentrated on these, thus decreasing the risk of a funding gap.

Strategic implication of core competencies

The overlapping of organisational core competencies and core activities comes about because a business should focus on the activities at which it is most competent. For example, a group of investment bankers setting up a new specialist investment bank may be excellent bankers, but they may have little knowledge of running an office, or payroll and IT systems. They may decide to outsource these non-core activities and concentrate on doing what they are most competent at: the business of investment banking.

If a business's core activity is closely aligned with its core competencies, these become a factor that enables it to achieve competitive advantage. In contrast, non-core activities cannot leverage core competencies.

CONFIGURATION OF RESOURCES

Competitive advantage is also derived from the configuration of resources rather than simply the uniqueness of those resources. Therefore the analysis of a firm should investigate the linkage between resources and how they form part of a system with the objective of adding value. The techniques used to analyse how resources in a business are configured and utilised are described below.

Value add analysis

Value added is the amount by which the selling prices exceed input costs. Input costs include bought-in products and services, payroll costs and the cost of capital equipment. Businesses exist to add value to a product or service. The ability to add value is closely linked to profitability. At a company level, the value added is broadly represented by earnings before interest and tax (EBIT).

At a unit or component level, the calculation of value added becomes more complex. Where fixed costs account for an important element, or where assets are used to produce a range of products and services, common costs must be allocated to different products or activities. The cost of administration and other support functions must also be allocated. All this involves a considerable degree of judgment, but it is still a worthwhile exercise because all costs and revenues have to be allocated somewhere. This is a requirement for the Hofer and Schendel value chain (see Chart 6.6 on page 49).

The identification of value added will allow a business to focus improvements or strategic change on areas where little value is added. For example, if a business discovers it is making a loss on delivery, it may decide to outsource delivery.

The value chain

The concept of the value chain developed by Michael Porter, a professor at Harvard Business School, is used in most businesses. Managing the value chain can produce sustainable competitive advantage:

> *Competitive advantage results from the business's ability to perform the required activities at a collectively lower cost than rivals, or perform some activities in unique ways that create buyer value and hence allow the business to command a premium price.*[3]

The value chain identifies five primary and four support activities (see Chart 6.5).

Chart 6.5 **The value chain**

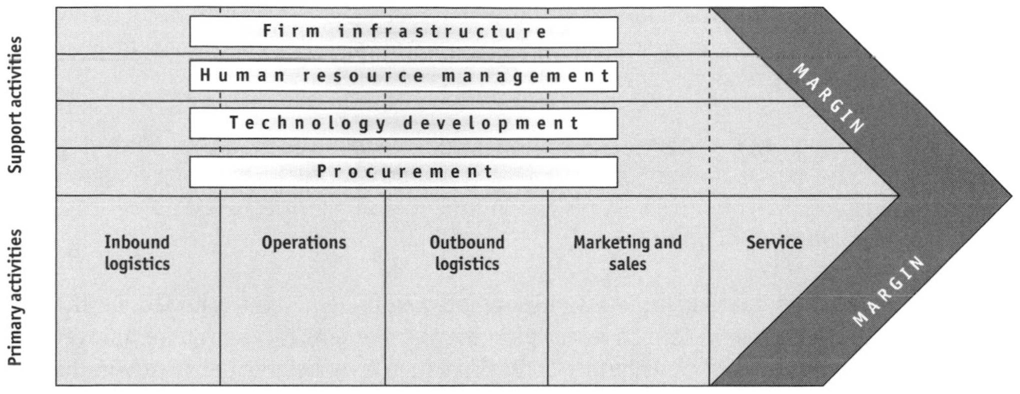

Source: Porter, M.E., *Competitive Advantage: Creating and Sustaining Superior Performance*, Free Press, 1985

The five primary activities are the sequential logistics, production and marketing processes. The primary activities can also be thought of as the main vertical functions of a business:

- Inbound logistics is the activity of receiving goods or services from suppliers and moving them on to the operations activity.
- Operations is where the production of the product or service takes place. Production may be broken down into further steps, for example producing intermediate goods from raw materials and then turning intermediate goods into the final product. Make or buy decisions can be made at every stage.
- Outbound logistics covers order fulfilment; that is, the warehousing of finished goods and the distribution of the products or service to the customer. This is often outsourced.
- Marketing and sales includes pricing, packaging and advertising as well as market research.
- Service refers mainly to after-sales service.

Support activities are horizontal; that is, they contribute to the different primary activities. For example, the human resources department will handle staffing for all functions. The value chain has four support activities:

- Firm infrastructure includes activities such as accounting, facilities, planning and control, and general administration.
- Human resources management covers recruitment, training, labour relations and salaries.
- Technology development includes the development of new products or services or enhancement of existing products and services. In some companies, research and development is a primary activity, for example in the pharmaceuticals industry.
- Procurement includes the purchasing of raw materials or intermediate goods as well as vehicles, office supplies and electricity. Again, because of its impact on input costs this activity may be considered primary.

A principal use of value chain analysis is to identify a strategy mismatch between different elements of the value chain. If a company competes on the basis of low costs, then every part of the value chain should be geared towards low cost. For example, low-cost airlines have looked at every aspect of the value chain and taken out costs at all stages. Bookings are taken only via the internet rather than through travel agents; seats cannot be reserved; there are no paper tickets, free meals and drinks, or lounges; and flights depart from secondary airports with lower landing fees.

An important aspect of the value chain is the linkage between the elements. For example, if stocks are to be kept to a minimum in order to respond quickly to changing consumer tastes, the business has to move towards just-in-time manufacturing, invest in logistics and pay particular attention to procurement.

The value chain is useful to identify activities where insufficient value is added, i.e. the return on capital employed is much lower than the average return on capital employed for the company as a whole, and to identify activities which may be cheaper to buy in than to produce in-house. For example, a manufacturing business has a return on average capital employed (ROACE) of 18%. Part of its operation is a chain of retail outlets. The ROACE from retailing is only 10%. The business could decide to withdraw from retailing and sell off the shops, thus releasing capital and generating a higher ROACE for the remaining business. As regards using the value chain analysis for cost reduction, it may be possible identify vertical activities that can be outsourced rather than produced in-house. Typical examples are call centres and logistics. Many banks outsourced call centres to low-wage countries such as India. Some major retailers decided that specialist logistics companies could transport goods to stores more efficiently. The value chain can also be used to examine whether a product should be made or bought in. In a particular strategic business unit the strength may be in marketing and sales and not in production.

The value chain as described by Porter has its limitations and should not be used slavishly. Your business may have a different value chain. For example, a trading business may just buy and sell and never handle any physical goods. Porter's value chain provides a framework for analysis that can be adapted to your particular business.

Charles Hofer and Dan Schendel[4] proposed a different value chain, which adds the dimension of value added (see Chart 6.6). The approach makes the value added by each element of the value chain explicit. The original model was geared towards a traditional manufacturing company. Again, the steps can be adapted to meet the needs of your business. The height of each function (R&D, inbound logistics, and so on) indicates the proportion of total value added.

Chart 6.6 **Value chain based on Hofer and Schendel**

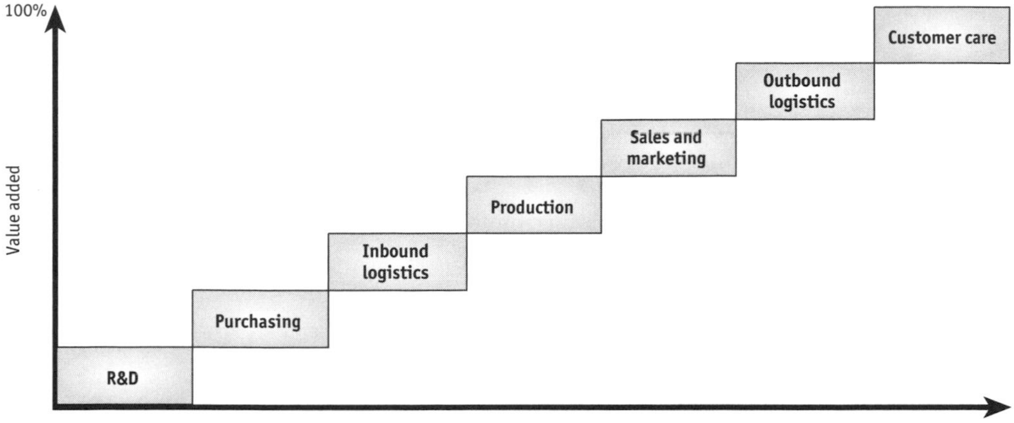

100%
Value added
R&D
Purchasing
Inbound logistics
Production
Sales and marketing
Outbound logistics
Customer care

Source: Hofer, C. W. and Schendel, D., *Strategy Formulation: Analytical Concepts*, 1978

Value system

The value system extends the value chain beyond the boundaries of the business and recognises that a business is dependent on relationships with suppliers and buyers. Competitors may have organised their value chain differently, for example they may have a lower degree of vertical integration, which could give them a cost advantage or make them more vulnerable.

Analysis of the value system may reveal that a source of competitive advantage for your business could be a better selection of suppliers, for example suppliers that have a labour cost advantage. Make or buy decisions are also affected by a downstream analysis of the value system, and the distribution strategy can be optimised by understanding the distribution value chain. For example, some manufacturers have their own retail outlets but also supply competing retailers. The question is whether or not such an arrangement produces competitive advantage.

Chart 6.7 **The value system**

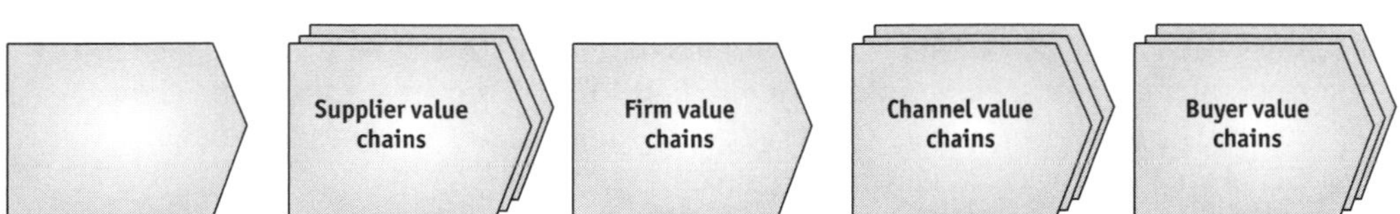

Source: Porter, M.E., *Competitive Advantage*, 1985

RESOURCE AUDIT

The resource audit should be undertaken in the context of the value chain. A business that makes optimum use of its operational, human, organisational and financial resources will gain competitive advantage.

The analysis of resources would encompass all or some of the following:

- Level of investment
- Utilisation
- Efficiency
- Stock levels
- Quality
- Lowering costs
- Degree of obsolescence because of technological or market change
- Scope for redeployment
- Flexibility, market adaptability

Operations resources

Operations resources, which consist of a variety of assets, not all of which may be recognised in the balance sheet, include:

- tangible assets such as plant and equipment, a branch network, office buildings;
- intangible assets such as brand names, rights, patents;
- operational methods and systems, for example a just-in-time manufacturing system or a flexible manufacturing system.

The identification of resources and whether they are put to good use may reveal astonishing waste. For example, in recent years, businesses have looked critically at the land and buildings they own. Leaseback deals and sell-offs have freed up substantial amounts of capital, and in some cases additional uses have been found for land and buildings.

An important task is to identify all resources that are not listed as assets on the balance sheet. There may be unused patents or rights, which could be employed in the value chain, licensed or sold off. In May 2003, for example:

> *Scottish Radio Holdings announced a multi-million pound recording deal with Universal Music after a spring clean turned up 600 forgotten recordings from artists such as U2, Rod Stewart and Elvis Costello. The archive consists of concert recordings broadcast by one of its stations, Radio Clyde, during the 1970s and early 1980s. The arrangement with Universal gave Scottish Radio Holdings royalties on CDs sold and provided a new income stream.*[5]

Human resources

As businesses become more knowledge based and dependent, human resources are increasingly viewed as a strategic asset. Annual reports of larger companies include information on human resources in an increasingly formalised manner. For example, in 2003 the Chartered Institute of Personnel and Development in the UK published a reporting framework on the value of human resources.

All businesses depend on their staff to succeed. For example, well-trained and motivated employees can make the difference between losing and retaining customers, and the cost of replacing lost customers can be high. An increasing number of businesses depend for their success on attracting and retaining a pool of increasingly talented people. To take account of these people assets, a human resource audit should be part of an analysis of the firm.

Chart 6.8 provides a checklist of the information you should collect about staff and managers and the impact they have on the business. The checklist should be used in conjunction with other elements of the resource audit, such as critical success factors.

The analysis may help to identify false economies, such as not investing in the training and retention of customer-care staff. For example, some businesses view sales as a profit centre but customer care as a cost centre, when, in most cases, it is cheaper to retain an existing customer than to acquire a new one. The human resource audit together with a value add analysis will bring this to light and allow a correction of strategy, allocating more resources to customer retention than to customer acquisition.

Chart 6.8 **Elements of human resource audit**

Staff and managers	*Organisational impact*
Recruitment	Leadership
Staff size	Know-how (core competencies)
Skill levels	Productivity
Leaders	Representation
Structures	Dependency
Labour relations	Culture
Salaries	Generation of new ideas
Training	Organisational change
Staff turnover	

The core competencies (see page 44) of a business may be embedded in its management and staff; in other words, the business is more successful than others because of its human capital. Skills are acquired over time and enhanced with investment in training. Concepts such as the "learning organisation" are based on this observation and underline the importance of human resources as part of an overall resource analysis.

Organisational resources

Organisational resources comprise the departmental structures and reporting systems of a business. A clearly set out organisation chart is a prerequisite for a good business plan. It is not possible to build a business plan without an organisational plan, which includes staffing and management control assumptions. In many businesses, staff and associated costs constitute the single biggest operating expense.

The purpose of analysing an organisation is to ensure that it can carry out its function, and that it is fit for its purpose and geared towards delivering value. Ideally, it should be possible to overlay or link the organisational structure with the objectives and the value chain.

Chapter 4 deals with the setting of objectives by which success or failure can be measured. Responsibilities have to be assigned to a person whose task it is to deliver the objectives. Responsibility for delivering value must be made visible in the organisation chart. For example, if the value chain shows that 30% of value added arises from a particular activity but no manager has been allocated direct responsibility for it, this must be corrected.

Different organisational forms and related aspects of the operational plan are covered in more detail in Chapter 13.

Financial resources

Financial resources include all forms of funding: capital, debt, loans, vendor finance and creditors. Return on capital employed is perhaps the final arbiter of how successful a business is. Financial resources are crucial to the development and survival of a business. Most strategic plans have some kind of growth objective. Any new business activity, even within an existing business, requires funding. Growth, even organic growth, usually results in a need for funding, if only increased working capital.

The different sources of finance and the optimisation of financial structures are covered in detail in Chapter 19.

Resource utilisation

Gerry Johnson and Kevan Scholes (1989)[6] pointed out that the operations resource audit must measure how efficiently resources are used and whether they are optimally configured to deliver value. The latter point relates to the value chain and is concerned with the effectiveness of resources.

Efficient use of operational resources

There are a number of measures of efficient utilisation of resources, such as capacity utilisation, stock turnover, yield, damage, sales per outlet or per salesperson, labour productivity, span of control, and so on.

- For many businesses, fixed assets are the most substantial part of the balance sheet. Fixed assets imply fixed costs and profitability becomes a function of utilisation. In industries such as passenger and freight transport, capacity utilisation is the single biggest factor in determining profitability.
- The efficiency of utilisation of inputs is important in certain types of industry. Measures could include energy efficiency, yield from raw materials or damage during transit. Energy efficiency is also important because it is part of the environmental responsibility statement.
- Labour productivity has a huge impact on producing competitive advantage. It is often cited as the single biggest factor in determining the competitiveness of countries. Measures can be specific to functions, for example turnover per salesperson, calls answered per call-centre operator, or units produced per production worker. Span of control (how many subordinates one manager controls) is a measure of management efficiency.
- Utilisation of overall financial resources is measured as return on capital employed

(see Chapter 17). Measures of working capital utilisation include stock turnover, how many days it takes to collect sales revenue from debtors (debtor days), and how many days' credit is taken from creditors (creditor days).

Once you have calculated the different measures of efficiency, you can set targets for improvement (setting targets is an important part of business planning) and, when the business is operating, track change. In doing this, you will want to know how efficient your business is relative to other businesses, which you can do by benchmarking (see Chapter 7).

Effective use of operational resources

When a resource is used effectively, it is much more valuable to the business. Some aspects you might investigate to determine how effectively resources are being used are as follows:

- Are intangible assets such as patents, rights and brands being used to their best advantage?
- Are any staff engaged in work below their level of capability or qualification (and consequently below their level of remuneration)? Redeployment could make effective use of their skills.
- Are you being too efficient? For example, you may have an excellent logistics system that delivers goods to customers within 24 hours of the order being placed. But if market research shows that customers would be happy if it took three days, you might consider reducing delivery resources.
- All aspects of the value chain must be working towards the same generic strategy (see Chapter 10). For example, if your business competes on the basis of cost leadership, then those involved in R&D should spend most of their time finding ways of making products cheaper rather than developing differentiated product features.

USES OF OUTCOMES IN THE BUSINESS PLAN

The analysis of the firm identifies the resources that are most important to the business and allows you to focus on the resources that are a source of competitive advantage. The value chain identifies how these resources are configured in order to ensure that resources are applied to maximise value added. The resource audit identifies unused and underused resources and provides measures of how efficiently and effectively resources are used.

Competitive advantage can only be achieved if resources are matched to the business environment. This means the analysis of a firm's resources is a requirement for strategy formulation. It enables you to identify resources that will have to be acquired in order to reach the objectives of the business plan.

The analysis of the firm is a prerequisite for strengths, weaknesses, opportunities and threats (SWOT) analysis and also many of the strategic management techniques that will be discussed in subsequent chapters.

References

1 Barney, J.B., "Firm Resources and Sustained Competitive Advantage", *Journal of Management*, Vol. 17, No. 1, 1991.

2 Dosi, G., Teece, D.J. and Winter, S., "Toward a Theory of Corporate Coherence: Preliminary Remarks", Working Paper, Center for Research in Management, University of California at Berkeley, 1990.

3 Porter, M.E., "Towards a Dynamic Theory of Strategy", *Strategic Management Journal*, Vol. 12, 1991.

4 Hofer, C.W. and Schendel, D., *Strategy Formulation: Analytical Concepts*, West Publishing Co., 1978.

5 *Financial Times*, May 15th 2003.

6 Johnson, G. and Scholes, K., *Exploring Corporate Strategy*, Prentice-Hall, 1989.

7 Industry and competitor analysis

OBJECTIVES

To develop a sound strategic plan for an existing or a new business it is necessary to understand the industry in which the business will operate and the competitive forces within that industry. Questions to be answered include the following:

- What is the current size and what are the major trends in the industry?
- What are the main competitive forces?
- Who are the competitors and what are their relative strengths?
- How should the strategy be adapted to respond to changes in the industry?

This chapter introduces different concepts and frameworks for industry and competitor analysis. These can be used at different levels of detail. The industry overview sets the scene for the readers of the business plan. The industry life cycle analysis provides an understanding of the degree of maturity of the industry. Structural analysis should include at least a short review of suppliers, buyers and the threat from new entrants and substitution, as well as a scan of competitors together with their strengths and weaknesses. Lastly, the main competitors should be analysed in more detail using a key success factor ranking.

INDUSTRY OVERVIEW

The first task is to collect some basic data about the sector you plan to operate in, including such relevant metrics as:

- annual sales in value for the last three years;
- annual unit or volume sales for the last three years;
- trend in prices for the last three years;
- a measure of capacity and possibly capacity utilisation.

Competitors should be identified by name and website and their market share should be listed. This should be combined into a measure of concentration, such as "the top 20% of competitors serve 80% of the market".

Broad industry information is often available from government statistics, including import and export figures. It is also useful to list relevant associations that have an impact on or seek to shape the future of the industry. Industry associations are often a convenient, low-cost source of information about the industry.

This basic industry information sets the scene for the reader of your business plan and provides the raw material for more detailed structural and competitor analysis.

THE INDUSTRY LIFE CYCLE

Industries evolve over time, both structurally and in terms of overall size. The industry life cycle (see Chart 7.1) is measured in total industry sales and the growth in total industry sales. The industry structure and competitive forces that shape the environment in which businesses operate change throughout the life cycle. Therefore a business's strategy must adapt accordingly. Chart 7.2 relates the industry life cycle to the five competitive forces:

- new entrants;
- buyers;
- suppliers;
- substitutes;
- rivalry among firms.

Chart 7.1 **Industry life cycle**

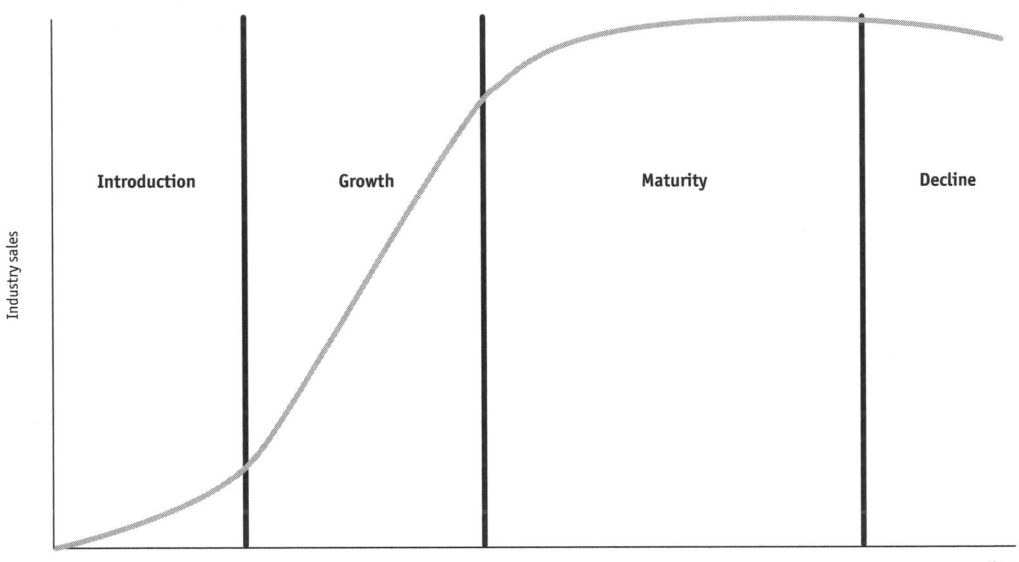

Chart 7.2 **Industry life cycle and competitive forces**

	Introduction	*Growth*	*Maturity*	*Decline*
New entrants	Few	Bandwagon effect	Consolidation	Exit
Power of buyers	Low	Very low, demand may be ahead of supply, it's a seller's market	Increasing	High, it's a buyer's market
Power of suppliers	Medium	High	Declining	Low
Threat from substitutes	Non-existent	Low	Growing	Substitutes may be the cause of decline
Rivalry among firms	Low	Low, focus on growth	Intense, as firms seek to continue to grow at the expense of rivals	Declining rivalry as some exit, firms realise that industry is declining

Introduction

In the introduction stage, there are few competitors and there is no threat from substitutes because the industry is so new. The power of buyers is low, because those who require the product are prepared to pay to get hold of the limited supplies. Suppliers exert some power, because volumes purchased are still low and the industry is relatively unimportant for suppliers.

Growth

In the growth stage, the number of competitors increases rapidly as other firms enter the growing industry. However, because at this stage growth in demand outstrips growth of capacity, rivalry among firms is kept in check. The power of buyers is still very low because demand exceeds supply. Often industry growth is associated with high profitability. Although at this stage firms may be profitable, they could still be cash absorbing and running risks as they jockey for position and market share.

Maturity

As the industry enters maturity, the power of buyers is increasing because capacity matches or exceeds demand. In contrast, the power of suppliers has declined because by now the volumes purchased by the industry are important to them. Losing a large customer could be very damaging to suppliers. The threat from substitutes is now growing. The industry will start to consolidate, possibly through mergers and acquisitions. Mature industries are settled, risks are low and cash is generated. However, rivalry among competitors is fierce and falling prices pose a serious threat to profitability.

Decline

The decline stage presents new challenges. Capacity exceeds supply thereby increasing the power of buyers. The weakest competitors will withdraw from the industry, leading to a decline in the rivalry among firms. At this stage firms may also combine forces to ask for government intervention or subsidies to help to protect the declining industry. The threat of substitutes is high; indeed substitutes are often the root cause of decline. However, if it is managed correctly, a slowly declining industry can produce attractive returns for investors because there is no new investment as the industry is gradually run down and milked for cash.

The industry life cycle is similar to the product life cycle (see Chapters 8 and 12) inasmuch as an industry is usually associated with a category of products. Industries such as shipbuilding grew to have enormous industrial importance, only to decline substantially as demand for ships fell.

The industry life cycle is not the same as the product life cycle, because within an industry there is a constant updating of products. For example, TV manufacturers first produced monochrome TVs and then colour TVs. Within the colour TV segment, the screen technology evolved from cathode ray displays to flat LCD or plasma screens and analogue receivers are being replaced by digital receivers.

ANALYSING THE STRUCTURE OF THE INDUSTRY

Understanding the structure of an industry is the basis for the formulation of competitive strategy. Michael Porter's work provides an analytical framework for the analysis of the structural factors that condition competition within an industry and suggests several generic competitive strategies, which are discussed in Chapter 10. Porter's 5 forces (see Chart 7.3) provide a framework for analysis of these structural factors.

Chart 7.3 **Forces driving industry competition**

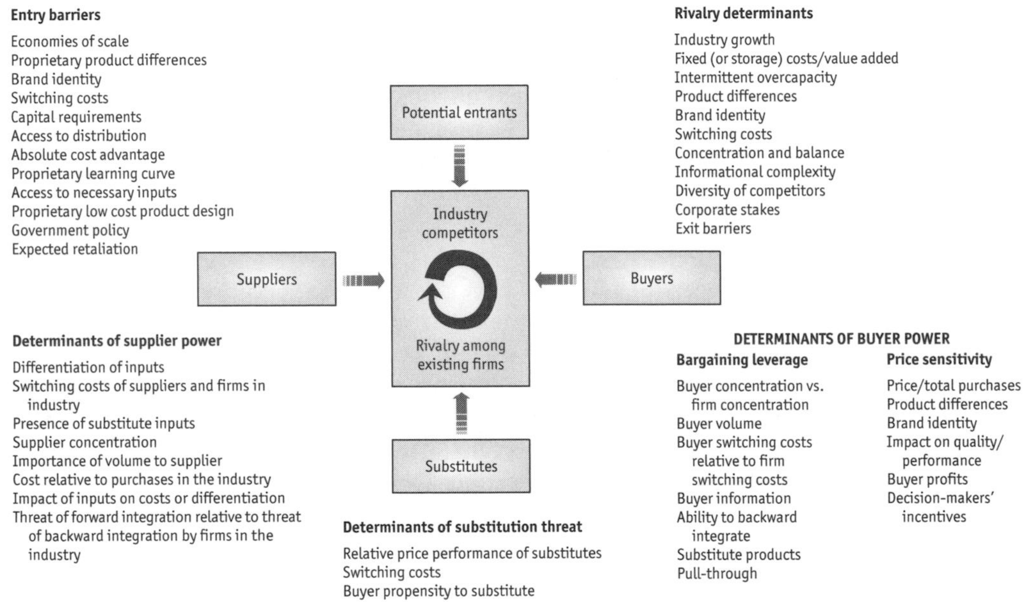

Source: Porter, M.E., *Competitive Advantage*, 1985

An industry is not a closed system. Competitors exit and enter, and suppliers and buyers have a major effect on the prospects and profitability of the industry. However, Porter points out that the structure of an industry will not change in the short term. Industry structure is something that irrespective of the general economic climate or short-term fluctuations in demand fundamentally affects return on investment. Structural change is slow and often associated with political and labour conflict. Structural factors are often cited as holding back development, and in some cases governments make funds available to mitigate social problems caused by structural change.

Rivalry among existing firms

The intensity of competition, or rivalry, will have a significant impact on the ability to generate adequate margins. The intensity of rivalry or competition among firms competing in the same industry depends on a number of factors:

- Industries with one dominant firm are generally more stable than fragmented industries where one competitor may try to achieve dominance.

- The degree of concentration or the extent to which the industry is monopolistic has an important effect on the behaviour of competitors. For example, in an oligopolistic situation price wars should be avoided. While avoiding price fixing, competitors can send out pricing signals to move towards a new level of lower or higher prices.
- If an industry stops growing, the only way any competitor can grow is by taking market share; in other words, competition will intensify until some competitors exit or consolidation takes place.
- In the case of commodity markets – those with undifferentiated products such as grain or computer RAM – competition focuses on price, which is particularly damaging to all manufacturers. Where there is scope for differentiation, price competition will be lower.
- In markets where products or services are perishable, competition becomes more intense when sales have to be made. An example is last-minute summer holiday bookings.

Potential entrants

New entrants to an industry add capacity, and if the capacity added is greater than growth in demand, this will reduce profitability. The threat of new entrants is low in cases where:

- industries are capital intensive;
- economies of scale are a key factor;
- access to resources is limited, for example mining concessions, limited radio spectrum, patents;
- access to distribution is problematic;
- buyers' switching costs are high.

New entrants may seek not to replicate the value chain of existing firms but to focus on certain activities where barriers to entry are lower. For example, a firm may enter the market for a product but subcontract the manufacturing to a low-cost producer and concentrate on R&D, sales and marketing, and distribution. A business that has achieved economies of scale in one industry may be able to apply these economies in another industry. An example would be an electricity retail distributor which starts to retail gas and telephone services, thus leveraging existing meter-reading staff and billing systems.

The objective of competitive strategy should be to deter new entrants if this is possible. Where scale economies matter, pricing is an important weapon. However, when pricing becomes predatory, regulators often step in to protect new entrants. In general, governments seek to foster competition and step in where structural factors prevent competition from emerging. An example is the ice cream industry in the UK, where certain manufacturers supplied freezers to retailers and prevented their use for other brands. Government intervention removed this barrier to entry. Incumbents must judge carefully how to use structural factors as a barrier to entry; used without political awareness, strategies that seek to prevent new entrants may backfire.

Substitutes

Substitute products are products that perform the same function or satisfy the same need as an existing product. The threat from substitute products is particularly severe if the substitute product is cheaper or more cost effective. Whole industries have been wiped out by substitutes, for example in Europe the silk industry was destroyed by viscose rayon.

A strategy to deal with competition from substitutes is to start making or supplying the substitute. A substitute may threaten only part of the value chain – actually making the product – but logistics, retailing and branding remain unaffected. Such a strategy is an option when dealing with manufactured products, but it can also work in the service sector. For example, on short intercity feeder routes such as Cologne to Frankfurt, the German airline Lufthansa offers a "flight" that is actually a train journey. Passengers find a fully functioning Lufthansa check-in counter at Cologne rail station where they receive their boarding passes to Frankfurt and onward airplane connections.

The definition of a substitute product can be wide and can include directly competing products and even unrelated products. Disposable incomes are finite, and all companies that sell products and services to consumers compete for the same limited pot of money. To deal with this, competitors in an industry may decide to pursue jointly a generic advertising campaign, such as a campaign for French wine in general rather than for any particular brand.

Bargaining power of suppliers

The balance of power between suppliers – which includes suppliers of labour – and the supplied industry is a function of the relative fragmentation. For example, in an industry with many small suppliers and few large buyers, the bargaining power of suppliers will be weak. Conversely, when there are few large suppliers their bargaining power will be strong.

In industries where inputs are commoditised and there is ample availability of substitutes, provided switching costs are reasonable, the ability of suppliers to raise prices is limited.

Certain strategies, such as just-in-time manufacturing, or even just holding low stocks, increase dependency on suppliers. To reduce the bargaining power of suppliers, strategies are to maintain a diverse base of suppliers or to make a few suppliers dependent on your business. But at the same time suppliers should not be squeezed too much. The relationship between the industry and its suppliers is symbiotic; it must work for both sides.

The operational expenditure of your profit and loss account (income statement) should be presented in sufficient detail to identify major expenditure categories. The bargaining power of suppliers for these services or goods should be addressed in detail, and ideally there should be an analysis of the trend in pricing.

Bargaining power of buyers

The prices you can obtain will have the biggest impact on the profitability of your business. In most cases, buyers shop around for best prices and thus exert downward pressure on prices. There are a number of factors that increase the power of buyers:

- Switching costs are low, which is generally the case with commodity products. Therefore the extent to which products can be differentiated will have a direct impact on prices. This is particularly true for consumer products where branding is a key differentiator.

- Buyers are large compared with the supplying industry. For example, farmers selling to a few big supermarket groups suffer from this.
- In business-to-business markets, buyers have the option of producing the product in-house; that is, they extend their value chain backwards. This is not only a credible threat, but it also increases a buyer's knowledge of the suppliers' costs. Knowledge of suppliers' costs considerably increases the bargaining position of buyers.

ANALYSING COMPETITORS

Rivalry among firms is the central force determining a business's competitive position. It is therefore necessary to analyse competitors in a similar way to how you would your own business. The elements of a competitor analysis are:

- current strategy or positioning;
- strengths;
- weaknesses;
- opportunities;
- threats;
- possible changes in strategy;
- reaction to changes in your business's strategy;
- financial strength;
- operational strength.

Of course, the analysis of competitors will be far less detailed than that of your own business, but any business strategy should demonstrate an awareness and understanding of the competition. Even if you are not yet in business, this analysis helps you and your investors to understand future rivals.

Analysis of direct competitors should start with a list of competing firms and their market share. This also provides a measure of industry concentration: what percentage of firms serve what percentage of the market. Your strategy will differ depending on whether the industry is fragmented or has two or three dominant players.

Profiles should be drawn up of the most important competitors. The current strategy or positioning of a competitor should be analysed by looking at the statement the company makes about itself and how it communicates with customers. Competitor positioning can be expressed in the context of Porter's generic competitive strategies; that is, does a competitor seek cost leadership? This analysis will also produce some insight into the strategic alternatives open to competitors and their possible reaction to your business's moves.

An important output of a competitor analysis should be a SWOT (strengths, weaknesses, opportunities and threats) analysis of the main competitors (see Chapter 9). Note that the opportunities and threats may not be the same as for your business. For example, increased regulation in the telecoms sector is aimed at large incumbent players, those deemed to have significant market power. It is a threat to the large incumbents but an opportunity for smaller players.

Competitor ranking by key success factors

David Aaker[1] proposed a model to rank a business against its competitors based on key success factors (KSF). He suggested that no more than ten KSFs should be used for which adequate information is available.

Once the KSFs are established they must be ranked. An importance weight should be assigned to each KSF with the sum of the weights adding up to 1. The weighting is judgmental and so requires a good understanding of the industry. Next, a strength rating is assigned to each KSF, ranging from 1 (weak) to 5 (strong). Again, this is a subjective process, but some proxies can be used if adequate numerical information is available. For example, the number of outlets a competitor has can be used as a proxy of relative strength in distribution. Lastly, the importance weight is multiplied by the strength rating to produce a score for each KSF for each competitor. Chart 7.4 shows an example for a hypothetical industry and gives an overall competitive strength score for each competitor (that is, the sum of the scores for each KSF). Because the importance weighting for the different KSFs totals 1, the maximum possible KSF score is 5.

Chart 7.4 **KSF competitor ranking**

		— Own business —		— Competitor A —		— Competitor B —		— Competitor C —	
KSF	*Importance weight*	*Strength rating*	*Firm strength*	*Strength rating*	*Firm strength*	*Strength rating*	*Firm strength*	*Strength rating*	*Firm strength*
Market share	0.25	4.0	1.0	3.0	0.8	1.5	0.4	1.2	0.3
Distribution	0.20	3.0	0.6	4.0	0.8	2.5	0.5	2.3	0.5
Brand image	0.16	4.0	0.6	3.9	0.6	2.0	0.3	5.0	0.8
Product quality	0.13	3.0	0.4	2.8	0.4	1.6	0.2	5.0	0.7
Product variety	0.11	5.0	0.6	3.9	0.4	3.0	0.3	1.0	0.1
Patents	0.08	4.0	0.3	4.0	0.3	2.0	0.2	4.0	0.3
R&D	0.04	4.0	0.2	4.0	0.2	2.0	0.1	4.0	0.2
Financial resources	0.03	5.0	0.2	4.0	0.1	3.0	0.1	2.0	0.1
Overall	1.00		3.8		3.6		2.1		2.9

The result of the KSF competitor ranking can be plotted on a chart (see Chart 7.5). The chart shows not only the relative overall competitive strength, but also the factors that contribute to it. In the example, your business could improve its competitive position dramatically if distribution was improved. Your nearest rival is weaker in almost all aspects except the second most important KSF, distribution. Management effort should therefore focus on this issue.

Chart 7.5 **KSF competitor comparison**

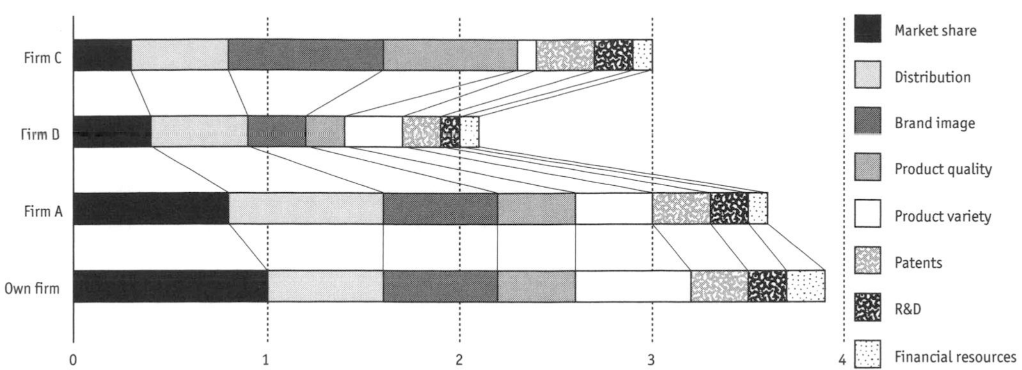

Sources of competitor information

It is easy to find information about competitors because they have to communicate with potential customers in order to sell to the market. The internet is a good place to start, enabling you to gather brochures, price lists, company reports, press cuttings, advertisements and so on. In many cases there will be too much information rather than too little.

Most small and medium-sized enterprises are incorporated and will have to file at least minimal accounts, which will be available from the relevant authority. For larger companies, annual reports and accounts and in many cases more detailed information such as analysis briefings are available on investor relations web pages. The information filed can be used to calculate key financial ratios and trends.

Do not forget to study the directors' report and other statements a competitor makes about itself. These often give a good picture of its corporate culture and overall strategic direction.

Benchmarking

The analysis of competitors also provides benchmarks against which a business plan can be measured. Benchmarks can be financial (balance sheet, profit and loss account) and operational ratios such as staffing ratios, number of sales per outlet and other relevant measures. Operational benchmarks are variables that are relevant to the industry in which a business operates, such as number of retail outlets, number of product lines, media advertising and so on. Some industries are driven by key ratios: for example, hotels measure occupancy rates, airlines measure load factors and TV channels measure viewer ratings.

Benchmarking is useful both for business planning and to develop strategic objectives:

- Typically, bankers and other financial investors will evaluate your business against known numbers from your competitors. If key ratios in your business plan are substantially different from the industry norm, you must provide a good reason for this.
- Competitor benchmarks can provide inputs for your business plan if you are unsure of what values to use.

- Benchmarks identify a best of class competitor and provide you with a target for improvement. For example, if a competitor achieves higher annual sales per retail outlet, this higher number can become an objective in your strategic plan. You know that it is achievable because a competitor has achieved it.

There are companies that specialise in providing industry financial ratios, such as Datastream, Dun & Bradstreet (Key Business Ratios), ValuationResources.com (www.valuationresources.com), BPIR.com (www.bpir.com) or BizMiner (www.bizminer.com). Banks and stock analysts also produce industry reports with benchmark data, but mostly on publicly quoted companies.

In some cases, competitors within an industry have formed a "benchmarking club". Benchmarking clubs are usually operated by a trusted third party. Typically, competitors would supply agreed operational statistics at certain intervals to the trusted third party. The trusted third party would compute values for the "best in class", the average and the worst, without identifying the company to which the data relates. This amalgamated data is fed back to all club members so that they can make a comparison on how well they are doing against competitors. The advantage is that the benchmarks are well defined and usually not available from any other source. The disadvantage of the approach is that the competitors are not identified.

The "Global Benchmarking Network" is another useful resource. It was established in 1994 by a group that includes the UK Benchmarking Centre, the SPI (USA), the SIQ (Sweden), the IZB (Germany) and the Benchmarking Club Italy "with the objective to achieve a consistent understanding of benchmarking as a management method and to promote its worldwide spread and utilisation". There are links to a number of benchmarking organisations and clubs around the world.

USES OF OUTCOMES IN THE BUSINESS PLAN

A business plan must demonstrate an awareness of the wider industry, the threats from new entrants and substitutes, and the competitive environment. An understanding of the strengths and weaknesses of your competitors will help to define your business's strategic options.

At the very least your business plan should contain all relevant metrics, such as total industry sales value and volumes for the size of the industry and the trend, as well as a list of competitors and their market share.

Detailed financial and operational ratios from competitors will provide a set of benchmarks that can be used to make comparisons with your own business plan and eliminate any assumptions that are implausible. Benchmarks can also be useful in quantifying objectives for your business.

Reference

1 Aaker, D., "How to select a Business Strategy", *California Management Review*, Vol. XXVI, No. 3, 1984

8 Product and portfolio analysis

OBJECTIVES

To investigate the competitive position of your business's products or strategic business units (SBUs) in the context of market development. By displaying products or a portfolio of products in a matrix fashion, insight is gained into the strategic position of the products, the likely direction in which they are developing, the cash flow implications and pointers as to what strategies should be pursued.

The analytical approaches covered in this chapter are:

- Experience curve and scale economies
- Product life cycle stage analysis
- Growth-share matrix
- Directional policy matrix
- Hofer matrix

Portfolio analysis is mostly relevant for existing, larger businesses with multiple products. For such businesses, matrix displays are helpful in making strategic decisions about the allocation of limited cash resources among a portfolio of products. Some products require further cash investments, some generate cash and others may have to be divested. This is an input into the generation of strategic options, which is addressed in Chapter 10.

Matrix displays can be generated for your business as well as for competitors. The displays can be used to make strategic comparisons between your business and competitors. This allows you to anticipate likely strategic moves by competitors and plan your own moves.

THE EXPERIENCE CURVE AND ECONOMIES OF SCALE

In most businesses, there is a relationship between volume and cost as a result of two factors: the experience curve and economies of scale effects.

Research by the Boston Consulting Group, a business consulting firm, showed that there is a relationship between cumulative production volume and unit costs. Unit costs decline in a predictable manner as the cumulative quantity produced over time increases. The mathematics of the experience curve and its application in forecasting are discussed in Chapter 12. The main reason for the experience curve effect is that the organisation and people within the organisation learn how to do things better. Initially, substantial benefit is derived from this learning process, but it diminishes over time. It should be noted that this effect does not depend on production volumes increasing. Even if production remains static, over time costs will decline.

Economies of scale effects occur when production volumes increase. There are several reasons for scale effects:

- Fixed and overhead costs can be distributed over a larger number of units.
- Plant and machinery may operate more efficiently at larger volumes.
- Increased bargaining power vis-à-vis suppliers.
- Increased specialisation.
- Potentially a higher utilisation of capacity.

In practice, the experience curve effect and the economies of scale effect work together. When a new product is launched volumes are small, but they increase rapidly. If a company achieves higher production volumes more quickly than its rivals, it will experience lower unit costs. As a result, it could offer lower prices, thus increasing market share even further (see Chart 8.1). Therefore market share is of overriding importance when assessing the strategic imperatives of product life cycle, portfolio and matrix analysis.

Chart 8.1 **The virtuous circle of volume and cost**

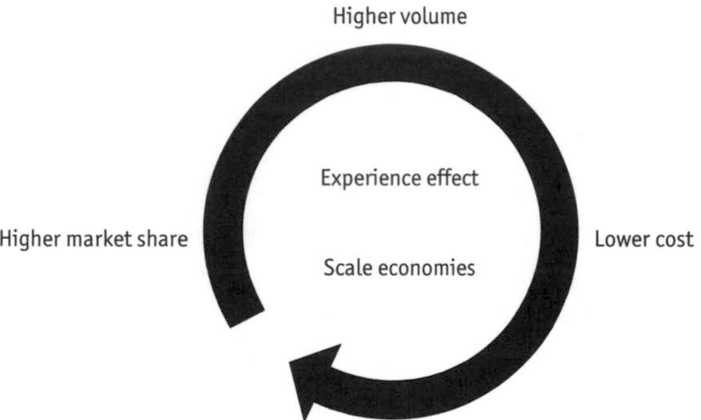

An important aspect of portfolio analysis, which is discussed in detail below, is market share. The importance of market share in a mass market derives from the ability to pursue a cost leadership strategy and thus achieve higher overall returns on investments because of high-volume sales. Market share is therefore a key determinant of business position.

PRODUCT LIFE CYCLE STAGE ANALYSIS

The growth pattern for many products follows an s-shaped curve, from an introduction stage, through growth, then reaching maturity and eventually declining when the product is being replaced with substitutes. A similar life cycle can be observed for whole industries (see Chapter 7). The product life cycle concept has several uses, notably for market forecasting, which is covered in Chapter 12. This chapter discusses the product analysis and business planning implications of the product life cycle concept.

From the introduction to the withdrawal of a product, customer, demand, marketing, competitive and resource factors generally follow a pattern that is driven by the product life cycle. Knowing where a product is in the product life cycle allows you to anticipate and plan for the next stage. Chart 8.2 summarises the product life cycle characteristics and the impact on strategy.

Chart 8.2 **Product life cycle characteristics and strategies**

	Introduction	*Growth*	*Maturity*	*Decline*
Users/sales	Few	Increasing rapidly	Settling in	Declining
Costs	High R&D, unit and launch costs	Falling rapidly, utilisation, scale and experience effects	Declining production costs but higher marketing costs	Stabilising
Competitors	Few	New entrants, innovator may sell out	Consolidation	Some exit
Marketing objective	Successful introduction, gain opinion leader endorsement	Build market share by focusing on new customers and creating distinct brand image	Retain customers, get customers to switch, renewals and upgrades, extend life cycle, increase frequency of use, new product uses, cost reduction	Further reduce costs and exploit product or brand
Product	Basic, little variety, quality not high, frequent design changes	Increasing variety and features, good quality and reliability	Stable, standardisation, some tinkering, eg, "new improved xyz"	Declining variety, no further development
Prices	High, price-skimming strategy, introductory offers	Falling slowly, supply constraints may keep prices high	Falling rapidly, discounts, price competition	Stabilising, increasing in late decline stage
Promotion	Promote product, build awareness, user education, press relations, high advertising to sales ratio	Mass-market advertising, increased focus of brand	Focus on brand and its advantages, loyalty, bundling, affinity	Scaled down brand promotion
Place	Specialist retailers, dealers who can give advice, exclusivity deals	Mass-market channels, large multiples	Mass-market channels, large multiples, power of channels increases	Phase out marginal outlets, some multiples may de-list, specialisation
Cash flow	Negative	Break even	Positive	Positive, but declining
Profitability	Losses	Profitable	Margins decline, but offset by volume	Declining margins offset by low depreciation charges, possible write-downs
Risk	High business risk	Low demand side risk, but cash flow risks	Low business risk, cyclical factor impact	Low business risk, labour conflict in unionised industries

Introduction

The introduction stage is the period before sales start to increase exponentially. It is the riskiest stage and requires most management effort. The business will have already committed substantial resources. Despite convincing market research, the product may fail the test of the real market. There is still the opportunity to fine-tune the marketing mix or even relaunch the product. If there are early signs of success and sufficient resources are available, managers may opt for penetration pricing, thereby driving up volume and capturing market share before competitors enter the market. However, this increases risk and failure will be catastrophic.

Growth

A rapid acceleration of sales signals the start of the growth stage, which can be divided into the accelerating growth stage and the decelerating growth stage. In the accelerating growth stage, the incremental year-on-year sales increase. In the decelerating growth stage, sales are still growing but year-on-year incremental sales decline. The dividing point between the two is the point of inflection in the s-shaped product life cycle curve.

As the business changes to become more volume driven, the risks profile changes. Demand for the product is now proven and competitors enter the market. The expansion requires investment in capacity and working capital. The early growth stage may coincide with the highest funding requirement. Many businesses fail during the expansion stage, not because they are unprofitable but because they become insolvent. A strategy for a smaller entrepreneur may be to sell out to a larger, later entrant. The rationale for seeking a buy-out is not just access to resources. The introduction stage and the growth stage require different kinds of organisation and skills. Indeed, many business plans have an explicit exit strategy, seeking to sell out once the business is in the early growth stage.

In the early growth stage the focus is usually on winning new customers. This stage is crucial to positioning the product as a market leader. In the late growth stage more attention is given to customer retention.

Maturity

At this stage the focus shifts to a fight for market share and cost reduction. Some consolidation may take place. Because growth objectives remain, businesses may seek to increase sales through a higher repeat sales rate, increased frequency of use or finding new uses for an existing product. For example, faced with declining sales in an ageing market, Cognac producers started to promote drinking Cognac on ice (much to the horror of traditionalists) as an aperitif rather than a digestif. This rejuvenated Cognac by making it attractive to younger drinkers and gave Cognac a new use.

Decline

When decline sets in, the time for consolidation is probably past. The least efficient competitors will gradually exit the market. Management is likely to focus on cost reduction in order to maintain profitability despite declining sales. Some assets may be reallocated. Businesses can become highly cash generating, because capital investment is low and some working capital is freed up. A re-reorganisation and change of management style are likely. In moribund, large, unionised businesses it may be extremely difficult to exit profitably because exit costs are high. Demand for some products does not die away completely but settles down at a low level. This can constitute an extremely profitable niche business.

Product life cycle and competitive position

Arthur D. Little, a management consulting firm, suggested using the product life cycle analysis in combination with the competitive position. This yields pointers as to what strategies should be pursued for the business or the SBU (Chart 8.3). In this analysis, the product life cycle stages are replaced by industry maturity stages – embryonic, growth, mature and ageing – which correspond to the product life cycle stages identified above. The competitive position is measured as dominant, strong, favourable, tenable and weak. A dominant position implies a near monopoly whereas a weak position means that a business's long-term survival is threatened as a result of low market share.

Conceptually, the matrix is similar to the growth-share matrix and directional policy matrix (see below), inasmuch as the market growth rate is an indication of industry maturity and market share is one factor in determining the business position. The strategies suggested by the industry maturity/competitive position matrix are also similar to the implication of the directional policy matrix and are discussed in more detail below.

The fact that strategic choice is more complex than the strategies suggested by the matrix analysis is captured by the fact that each box contains multiple options in descending order of suitability. There may well be overriding reasons, not captured by the two-factor matrix, for a business to pursue one strategy rather than another.

Chart 8.3 **Industry maturity: competitive position matrix**

	STAGES OF INDUSTRY MATURITY			
COMPETITIVE POSITION	Embryonic	Growth	Mature	Ageing
Dominant	Fast growth Start-up	Fast growth Attain cost leadership Renew Defend position	Defend position Attain cost leadership Renew Fast growth	Defend position Focus Renew Grow with industry
Strong	Start-up Differentiate Fast growth	Fast grow Catch-up Attain cost leadership Differentiate	Attain cost leadership Renew Focus Differentiate Grow with industry	Find niche Hold niche Hang in Grow with industry Harvest
Favourable	Start-up Differentiate Focus Fast growth	Differentiate Focus Catch-up Grow with industry	Harvest, hang in Find niche, hold niche Renew, turnaround Differentiate, focus Grow with industry	Retrench Turnaround
Tenable	Start-up Grow with industry Focus	Harvest, catch up Hold niche, hang in Find niche Turnaround Focus Grow with industry	Harvest Turnaround Find niche Retrench	Divest Retrench
Weak	Find niche Catch up Grow with industry	Turnaround Retrench	Withdraw Divest	Withdraw

Source: Johnson, G. and Scholes, K., *Exploring Corporate Strategy*, Prentice-Hall, 1989, from Arthur D. Little

GROWTH-SHARE MATRIX

The original growth-share matrix was developed by the Boston Consulting Group and is also referred to as the BCG box. The purpose of the matrix is to analyse a firm's product portfolio or portfolio of SBUs. The matrix relates market growth (the key variable in the product life cycle stage analysis) to relative market share. The objective of the analysis is to gain strategic insight into which products require investment, which should be divested and which are sources of cash.

The growth-share matrix (Chart 8.5) is constructed by plotting the market growth rate as a percentage on the vertical axis and the relative market share on the horizontal axis. Relative market share rather than absolute market share is used because it gives a better representation of the relative market strength of competitors. For example, if company A has 50% of the market for a particular product and there are two competitors, B with 40% and C with 10%, relatively speaking B's position is close to A. The relative market share for a business is calculated by dividing the sales of the business by that of its largest competitor. In the example, A's relative market share is 1.25 and B's is 0.80. A firm's portfolio of products is represented as circles, where the area of the circle represents annual sales of a product. Most spreadsheet programmes have the facility to create a growth-share matrix. Chart 8.5 was generated with the data shown in Chart 8.4 using the bubble chart option in Excel.

Chart 8.4 **Chart data for the growth-share matrix**

Product	*Relative share (%)*	*Market growth (%)*	*Annual sales ($m)*
Sky blue	4.0	4	100
Dark blue	0.2	1	50
Red	2.0	10	110
Purple	0.4	8	170
Green	0.6	18	40
Yellow	6.0	18	180
Orange	0.2	13	15

Chart 8.5 **Growth-share matrix**

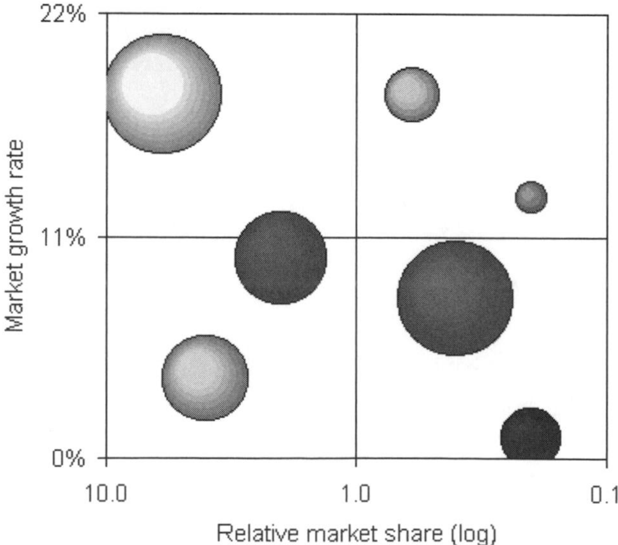

Using the growth-share matrix for strategic planning

The growth-share matrix allows you to visualise which products are cash generating and which are cash-absorbing. This is helpful to understanding where resources should be allocated to change the strategic position of products or which products should be divested. Depending on the position of the products, they are classified as stars, problem children, dogs or cash cows (see Chart 8.6).

Chart 8.6 **Cash characteristics and classification of product portfolio**

RATE OF MARKET GROWTH %

	High relative market share	Low relative market share
High	CASH NEUTRAL Star	CASH ABSORBING Problem child
Low	Cash cow CASH GENERATING	Dog CASH NEUTRAL

High Low
RELATIVE MARKET SHARE (LOG)

Star

Stars have a high relative market share in a rapidly growing market; they are in the introduction or growth stage of the product life. Although gross margins are likely to be excellent and generate cash, the rapid growth means more cash is required to fund marketing and capacity additions. This means cash outflows and inflows are roughly balanced. If the business fails to spend to keep pace with market growth, the product will lose market share and become a problem child and eventually a dog. However, if the position is maintained through continued investment, the product will turn into a cash cow when market growth slows down.

Problem child

A problem child product creates a dilemma. The rapid market growth means investment is required. However, if investment is made only to keep up with market growth, the competitive position of the product will not be improved. In order to gain relative market share, additional cash is required, making problem children highly cash absorbing. The alternatives are to divest or to do nothing. Divestment will generate cash, which can be used, for example, to transform other problem children into stars. Although the market is still growing rapidly, it may be possible to sell the problem child for a good price to a rival who is in the same position. The combined market share may turn two problem children into one star. Doing nothing is probably the worst choice, because eventually the product becomes a dog.

Dog

Dogs are products with a low market share in a market that has reached maturity. Profits will be relatively low. At this stage it will be difficult to find a buyer for a reasonable price. As long as the product is slightly cash generating or cash neutral, the temptation may be to keep it going, but of course it ties up capital. Another strategy might be to reposition the product into a particular niche, where volumes may be even lower but a premium price can be obtained.

Cash cow

Cash cows are products with a high market share in a relatively mature market. No further investment in growth or product development is required, and the dominant market position means margins are likely to be high. This makes the product cash generating. Some funds are likely to be returned to investors in the form of dividends or by paying back debt, but a substantial part of the cash should be used to fund new product development, stars or problem children. However, as decline sets in, cash cows will become less cash generating and may eventually die.

Portfolio strategy

Fundamentally, there is little businesses can do about the market growth rate. This is implicit in the product life cycle curve. In other words, movement along the growth axis is an externality. However, position and movement along the relative market share axis is the result of management action relative to the action of rivals. Ideally, a product enters the matrix on the upper left-hand corner and gradually moves to the lower left-hand corner.

The growth rate is highest in the early stages of the product life cycle (see Chart 8.7), so all products start at the top of the matrix. Ideally, products are first stars and then become cash cows. During the introduction stage of the product life cycle, growth rates are high and continue to be relatively high during the early growth stage. The early growth stage is defined as the period between the introduction and the point where volume growth is no longer increasing but starts to decrease. It is important to distinguish between the percentage growth rate and growth in absolute terms. The growth rate declines throughout the product life cycle, but growth in volume terms increases to a peak before declining (see Chart 8.8). This is the point of inflection in the product life cycle curve.

Chart 8.7 **Sales volume and growth rate**

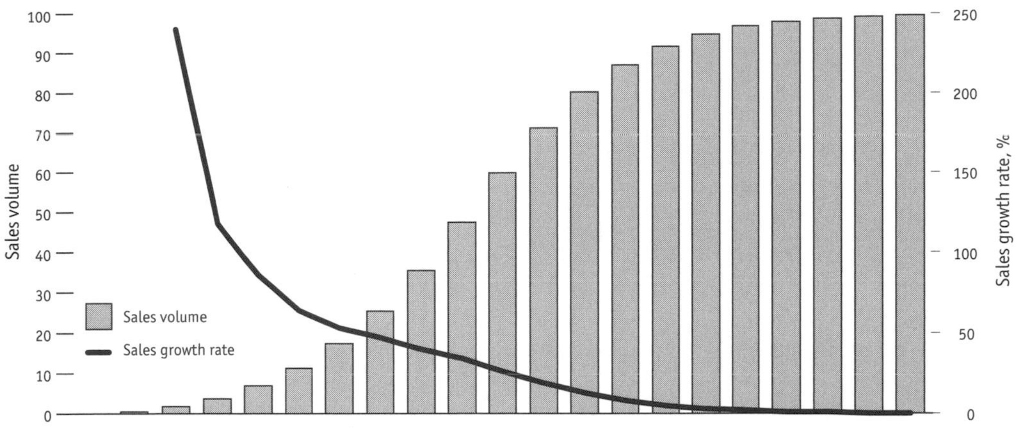

Chart 8.8 **Point of inflection in market growth**

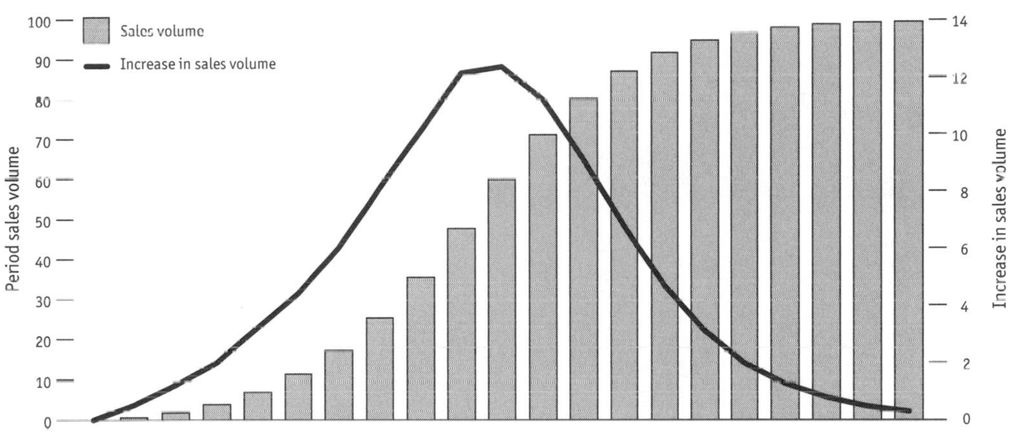

While markets are growing rapidly and overall volumes are still small, differences in market share are not very important. However, as the market moves into the late growth stage, it becomes increasingly more difficult to win market share. You should therefore have manoeuvred the product into a star position before reaching the point of inflection, or it will be in danger of becoming a problem child and eventually a dog.

Irrespective of your efforts, some products may become problem children. If a business also has cash cows, funds can be used to transform a problem child into a star (see Chart 8.9 on the next page). Alternatively, the problem child can be divested and the funds used to grow a new star. Most products will eventually reach the decline stage of the product life cycle. This means standing still is not an option for most businesses. A balanced product portfolio should include cash cows and stars, and possibly problem children that can be turned into stars. The cash generated from cash cows funds stars and problem children as well as returning money to shareholders and bondholders.

Because cash cows will eventually enter the decline stage of the product life cycle where they no longer generate much cash, there must be a flow of new products. The development of new products is financed by cash cows. Given that funding is a significant constraint, maintaining a balanced portfolio must include a product development pipeline or the business will cease to exist.

Generally, cash cow products will have a large sales volume (represented by a larger than average circle in the matrix), because the market is mature and because the product has a high relative market share. This means the volume of cash generated will be correspondingly large. This needs to be the case because one cash cow has to fund several new products, of which some may not make it to launch and others may become dogs.

Chart 8.9 **Strategic movement of portfolio products and cash**

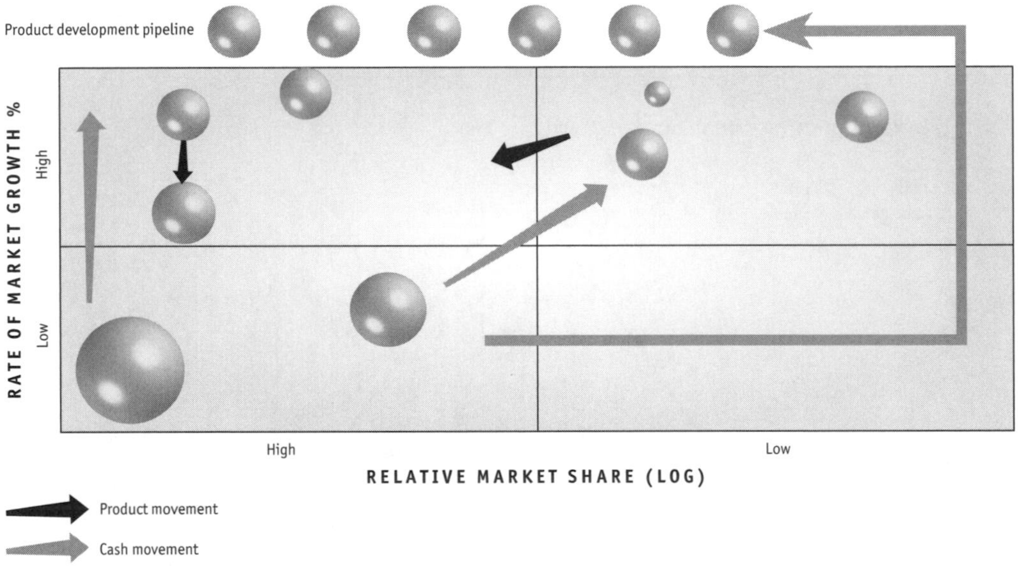

Plotting product movements over time

Ideally, you will carry out an annual strategic planning exercise so you should have a time series of matrix displays. This means you will be able to track the movement of your portfolio over time and thus obtain feedback on how well strategies have been working. This can lead to a reappraisal of strategic choices.

DIRECTIONAL POLICY MATRIX

A limitation of the growth-share matrix is that it relies only on two factors: the market growth rate and relative market share. Market growth is only one factor that affects business prospects. Similarly, relative market share is only one aspect of the business position. The directional policy matrix seeks to overcome this limitation by including many more factors (see Chart 8.10 on page 76). In doing so, the exercise becomes less numerical and involves judgment.

Joseph Guiltinan and Gordon Paul developed the directional policy matrix while working at Shell Corporate Planning during the late 1970s. It is based on the growth-share matrix (see above), originally developed by the Boston Consulting Group, but the work done at Shell enhanced the perspective specifically with a view to managing a portfolio of products competing for limited funds within Shell. The method of developing a directional policy matrix shown here is based on Patrick McNamee's *Tools and Techniques for Strategic Management.*[1]

In the directional policy matrix, the vertical axis is used to map business-sector prospects and the business position is plotted against the horizontal axis. Completion of a directional policy matrix involves considerable environmental and resource analysis. The evaluation factors used to generate the data for the directional policy matrix could be limited to the critical success factors or could be a broader collection of factors. The list provided in Chart 8.10 is only indicative and should be adapted to meet the industry's and your firm's particular circumstances.

Quantification of business-sector prospects and business position

The factors identified in Chart 8.10 on the next page must be converted into values so that the products or SBUs can be positioned in the directional policy matrix. This requires judgment, so this method is more subjective than the growth-share matrix. Subjectivity is not necessarily a bad thing, because it involves thinking through the issues affecting the business in a structured manner. Clearly, businesses are not managed by just two numbers but by an understanding of the wider environment and the business position in that environment.

The same method is used to quantify the business-sector prospects and the business position.

1 An importance score is assigned to each factor. The importance scale ranges from 0 to 5. A factor with a zero importance score could be omitted for the purposes of the calculation, but it is still valuable to record the fact that a particular factor is of no importance and has not just been missed.
2 A score is assigned to indicate the strength of the influence of the factor on your firm's product or SBU. The scale ranges from –5 to +5. A negative number indicates a negative influence.
3 The two scores for each factor are multiplied to produce a total score for business-sector prospects and the business position for your firm's product.
4 The score achieved by your firm's product is expressed as a percentage of the maximum score (all scores set to +5 and totalled). This produces the co-ordinates to position the product on the matrix. The area of the circles should be proportional to the annual sales value of the product.

The scale on the axis of the matrix ranges from –100% to +100%: –100% is the worst possible business-sector prospect and –100% is the worst possible business position; +100% indicates the best business-sector prospect and strongest business position. Charts 8.11 (page 77), 8.12 (page 78) and 8.13 (page 79) provide an example of how to calculate and display a particular product for a company.

Chart 8.10 **Factors for evaluation in a directional policy matrix**

Business sector prospects

Market factors

Market size
Market growth
Price elasticity
Product life cycle stage
Cyclicality
Bargaining power of suppliers
Bargaining power of buyers

Competitive environment

Degree of concentration
Threat from new entrants
Exits
Consolidation
Vertical integration
Threat from substitutes

Technology factors

Scope for innovation
Speed of change
Product diversity
Complexity
Differentiation
Flexible manufacturing
Capacity utilisation
Patents and copyrights

Financial and economic factors

Margins
Fixed versus marginal costs
Trend in input costs
Capital intensity
Contribution
Share prices
Cost of capital
Synergies

Political factors

Social trends
Barriers to exit
Subsidies
Regulation and legislation
Environmental impact
Threat of litigation
Pressure groups

Business position

Marketing factors

Market share
Relative market share
Sales growth
Relative product quality
Image
Brand
Product diversity
Relative maturity
Positioning
Distribution strength

Technology factors

R&D strength
Product development pipeline
Patents and rights
Manufacturing technology
Degree of flexible manufacturing
Scalability

Production

Cost relative to competitors
Scope for cost reduction
Capacity utilisation
Inventory
Degree of vertical integration

Organisational factors

Relative skill level
Stakeholder interest and backing
Attitude to risk
Strategic interests
Union reaction

Financial factors

Margin
Contribution to profit
Cash flow
Cost of capital
Access to funding
Capital structure
Capital intensity
Fixed versus marginal costs
Potential impairment charges
Taxation

Chart 8.11 **Quantification of business-sector prospects**

Factor	*Importance*	*Strength*	*Score*
Market factors			
Market size	5	2	10
Market growth	4	3	12
Price elasticity	2	–3	–6
Product life cycle stage	4	2	8
Cyclicality	0	0	0
Bargaining power of suppliers	2	3	6
Bargaining power of buyers	3	–1	–3
Competitive environment			
Degree of concentration	3	–2	–6
Threat from new entrants	1	–1	–1
Exits	1	2	2
Consolidation	2	–4	–8
Vertical integration	2	1	2
Threat from substitutes	5	–4	–20
Technology factors			
Scope for innovation	1	1	1
Speed of change	2	–2	–4
Product diversity	3	2	6
Complexity	4	5	20
Differentiation	3	–2	–6
Flexible manufacturing	3	–5	–15
Capacity utilisation	4	4	16
Patents and copyrights	0	0	0
Financial and economic factors			
Margins	4	3	12
Fixed versus marginal costs	5	5	25
Trend in input costs	4	–1	–4
Capital intensity	5	5	25
Contribution	5	3	15
Share prices	3	2	6
Cost of capital	3	2	6
Synergies	0	0	0
Political factors			
Social trends	3	5	15
Barriers to exit	4	–3	–12
Subsidies	0	0	0
Regulation and legislation	2	–1	–2
Environmental impact	2	–1	–2
Threat of litigation	1	–1	–1
Pressure groups	1	–1	–1
Total score			96
Maximum possible score			480
Percentage score			20

Chart 8.12 **Quantification of business position**

Factor	*Importance*	*Strength*	*Score*
Marketing factors			
Market share	5	5	25
Relative market share	4	–1	–4
Sales growth	1	1	1
Relative product quality	4	2	8
Image	3	1	3
Brand	3	3	9
Product diversity	0	0	0
Relative maturity	5	2	10
Positioning	4	3	12
Distribution strength	2	1	2
Technology factors			
R&D strength	2	1	2
Product development pipeline	1	0	0
Patents and rights	0	0	0
Manufacturing technology	4	3	12
Degree of flexible manufacturing	5	5	25
Scalability	3	–2	–6
Production			
Cost relative to competitors	5	2	10
Scope for cost reduction	5	4	20
Capacity utilisation	5	2	10
Inventory	2	–2	–4
Degree of vertical integration	0	0	0
Organisational factors			
Relative skill level	2	0	0
Stakeholder interest and backing	3	–2	–6
Attitude to risk	2	–4	–8
Strategic interests	3	–2	–6
Union reaction	2	–4	–8
Financial factors			
Margin	3	–2	–6
Contribution to profit	4	1	4
Cash flow	3	–1	–3
Cost of capital	3	–2	–6
Access to funding	1	–2	–2
Capital structure	0	0	0
Capital intensity	4	–2	–8
Fixed versus marginal costs	4	2	8
Potential impairment charges	0	0	0
Taxation	0	0	0
Total score			94
Maximum possible score			485
Percentage score			19

Chart 8.13 **Directional policy matrix**

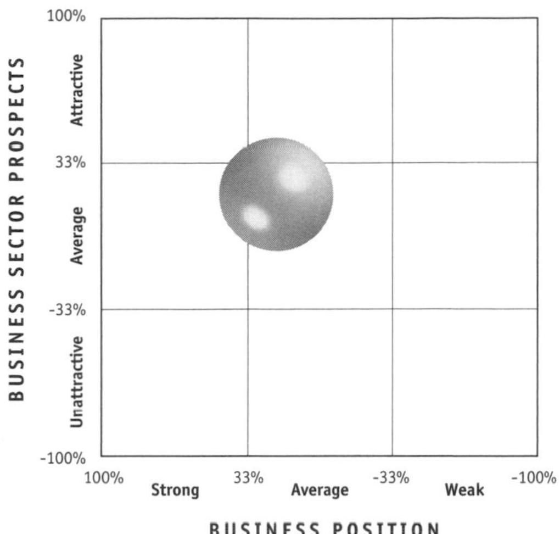

Using the directional policy matrix to develop strategic direction

The nine squares in the directional policy matrix and the labels assigned to it (see Chart 8.14) are similar to those in the growth-share matrix, but they provide a finer degree of analysis. The labels provide an indication as to what strategic directions may be most appropriate for a particular product or SBU.

Chart 8.14 **Strategic directions**

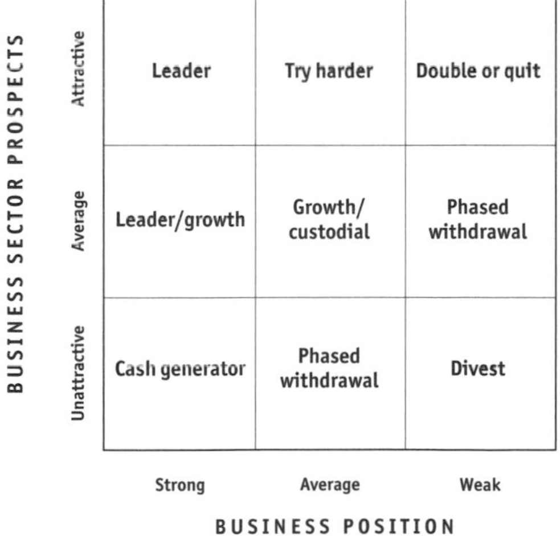

Leader

This is the position that is most likely to generate the highest return on investment in the longer term. It is similar to the star in the growth-share matrix. A product in this category is well positioned with regard to the most important industry attractiveness factors. Rapid market growth is probably one of the reasons for its attractiveness, so the product will require investment in capacity and marketing, for example brand building and distribution channel development. If the position as leader is maintained, the product will become a cash generator.

Try harder

A product in this category is not the market leader but it has a good chance of catching up. The market is still growing fast and positions can change. To move the product to the leader box, additional cash above that required to keep up with market growth is required.

Double or quit

Here the chances of catching up with the market leader are slimmer. The product is in an attractive market but its position is weak. Substantial investment is required to improve the business position and success is not guaranteed. The easier option may be to divest, by selling out to a competitor whose product is in the try harder box, for example. It is highly likely that the net present value of a product to a competitor is higher than it is to your business. In other words, you would maximise your return on investment by selling out.

Leader/growth

These products are leaders in a market of medium attractiveness. To ensure that they do not lose their business attractiveness, some investment is required. If the position is maintained, they are likely to become cash generators.

Growth/custodial

A product in this category has good business-sector prospects and there are no particular business advantages. Sales are likely to be too large to reposition the product as a niche player. Given that sector prospects are only average, a holding strategy may be appropriate. This is likely to release some cash, but returns will be below average.

Phased withdrawal

Products that are either in an unattractive market and have only an average business position or in an average market but with a weak business position fall into this category. In both cases returns are below average. Although these products are probably cash generating, they can easily turn into the growth-share matrix dog and become a drain on resources. The best strategy may be to withdraw the product and reallocate resources.

Cash generator

Products in this category are similar to the cash cow products. They are in a relatively unattractive market but with an excellent competitive position. Because business prospects are not good, making further investments is not recommended. The strong competitive position means that cash flow will be highly positive. However, in the directional policy matrix the business prospect does not depend on growth rates alone. Other factors may be responsible for the unattractive business prospect, such as a reduction in import tariffs which may allow the market to be flooded with cheap imports.

Divest
This is the least enviable position. The product's business-sector prospects are bleak, its business position is weak, and it is likely to lose money. This is a true dog identified in the growth-share matrix. The best strategy is to divest the product. It is unlikely that a high price could be obtained in these circumstances, but at least the cash haemorrhage could be stopped. Shutdown and write-off may be the only alternative.

THE BUSINESS/INDUSTRY ATTRACTIVENESS SCREEN

Following the development of the directional policy matrix, McKinsey & Co, a management consultancy, developed a similar approach working with General Electric (GE). The matrix is commonly known as the GE business/industry attractiveness screen (see Chart 8.15) and the approach is similar to the directional policy matrix. It comes in several versions, but they all have the same basic structure and strategy implications.

The version shown in Chart 8.15 is based on the work of Charles Hofer, Dan Schendel and Michael Porter. The competitive position of the SBUs to be analysed is plotted on the horizontal axis and the industry attractiveness on the vertical axis. The criteria used to quantify the position are similar to those in the directional policy matrix and can be selected according to what is relevant for your industry.

SBUs in boxes 1, 2 and 4 are those that should be protected or developed (they require funding), those in boxes 6, 8 and 9 should be carefully managed, harvested or even divested (they provide cash), and those in boxes 3, 5 and 7 should be managed in a cash flow neutral manner.

Chart 8.15 **Industry maturity: competitive position matrix**

		COMPETITIVE POSITION		
		Strong	Average	Weak
INDUSTRY ATTRACTIVENESS	High	**1 Protect position** ▪ Invest to grow at maximum rate ▪ Focus effort on maintaining strength	**2 Invest to build** ▪ Challenge for leadership ▪ Built selectively on strengths ▪ Reinforce vulnerable areas	**3 Built selectively** ▪ Specialise around limited strengths ▪ Seek ways to overcome weaknesses ▪ Withdraw if indications of sustainable growth are lacking
	Medium	**4 Built selectively** ▪ Invest heavily in most attractive segments ▪ Built up ability to counter competition ▪ Emphasise profitability by raising productivity	**5 Selectivity/manage for earnings** ▪ Protect existing programme ▪ Concentrate investment in segments where profitability is good and risks are relatively low	**6 Limited expansion or harvest** ▪ Look for ways to expand without high risk; otherwise minimise investment and rationalise operations
	Low	**7 Protect and refocus** ▪ Manage current earnings ▪ Concentrate on attractive segments ▪ Defend strengths	**8 Manage for earnings** ▪ Protect position in most profitable segments ▪ Upgrade product line ▪ Minimise investment	**9 Divest** ▪ Sell at time that will maximise cash value ▪ Cut fixed costs and avoid investment

THE HOFER MATRIX

Hofer's product market evolution matrix adds an additional dimension to the display of market evolution and business position and uses a finer grid. The competitive position is plotted on the horizontal axis and the stage of product or market evolution on the vertical axis. The competitive position, which is similar to the business position in the directional policy matrix, can be calculated in the same way as for that matrix. The market evolution axis is similar to the product life cycle, where development equates to the introduction stage, growth to the accelerating growth stage and shake-out to the decelerating growth stage. The products or SBUs are shown as circles and, unlike in other matrixes, the area of the circle represents total product turnover. Within the circle the share of a firm's product is shown as a slice of the circle.

The Hofer matrix includes more information, but is also more difficult to construct and exceeds the capabilities of Excel. However, there are specialist software tools (see below) to facilitate the creation of matrixes such as this.

Chart 8.16 **Hofer matrix**

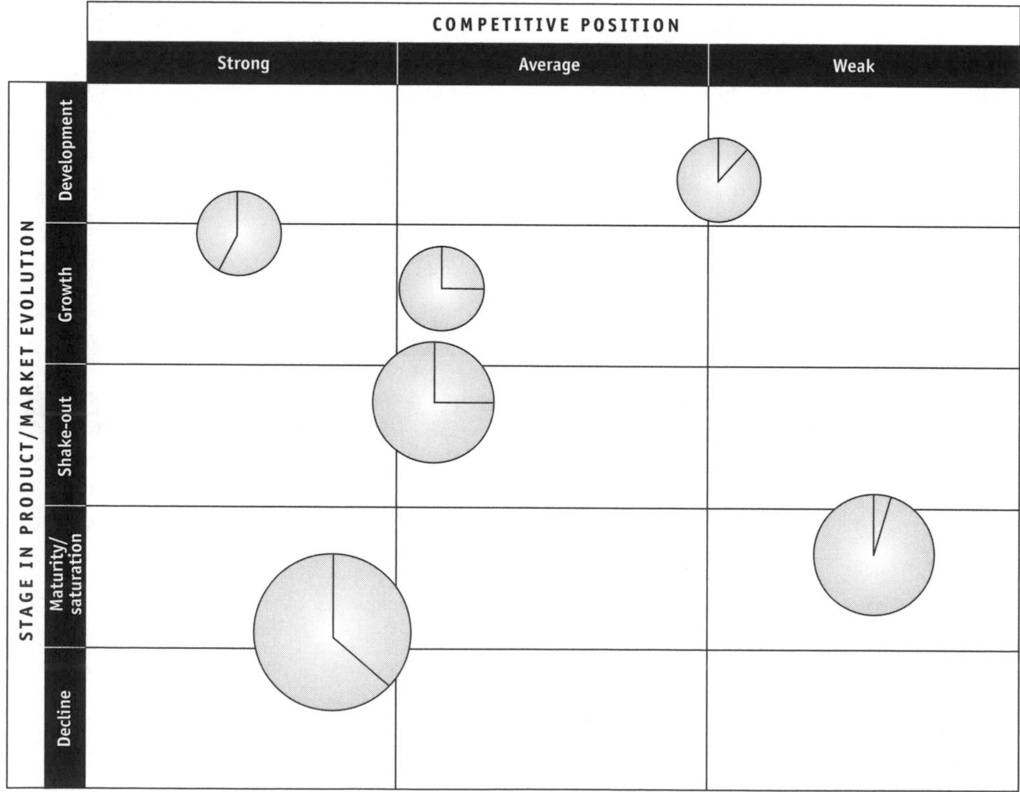

Source: Hofer, C. and Schendel, D., *Strategy Formulation: Analytical Concepts*, West Publishing Co, 1978, p. 34

USING SOFTWARE FOR PRODUCT LIFE CYCLE AND MATRIX ANALYSIS

Many of the diagrams in this chapter can be created using Excel, but it has charting limitations. There are specialist PC-based software tools that facilitate the task of analysis and create the associated charts as an output. Some of the programmes can be interfaced with Excel, so that your projections can be made in Excel and then read into the specialist software. For example, Market Modelling Ltd (www.market-modelling.co.uk) has developed an easy-to-use set of software tools for strategic marketing analysis.

LIMITATIONS OF MATRIX PORTFOLIO ANALYSIS

Product life cycle stage and portfolio and matrix analysis provide a structured approach to the analysis of products, particularly for larger, multiple product businesses. They should be part of a strategic and business planning process. If a business plan includes some of the above diagrams, it will gain credibility. This is not because fancy charts impress people, but because it demonstrates that you have gone through the strategic planning process and thoroughly researched and thought through the strategic implications before presenting the business plan.

Any such tool or model is only an abstraction of the real world, which is extremely complex with diverse influences. It may not always be possible to capture these in a matrix. For example, the cash flow issues, which are central to the growth-share matrix, depend on much more than the market growth rates and relative market share. Matrices should not be used blindly for strategy formulation but as a key input into strategic thinking and business planning.

Lastly, the models need not be used in exactly the way they have been devised by the authors; often it will be better to take the basic ideas and adapt them to the circumstances of the business that is planned.

USES OF OUTCOMES IN THE BUSINESS PLAN

One of the main outputs of product life cycle and portfolio analysis is the insight into cash flow implications. Funding is central to any business plan. It may not be possible to develop all products in the manner planned, because access to funds is limited. If a business embarks on an ambitious strategy to turn "problem children" into "stars", it must ensure adequate funding. The portfolio analysis should be checked against funding plans.

The analysis helps to ascertain the need for future product development to maintain the business as a going concern. If there are no stars or problem children to be developed, turnover will decline in the medium to long term. A business that consists mainly of cash cows but does not see an opportunity to develop products internally may embark on an acquisition strategy or, although this is rare, return funds to shareholders, for example through a share buy-back plan.

The matrix analysis produces recommendations on the strategic direction in which products should be developed. The prescriptive aspects of matrix analysis, such as "build" or "harvest", are an input into the generation of strategic options. This is discussed fully in Chapter 10.

If the portfolio analysis is carried out not only for your business but also for competitors, this provides useful insight into the strategic direction your rivals may take and is therefore an input into the competitor analysis.

Reference

1 McNamee, P.B., *Tools and Techniques for Strategic Management*, Pergamon Press, 1985.

9 SWOT analysis

OBJECTIVES

The analysis of strengths, weaknesses, opportunities and threats brings together the results of the analysis of the firm (internal), the environmental analysis (external) and the portfolio analysis. A SWOT analysis allows you to look at the strengths and weaknesses in the context of the opportunities and threats.

Implicit in the SWOT analysis is the aim of achieving the optimum match of a firm's resources with the environment in order to gain sustainable competitive advantage by:

- building on a firm's strengths;
- reducing weaknesses or adopting a strategy that avoids weaknesses;
- exploiting opportunities, particularly using the firm's strengths;
- reducing exposure to or countering threats.

A SWOT analysis used on its own is a crude, rather subjective tool. However, this is also an advantage because it can be done quickly. In any event, a SWOT analysis should be short and simple; complexity and over-analysis are to be avoided. This means a SWOT analysis is easily understood and communicated and can fit on one page. Therefore you could use a SWOT analysis to carry out a quick strategic review.

The process of creating a SWOT analysis is valuable because it involves discussion among managers or key people in a business. This stimulates thinking in a way that is not too structured or restrictive.

CONDUCTING A SWOT ANALYSIS

A SWOT analysis (see Chart 9.1 on the next page) could be viewed as bringing together the outputs from the strategic review, in particular:

- the analysis of the firm (internal elements);
- the market analysis (internal and external elements);
- the product, portfolio and matrix analysis (internal and external elements);
- the analysis of the general environment (external elements).

The first step of the SWOT analysis is to list strengths, weaknesses, opportunities and threats. Only important factors should be included, but some factors will invariably be more important than others. Factors should be listed in order of importance or ranked, and an importance score could be assigned to each factor.

Each factor should be a short bullet point, so that the SWOT analysis fits on one page. Assertions should be specific and if possible include some quantification. For example, a statement about strength in distribution might say: "Our products are distributed through

1,000 outlets, compared with our nearest rival's 400 outlets." Some explanation may also be required, but this can be provided in a supporting paragraph on a separate sheet. This could include a more detailed quantification of factors, such as demand growth projections or the number of pieces of environmental legislation under discussion. It is not necessary to provide a long list of all possible factors. It is better to focus on factors that really matter and follow a rationale that links factors, for example weaknesses in the context of identified threats.

In a larger business, ideally the SWOT analysis is carried out by a multi-disciplinary team in a workshop dedicated to producing such analysis. The workshop techniques suitable for this process are the same as for the political, economic, social and technological (PEST) analysis (see Chapter 5).

Chart 9.1 **SWOT analysis**

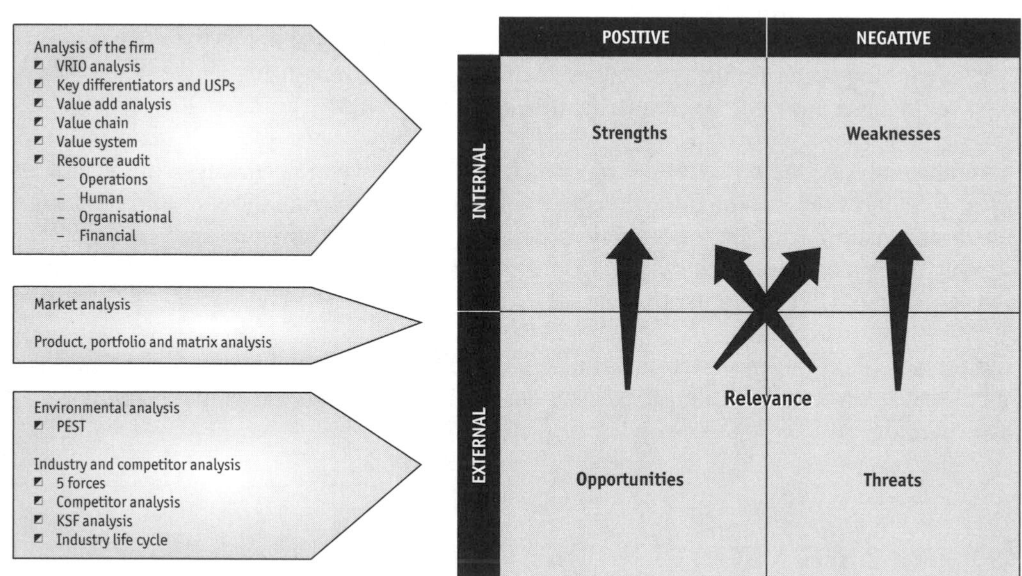

Strengths and weaknesses

The strengths and weaknesses analysis should be closely related to the analysis of the firm, which is an input into the strengths and weaknesses analysis. However, it is important to look at strengths and weaknesses in the context of opportunities and threats. The crucial question is relevance.

Strengths matter only if you can use them to exploit an opportunity or counter a threat. Similarly, a weakness is problematic if it relates to a threat. Thus an external factor can be an opportunity or a threat. For example, if new technology is becoming available and a business has an excellent product-development department that can take advantage of the new technology to develop products, this is an opportunity. In contrast, if a business cannot make use of the new technology, there is a threat from substitution if rivals make use of the technology.

The analysis should be made bearing in mind the objective of strategic planning: to gain sustainable competitive advantage. A strength is a potential source of competitive advantage, such as core competencies or financial strength.

Because competitive advantage can only be sustained if customer needs are addressed, the market analysis is an important input into the SWOT analysis. Enormous marketing strength is derived from a well-positioned product. This means a SWOT analysis should, like your business, have a customer focus. To derive real advantage from a strength, it must be useful in satisfying the needs of customers. Similarly, a weakness that relates to specific customer needs should be addressed as a priority.

The analysis of the firm focuses on resources and does not address weaknesses. Entrepreneurs and managers generally find it easier to think of strengths rather than weaknesses. Weaknesses may not be immediately apparent, so considerable time should be spent on identifying potential weaknesses. After an initial pass and following the listing of threats, the list of weaknesses should be revisited. The inability to neutralise or sidestep a threat is a fundamental weakness.

The matrix analysis of products may also identify weaknesses, such as an unbalanced portfolio with too many products in the mature stage of the product life cycle, or too many SBUs with a weak business position. Carrying out a SWOT analysis for competitors is recommended. A competitor's strengths may well be a potential weakness for your business.

Chart 9.2 on the next page provides a non-exhaustive checklist of factors that may be relevant to your SWOT analysis. However, since these are specific to each business and environment you may use other factors. You can also use Chart 8.10 on page 76 as a checklist.

Opportunities and threats

An essential input into the analysis of opportunities and threats is the PEST analysis (see Chapter 5). You must be aware of the major changes in the environment in which your business operates.

Again, opportunities and threats should be considered in the context of strengths and weaknesses. For example, there may a new market opportunity but at present your business does not have the resources to exploit it. Indeed, you may be preparing a business plan to raise funds for this purpose. To be successful in this, you must use resources to acquire the strengths that are necessary to exploit the opportunity.

Changes in the competitive environment may pose a threat. Therefore the industry and competitor analysis is an input into the analysis of opportunities and weaknesses. For example, a business could be threatened by consolidation taking place in the industry which may relegate the business to a secondary position unless that business also becomes part of the consolidation process.

Chart 9.2 **Checklist for SWOT analysis**

Strengths	Weaknesses
Internal	
Strengths	***Weaknesses***
Market dominance	Low market share
Core competencies	Few core competencies
Economies of scale	Old plant
Low-cost position	High cost base
Leadership and management skills	Weak balance sheet and cash flow
Financial resources	Low R&R capability
Manufacturing skills and technology	Undifferentiated product
Research and development	Weak positioning
Brand and reputation	Quality problems
Differentiated products	Lack of distribution
Patents and copyrights	Skills gap
Distribution network	
External	
Opportunities	***Threats***
Technology innovation	New market entrants
New demand	Competitive price pressure
Diversification opportunity	Higher input prices
Market growth	Changing customer needs
Demographic and social change	Consolidation among buyers
Favourable political support	Threat from substitutes
Economic upswing	Capacity growth outstrips demand growth
Acquisition and partnerships	Cyclical downturn
Cheap funds	Demographic change
Trade liberalisation	Regulation and legislation
	Threat from imports

Source: Based on Lynch, R., *Corporate Strategy*, Prentice Hall, 2000

USES OF OUTCOMES IN THE BUSINESS PLAN

A SWOT analysis is a snapshot of a business's position and provides an input into the generation of strategic options. It gives management an outline of the major issues affecting the industry and the business and identifies the basis for developing strategies.

A SWOT analysis is well understood and easily communicated. Of particular value is the identification of weaknesses and threats. In addressing these realistically, a business plan will become more plausible and robust. It demonstrates that you are not just looking at the upside but are aware of the challenges that face your business.

10 **Generating strategic options**

OBJECTIVES

This chapter addresses the generation of strategic options based on the analysis covered in previous chapters. Chapter 18 covers the evaluation and selection of options.

The discussion of the generation of strategic options is approached in three steps:

- The basis for achieving competitive advantage (Michael Porter's generic strategies).
- Exploring alternative strategic directions.
- Alternative methods to employ in pursuit of a strategic direction.

This methodical approach suggested by Garry Johnson and Kevan Scholes has been adapted by the authors and is shown in Chart 10.1. Chapter 18 also explains the linkage between the portfolio and matrix analysis covered in Chapter 8 and in this chapter.

Chart 10.1 **Generating strategic options**

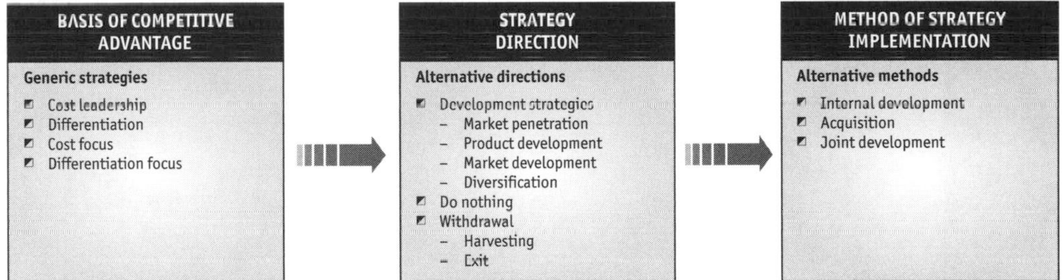

Source: Adapted from Johnson, G. and Scholes, K. *Exploring Corporate Strategy*, Prentice-Hall, 1989

LINKAGE TO PORTFOLIO AND MATRIX ANALYSIS

The industry maturity-competitive position matrix, the growth-share matrix, the directional policy matrix and the GE business/industry attractiveness screen not only analyse the position of products or strategic business units, but also provide recommendations as to the strategic directions in which strategic business units (SBUs) should be developed.

For example, the recommendation for a problem child SBU is either to develop it by means of heavy investment or to withdraw it before it becomes a dog. In other words, there are two strategic options. The GE business/industry attractiveness screen with a three-by-three matrix is even more prescriptive, suggesting only one strategic direction is suitable in some cases.

Matrix analysis is therefore a useful tool in helping to generate strategic options and understand the cash flow implications of strategic decisions for a portfolio of products. The advantage is that the strategies for several products or SBUs are looked at not in isolation but in the context of a business with limited resources, which should be allocated to the products or SBUs that produce the greatest return on investment.

BASIS OF COMPETITIVE ADVANTAGE

Generic strategies

Michael Porter[1] identified three generic strategies: cost leadership, differentiation and focus. The focus strategy has two variants: cost focus and differentiation focus (see Chart 10.2).

Chart 10.2 **Generic strategies**

COMPETITIVE SCOPE		COMPETITIVE ADVANTAGE	
		Lower cost	Differentiation
	Broad target	1. Cost leadership	2. Differentiation
	Narrow target	3a. Cost focus	3b. Differentiation focus

Source: Porter, M.E., *Competitive Advantage*, Free Press, 1980

Cost leadership

Cost is of overwhelming strategic importance. This is implicit in many of the portfolio or matrix models. Cost leadership strategy aims to reduce the firm's costs at all stages of the value chain. This will allow it to earn a higher return on investment.

In the early stages of the product life cycle, experience-curve-driven reductions in costs are important for attaining cost leadership. For a cost leadership strategy to work in the longer term, volume is usually important. This means that products must address a wide market. Products are often standardised to bring down prices and appeal to a wide market. In industries where scale economies matter, market share will be a key objective. In terms of the growth-share matrix, a cost leadership strategy is an option for stars and cash cows.

In industries with high fixed costs, capacity utilisation has to be maximised. For example, a cellular mobile phone operator usually has to cover a whole country, so driving up customer numbers is of overriding importance in order to increase utilisation and bring down average costs. In the airline industry, low-cost carriers that apply yield-management techniques with the objective of full capacity and short turnaround times are more profitable than traditional full-service airlines.

True cost leadership can only be achieved by one firm in the industry. However, given the law of diminishing returns, once volumes exceed certain levels, cost differences among leading businesses will be small. In other words, once a certain scale has been reached no further cost advantages may be available. The scalability of a business is therefore an important issue.

Differentiation

A differentiation strategy is based on equipping a product or service with some perceived or tangible unique attribute that cannot be easily replicated by competitors. Perceived differentiation can be achieved, for example, through branding. High quality is a commonly used way to differentiate a smaller supplier from a volume-driven supplier. Again, the differentiation strategy must be applied consistently at all stages of the value chain. A quality product can lose its reputation if delivery and installation are shoddy, or if distribution is only through stores that are located in downmarket areas. In order to be of value, the cost of differentiation must be lower than the premium buyers are prepared to pay for the differentiated product.

Differentiation is a strategic option for followers, rather than for market leaders. For example, if a product is a problem child, the firm could invest to catch up with the leader. This strategy is more risky than investing to differentiate the product for two reasons. First, the market leader probably has a cost advantage, which will make it more difficult for the follower to catch up. Second, a differentiation strategy does not directly challenge the market leader and therefore reduces the chances of a damaging competitive response, such as cutting prices.

Focus

The objective of a focus strategy is to gain competitive advantage by building on advantages of segment-specific specialisation, such as a better understanding of the requirements of buyers in that segment and the ability to respond to particularities of buyers. It is also referred to as a niche strategy. Pursuit of a niche strategy amounts to choosing a competitive playing field where competitive advantage can be achieved. In pursuing this niche strategy, for this special group of buyers the firm aims to be the "best" supplier. Within the chosen segment, the firm can achieve competitive advantage either because it is the cost leader or because it offers a differentiated product. Hence the two variants of the focus strategy.

Skills required to pursue generic strategies

Depending on the characteristics of the firm, industry and markets, not all strategies may be a realistic option. In other words, the resources and the environment condition the ability of a firm freely to select its strategy. Porter produced a list of resources and organisational requirements commonly required to pursue the generic strategies (see Chart 10.3 on the next page).

Chart 10.3 **Strategies and required skills and resources**

Generic strategy	Required skills and resources	Organisation requirements
Overall cost leadership	▪ Substantial capital investment and access to capital ▪ Process engineering skills ▪ Intense supervision of labour ▪ Products designed for ease in manufacture ▪ Low-cost distribution system	▪ Tight cost control ▪ Frequent, detailed cost-control reports ▪ Incentives based on meeting strict quantitative targets
Differentiation	▪ Strong marketing abilities ▪ Product engineering ▪ Creative flair ▪ Strong capability in basic research ▪ Corporate reputation for quality or technology leadership ▪ Long tradition in the industry or unique combination of skills drawn from other businesses ▪ Strong co-operation from channels	▪ Strong co-ordination among functions in R&D, product development and marketing ▪ Subjective measurement and incentives instead of quantitative measures ▪ Amenities to attract highly skilled labour, scientists, or creative people
Focus	Combination of the above policies directed at the particular strategic target	Combination of the above policies directed at the particular strategic target

Source: Porter, M.E., *Competitive Strategy*, Free Press, 1985

Risks associated with generic strategies

For a strategy to be successful (that is, increase value), it must be sustainable. If other businesses can copy the strategy, the competitive advantage will be lost and returns will decline to the industry average. Depending on the strategy chosen, managers must carefully monitor what factors can challenge the business position.

For example, if a strategy of cost leadership largely succeeds because of volume production, the firm is particularly exposed to technological changes. A competitor with much lower volumes may be able to enter the market using new technology, whereas the incumbent would have to make massive investments to convert existing capacity to the new technology. In this situation, the incumbent may use its financial strength to acquire the newcomer and gradually introduce the new technology. Indeed, the new entrant may consider this the best option because expanding businesses are often financially vulnerable.

The risk of differentiation is that products become commoditised and customers no longer perceive or care about differences. This means there is no value in differentiation; the competitive advantage is lost. It may also be possible for volume-based manufacturers to use some aspects of their products to achieve a significantly lower cost base for differentiated products. For example, volume car manufacturers generally use the same platform for high-value, low-volume models and share research and development costs across the whole product range. As a result, many luxury car brands are now owned by volume manufacturers.

Focus brings with it the risk of specialisation. Highly specialised businesses may live profitably in their chosen niche. However, as businesses become more adapted to serve their niche market they also become less flexible. Small changes in demand or the competitive environment may lead to rapid failure. Other risks include imitation and a narrowing of differences between the niche and the general market.

ALTERNATIVE STRATEGIC DIRECTIONS

The alternative strategic directions for a business are to grow the business (that is, embark on a development strategy), do nothing or withdraw. Generally, you would be making a business plan in order to develop a business. However, among a portfolio of products or SBUs, it may be best to withdraw some problem children or dogs in order to concentrate resources on stars. This is also addressed in Chapter 8.

Development strategies

A business can be developed in four possible directions (see Chart 10.4):

- Market penetration – sell more of the same to the same market.
- Product development – sell new products to existing customers.
- Market development – seek out new markets for existing products.
- Diversification – sell new products to new groups of customers.

With all development strategies, the question of leverage of core competencies or resources is crucial. The scope for leverage is highest for a market penetration strategy and lowest for an unrelated diversification strategy.

Chart 10.4 **Alternative strategic directions for business development**

MARKET/CUSTOMER GROUPS	PRODUCT: Existing	PRODUCT: New	SCOPE FOR LEVERAGE
Existing	Market penetration	Product development	High
New	Market development	Diversification	Low
SCOPE FOR LEVERAGE	High	Low	

Market penetration

Selling more of an existing product to the same customers or market is generally regarded as the easiest development strategy. Products and markets are well known, and this strategy potentially provides the best scope for leveraging existing skills and assets.

In growing markets, all competitors to a greater or lesser extent pursue penetration strategies; they are jointly expanding the total market. Because market penetration increases overall volumes, the strategy is particularly relevant in industries with high fixed costs and low marginal costs, such as hotels, railways and utilities.

In markets that are in the maturity stage of the product life cycle, the pursuit of a market penetration strategy becomes more difficult. At its simplest, increased market penetration is a fight for market share, but this can be costly. However, increased market penetration can be achieved by selling more to existing customers or retaining customers longer.

- The rate of product innovation can be increased, inviting customers to upgrade more often. For example, Microsoft, which already dominates the PC operating-systems market, regularly brings out new operating systems, which leads to sales to customers who already have the previous version. Subsequently, application software such as Microsoft Office also has to be upgraded.
- The rate of use can be increased, for example increasing the visits to a cinema by people who are already cinema-goers. Also getting customers to buy double the quantity of a food product generally does not mean that it will take twice as long to consume, and the overall sales volume per buyer increases. Another example is telephone companies that encourage customers to make more calls.
- The uses or applications of a product can be multiplied, such as promoting cornflakes not just as a breakfast cereal but also as a snack to be eaten at any time of the day. Cable TV subscribers can be encouraged to use an existing cable subscription more by making it interactive so it can be used for shopping or by offering video on demand. The interesting point about using the TV for shopping is that increased revenue does not come from the shopper but from the retailer.
- Customers can be induced to trade up; instead of buying the standard version of a product they buy an enhanced version. This technique is commonly applied in restaurants, where diners are asked whether they would like extra toppings for a pizza or the waiter recommends an expensive wine. Another prime example is cars. The basic versions have a relatively low price to get customers interested, but optional extras often account for a disproportionately high share of the final sales price.
- In mature markets, it is particularly important not to lose customers. As long as a business retains customers and adds just a few more, market penetration increases. It generally costs far less to retain a customer than to acquire a new customer. For example, magazines seek to retain customers by inviting them to renew their subscription early, offering a higher discount for two- and three-year subscriptions, and encouraging automatic renewal by direct debit.

Product development

The basis of a product development strategy is to sell new products in addition to existing products into the same market or to the same customer groups. The term "new products" is used here to describe genuinely new products that satisfy different needs and generate incremental sales, not enhancements or new versions of existing products. Because the new products are sold into existing markets or to existing customers, some aspects of the value chain can be leveraged, notably distribution and customer knowledge. It may also be possible to leverage other aspects of the value chain such as manufacturing or warehousing.

If there is no possibility of further growth for an existing product, product development may be the only way to achieve growth. Because new product sales leverage existing assets, a contribution is earned and this reduces the cost base for existing products. This increases the competitive position for existing products, thus reinforcing a cost leadership strategy.

- Product development strategies are particularly relevant where a firm has acquired extensive market knowledge or has an established customer relationship. A prime example is database marketing. Profiling of customers on the basis of past purchases may allow the business to target new products at particular customer groups. Such methods achieve much higher conversion rates than generalised sales campaigns. For example, a firm selling car insurance may develop other products, such as home or travel insurance.
- Retailers continually extend their offerings, not only to meet the changing tastes of customers but also to induce customers to increase the average sales value per store visit. Some supermarkets are now selling credit and telephony services.
- A brand can be extended to new products, say Ferrari branded watches and men's toiletries. However, care must be taken not to overstretch the brand and dilute its value. In this case the strategy becomes merely a diversification strategy, which may lead to lower sales of existing products because the brand value has been diluted.

Market development

Here a business seeks to sell existing products to new markets or customer groups. A classic market development strategy is extending the geographic reach, either within the country or by exporting. This generally requires modifications to the marketing mix, such as adjustments to the products so that they appeal to new market segments, printing manuals in different languages and ensuring compliance with local standards.

- Many products are now sold globally. High R&D costs drive globalisation in industries such as electronics, cars and pharmaceuticals. In other cases, the engine for globalisation is the brand, for example Disney and of course Coca-Cola. In the media business, distribution can be the basis for globalisation. For example, the News Corporation satellite TV empire incorporates satellite platforms in Australia, Asia, Europe, the Middle East and the United States.
- Another way of developing the market is to extend reach by having a presence in more retail outlets or offering mail-order delivery to remote customers. A single-outlet sandwich bar can develop its market by offering delivery to offices that are not within walking distance. Adjustments as small as in-store shelf presence constitute market development. For example, an Italian sauce can be referenced in a supermarket's sauces and condiments section and in the pasta section.
- Market development can also mean targeting new market segments. For example, cosmetics companies now sell make-up targeted at men. Another common marketing theme of established products is to attract a younger clientele.

Diversification

Diversification offers the least scope to leverage existing competencies and resources. The strategy aims at selling new products into new markets. Diversification can be further distinguished into related or unrelated diversification.

Related diversification means that a business stays broadly within the industry but needs to acquire new competencies and resources:

- A firm can pursue a strategy of related diversification by means of vertical integration: extending the value chain backwards or forwards. For example, a manufacturing business can choose to make components rather than buying them from a supplier.
- A successful restaurant chain may decide to leverage its brand name to get into the frozen convenience-food business. The skills required to run a restaurant and manufacture ready meals for distribution in supermarkets are entirely different, but the brand and possibly some recipes or signature dishes provide the link between the two.

Unrelated diversification takes a business into a completely new field, a different industry. Because it is unrelated, it is often difficult to establish a strategic logic for such moves, other than perhaps a limited degree of synergy. Conglomerates are the archetypal diversified businesses, where a holding company manages a diverse collection of companies, acting almost like an investment fund. Although conglomerates and diversified companies do not find much favour with analysts and management gurus, they do have merits:

- The financial management and planning skills are core competencies of the head office, and this expertise can be applied to make portfolio companies in different industries more successful.
- Diversified companies are less affected by a downturn in one industry. For example, if a diversified company owns businesses in industries with opposing cycles, cash flow can be balanced between industries. The downturn in the telecoms industry in 2000 and 2001 adversely affected highly telecoms-focused companies such as Ericsson much more than it did diversified Siemens, which has substantial interests in telecoms, information technology, power generation and transmission, lighting, medical solutions, automotive technology, transportation systems and building technology.

Do nothing

In a constantly changing world, "do nothing" could hardly be termed a strategy option. However, Johnson and Scholes[2] point out that this option provides the base against which other strategic options can be evaluated.

Doing nothing does not imply that a firm ceases all activity; it simply means that it does not develop in any new direction. But, generally, standing still is not a realistic option. In terms of portfolio strategy, doing nothing in a growing market means the product or SBU will rapidly lose market share. In a slow-growing market, doing nothing is similar to harvesting (see below). Thus merely to maintain market share and competitive position, a firm will have to keep pace with market development, which will probably entail some investment. The closest a business can come to doing nothing and standing still is perhaps as the dominant player in a mature, stable industry that is not declining.

Withdrawal

In a portfolio-based business, withdrawal should always be actively considered. Even for a single SBU, business withdrawal should not be ruled out. In terms of the growth-share matrix, withdrawal may be the only shareholder-value-increasing option for problem children and dogs. What makes this option different from others is that it affects vested stakeholder interests in an organisation, and there may be high political and social exit barriers. In some cases, withdrawal is a deliberate strategy:

- To save a company from bankruptcy severe measures may have to be taken, such as selling off divisions and making a large part of the workforce redundant. In the United States, companies under Chapter 11 protection often go through this restructuring process in order to salvage profitable bits of the company.
- Entrepreneurs and venture-capital companies have a specific target to exit the industry once they have turned a new business into a self-sustaining going concern.

Withdrawal can take three forms:

- Harvesting involves the gradual running down of an SBU. Market share will be lost but cash is generated. In a declining market, harvesting may be the best option because if buyers cannot be found, the only means of releasing shareholder value is to release cash flow.
- Divesting is the outright sell-off of an SBU. This is a strategy that may be applied to a problem child, particularly if there are other SBUs competing for limited resources. Ideally, a sell-off should take place while the business is still of value to competitors. This will maximise shareholder value.
- Disintegration is the opposite of the integration path described as one of the options in a diversification strategy. This route has been taken by some major electronics manufacturers, which now no longer make products but just develop and market them. Manufacturers in low-cost countries take up the production part of the value chain.

ALTERNATIVE METHODS OF STRATEGY IMPLEMENTATION

Johnson and Scholes[3] identified three alternative methods by which to implement a strategy once it has been selected: internal development, acquisition and joint development. They describe the choice between the methods as a trade-off between cost, speed and risk.

- Internal development of products or markets takes more time but means the firm is fully in control and develops a detailed understanding. In terms of product development, companies such as Sony have built a reputation for internal R&D, thus turning the business into a technology leader. In some cases, companies grew overseas operations from a small sales office into a virtually autonomous business unit.
- Acquisitions can be a quick route for product and market development. Established companies often acquire smaller businesses to gain control of new technology and hence new products. Also, once the decelerating growth or shake-out stage of the product life cycle is reached industries often consolidate. This is an opportunity to

increase market share through the acquisition of competitors. Overseas acquisitions are a well-established way of building a foreign presence.

- Joint development is a co-operative form of development by which risks and rewards are shared between partners. Forms include joint ventures, licensing, franchising and the use of agents. In many cases, joint development is the only suitable form of export market development because local laws prohibit or discourage foreign investment. In cases where a small firm has a patent but cannot exploit it fully, licensing is the best method for product and market development. Licensing is also an excellent way of staving off competition from substitutes, because potential competitors will find it cheaper to license than to develop substitute technology.

USES OF OUTCOMES IN THE BUSINESS PLAN

When the options have been generated they should be screened (qualitative filtering), and those that survive the screening process should be subjected to detailed financial analysis (quantitative ranking). This is covered in Chapter 18. You should opt for the strategies that produce the greatest return on investment.

References

1 Porter, M.E., *Competitive Advantage: Creating and Sustaining Superior Performance*, Free Press, 1985.
2 Johnson, G. and Scholes, K., *Exploring Corporate Strategy*, Prentice-Hall, 1989.
3 Ibid.

11 Market analysis and strategy

OBJECTIVES

A central aspect of any business plan is the marketing strategy. To develop a marketing strategy (see Chart 11.1), the market and potential customers must be analysed. Marketing differs from selling in as much as marketing has a customer rather than product focus (see Chart 11.2). This means that customer needs should be analysed with a view to segmenting the market on this basis. From this flows the targeting of particular segments with a segment-specific marketing mix. This positions products in the market, based on an understanding of buyer needs, attitudes and behaviour.

The market analysis and strategy are an important part of the marketing plan within the business plan. The marketing plan includes qualitative aspects (covered in this chapter) and the quantification and forecast of demand and sales (covered in Chapter 12).

This chapter covers the most important aspects of market analysis and strategy, which should be sufficient for smaller businesses. Readers who require further information about marketing are advised to consult specialist marketing textbooks.

Chart 11.1 **Marketing strategy process**

Chart 11.2 **Selling versus marketing concept**

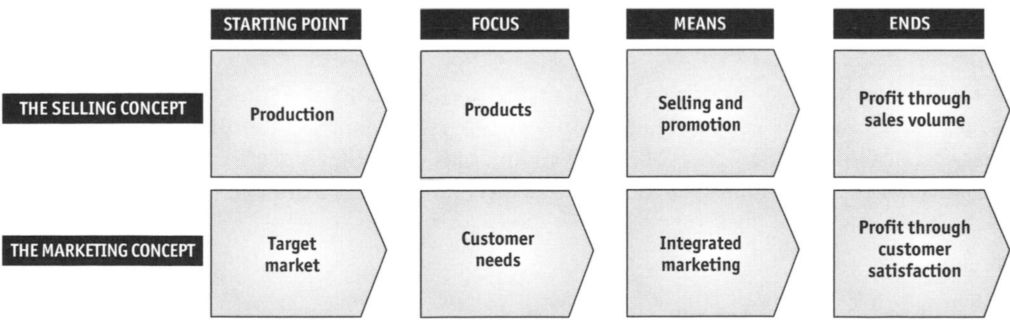

Source: Kotler, P., *Marketing Management*, Prentice-Hall, 1997

UNDERSTANDING MARKETS AND CUSTOMERS

To help them understand the market and buyer behaviour, marketers should answer the following questions:

- What market need does the business address?
- What products serve that need?
- Who buys the products?
- Why do customers buy?
- Who makes the buying decision?
- Where do customers buy?

The focus of understanding markets is the understanding of customers and buyer behaviour. Philip Kotler, professor of international marketing at Kellogg School of Management, devised a model of buyer behaviour (see Chart 11.3) in consumer markets emphasising the stimuli-response mechanism where buyers react to marketing and environmental stimuli. Depending on the personal characteristics of the buyer, the stimuli will result in a particular buying decision.

Chart 11.3 **Model of buyer behaviour in consumer markets**

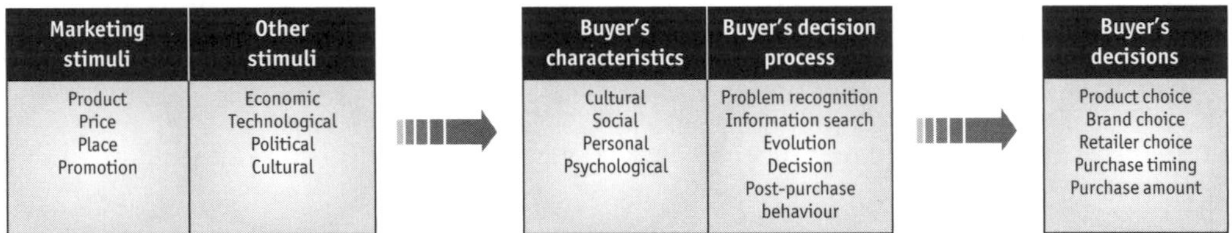

Source: Kotler, P., *Marketing Management*, Prentice-Hall, 1997

The value of the model of buyer behaviour is that it provides an explanation for the demand of a business's products, not just as a function of price, but also as a result of a host of other factors that are specific to individual consumers or groups of consumers. Demand for a product can be stimulated only by addressing all factors that finally result in a buying decision. For example, the price of a cup of coffee may be almost irrelevant in explaining why an individual goes to one coffee shop rather than another. Factors such as "feeling relaxed" or being able "to watch the world go by" can be far more important and would influence shop design.

When selling to businesses or government, the personal characteristics of a buyer are not entirely irrelevant, but rational factors outweigh personal factors. In business-to-business markets, environmental (demand, PEST) and organisational factors are far more important. However, an understanding of customer needs is more easily achieved by establishing a relationship with the decision-makers.

Market segmentation

A market segment is defined as a sufficiently large group of buyers with a differentiated set of needs and preferences that can be targeted with a differentiated marketing mix (see below). Fine-tuning the marketing mix to address the segment needs will lead to increased sales. However, adjusting the marketing mix for particular segments results in increased costs. To be of value, therefore, the benefits of segmentation must outweigh the costs.

A benefit of market segmentation could be a higher market share in the targeted segment or the ability to charge a higher price. For example, when analysing the tariff-plan preferences of mobile phone users, market research revealed that customers are prepared to pay a substantial premium in terms of the average per-minute price to have their preferred tariff plan. By offering a range of tariff plans aimed at segments with different preferences, a mobile phone company will not only win more customers but also reap a higher average revenue per minute.

For segmentation to work in practice, a segment must be identifiable and quantifiable, and it must be possible to address the segment effectively. Some buyers may be happy to pay a higher price for certain attributes. An example is air travel, where business travellers who attach value to flexibility are prepared to pay much more than they would for a non-flexible ticket. But discriminating between buyers can be problematic, inasmuch as a business traveller may buy a cheap, non-flexible return ticket and simply not use the return portion.

Segments must be measurable, in terms not just of potential market size but also of actual buying behaviour. It must be possible to attach segment flags to sales records in order to track segments. Simple information, such as gender, can be recorded at the point of sale, but factors used in psychographic segmentation schemes are difficult to record and it may be impossible to validate the success of the chosen segment scheme in a feedback loop.

Primary market research is the most appropriate tool to identify market segments. Typically, a market research questionnaire includes the demographics, questions relating to product attributes and their relative importance, brand preferences, usage patterns and willingness to buy, as well as attitudinal and lifestyle questions.

Segmentation methods

It is important to bear in mind that segmentation is not simply the act of dividing the market into categories, for example a breakdown of buyers by age. If age does not explain differences in buyer behaviour, it is not a useful variable for the purposes of market segmentation. There are several segmentation methods, each with advantages and drawbacks:

- Geographic segmentation is increasingly used with geo-marketing databases. Detailed information about the type of household in particular postcodes is available to marketers. Often geography is a proxy for a host of other variables (income, ethnicity, household size) because households with common attributes tend to cluster in certain areas.
- Demographic segmentation includes segmentation based on life-stage analysis, age, gender, income and social class. In saturated consumer markets, such traditional measures are often bad at explaining buyer behaviour because demographics do not necessarily explain needs.
- Psychographic segmentation is based on lifestyle, personal values and attitudes. It is better at identifying clients' needs or preferences than, for example, social class, but measurement and tracking are problematic.
- Behavioural segmentation is based on customers' knowledge of the product, point of purchase, purchase pattern and frequency, intensity of use, benefits and trade-offs, loyalty and other buyer behaviour factors.

Segmentation can be simple, using one variable (for example, business versus consumer market, male versus female), or based on preferences. Segments based on demographics are readily identifiable and quantifiable, but as mentioned previously, they may not be sufficient to explain differences in buyer behaviour.

Multivariate analysis uses more than one variable in the development of market segmentation and examines several elements simultaneously, for example age and gender. Multivariate segmentation can be imposed or evolved:

- Prescribed multivariate segmentation is based on identifiable attributes among existing and potential buyers. Life cycle stage analysis is a common form of prescribed multivariate segmentation. It is based on the mix of age, marital status and whether or not there are children in the household. Customers are placed into segments based on their life stage, on the basis that, at particular stages in life, people have similar needs that can be addressed.
- Evolved multivariate segmentation uses market research data in conjunction with cluster analysis to indicate the appropriate grouping of buyers based on common attitudes, behaviour and demographics. Once these groupings are established, it becomes possible to give meaningful labels to the clusters, such as "young aspirational urbanite" or "work hard, play hard". Such segmentation is generally better at explaining buyer behaviour, but measurement and tracking are notoriously problematic.

In business markets, segmentation is very different. Typical segmentation schemes are based on the size of the buying organisation or the industry sector, or a combination of both. Segmentation can also involve organisational functions or applications. For example, a wireless messaging service provider may segment the market by application, such as dispatch, e-mail, logistics and field sales. The basic messaging product will be adapted better to meet the functional needs of these segments.

A business plan becomes significantly more realistic and plausible if it matches the business's offer to segments and demonstrates a clear link between identified segment needs and the marketing mix targeting the segment. Making a demand forecast based on market segments (see Chapter 12) is also likely to increase the accuracy of the forecast.

Market targeting

In considering which segments to target, the attractiveness of the segment and the resources available to target it must be analysed. In general, if a segment can be served profitably it represents a potential target.

A business can concentrate on one segment or target several or all segments (see also Chapter 10). Even if all segments are addressed, this does not imply lack of market segmentation. Elements of the marketing mix can be adjusted to address particular segments.

An important aspect of market targeting is marketing communication. If a product is positioned to serve the needs of a segment, it may not be possible to serve simultaneously other segments with different needs. For example, if a product is positioned as a safe family-oriented product, this would be part of the brand value. Trying to promote the product to adventurous single people as well may dilute the brand value in the family market, while not generating many sales in the "adventurous single person" segment. It is therefore important to have a consistent segmentation strategy.

The segments targeted have operational implications, notably logistics, customer service, advertising and distribution. You must ensure consistency in your business plan. For example, if a product is aimed at the 16–24 age group, who by and large do not read newspapers but do watch a lot of TV, the media budget should not include newspaper advertising.

A key variable in any business plan is market share. Target marketing could explain convincingly why you hope to achieve a high share in certain segments but obtain hardly any sales in other segments. This level of detail in your forecasts shows that you have done your homework.

DEVELOPING THE MARKETING MIX

The marketing mix is a tool to position products in the target market. The marketing mix is defined by the four Ps: product, price, promotion, place (see Chart 11.4). Sometimes packaging is added as a fifth element, otherwise it is part of the product. All elements of the marketing mix together constitute the "offer".

Chart 11.4 **The marketing mix**

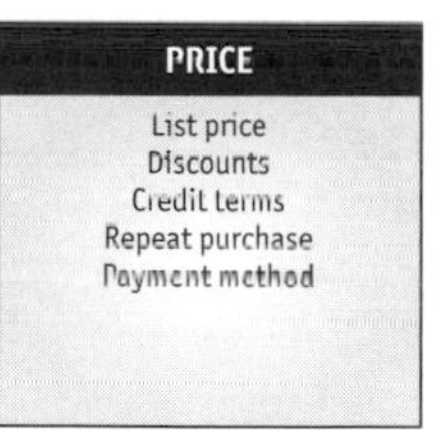

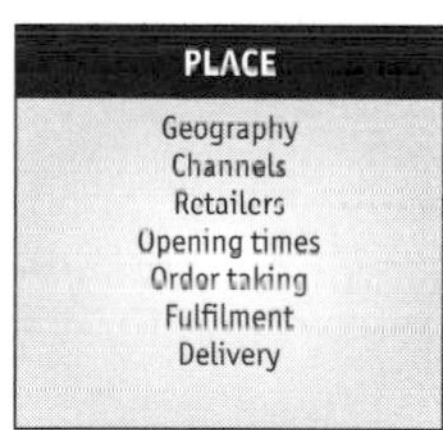

The offer is more than the product. It is a value proposition that satisfies customer needs. The attributes of the offer are defined by the marketing mix. The elements of the marketing mix should be adjusted so that the resulting value proposition is consistent. For example, skin-care products differ hugely in terms of pricing. The high price is not so much a function of the raw material and manufacturing cost, but mostly related to advertising, branding and retail channels. It does not make sense to sell an expensive face cream in a supermarket, so the manufacturer will restrict distribution to pharmacies and upmarket cosmetics stores.

PRODUCT POSITIONING AND THE VALUE PROPOSITION

To occupy a distinctive place in the market, businesses seek to differentiate their offer from that of competitors. This is achieved by positioning the product in such a way that customers readily perceive it as different. Any element of the marketing mix can be used to achieve a differentiated positioning.

Differences must be meaningful in the context of the market; they must satisfy the following criteria:

- The difference must be of additional benefit to the customer.
- A sufficiently large demand must exist for the benefit.
- The difference must be readily perceived.
- It must be easy to communicate the difference and the benefits associated with it.
- The difference must be an improvement compared with existing offers.
- The incremental cost of producing the difference must be lower than the incremental revenue.

In this context, the value of price, promotion and place should not be underestimated. Differentiation can be achieved for products that would otherwise only be commodities. For some products differentiated positioning is everything but the product:

- Mobile phone companies are selling essentially the same service to all customers. However, tariffs, distribution, bundling and options differ depending on the segment the particular offer is aimed at.
- Some manufacturers sell exactly the same physical product under two different brands with different packaging, distribution and pricing.

To show differences in positioning between competitors, a positional matrix (two dimensions) or a positional diagram (multiple dimensions) can be used. The objective is to compare how competitors are positioned relative to significant product dimensions. For example, cars may be positioned in a safety versus engine-power matrix (see Chart 11.5). This type of map is particularly useful if it is overlaid with a market segment analysis. This may show that there are a significant number of people who want safe cars with a small engine, but the segment is not served adequately by an existing offer.

Chart 11.5 **Product positioning map**

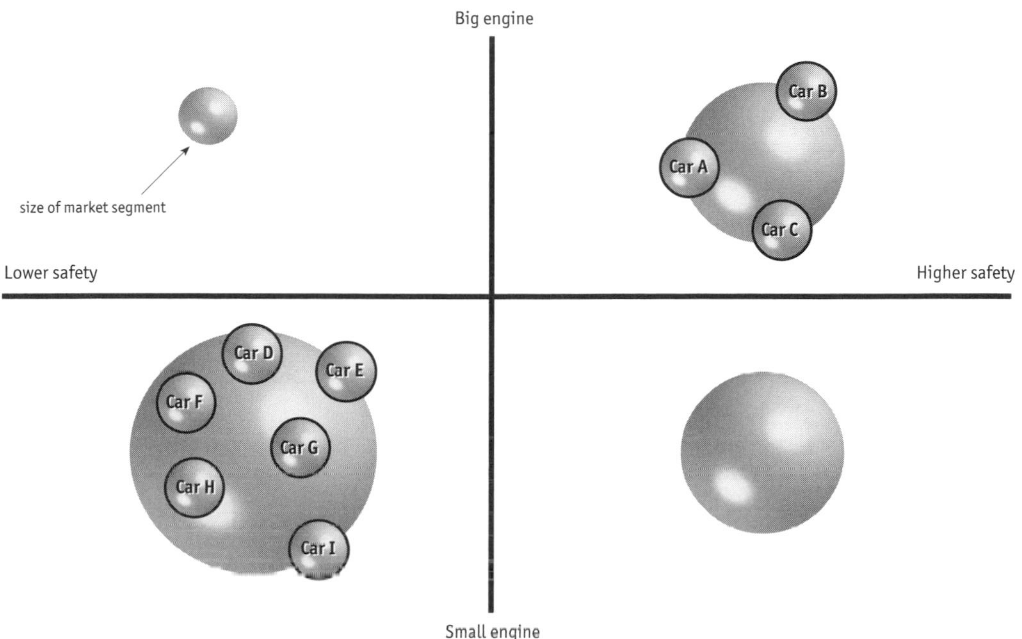

A positional diagram is often used to build a brand perception map (see Chart 11.6). This can be used to show how a brand or product appeals to a differentiated set of needs. If segmentation is needs-based, the product should score highly against the needs you are targeting. To create the diagram you must carry out a market research survey with a sufficiently large sample. For each criterion, respondents are asked how important it is in making the purchasing decision. Then they are asked to score each brand against the criteria. A scale of 1–5 is often used. However, because there can be a tendency to pick the middle number, a scale of 1–6 may yield a more differentiated result.

Chart 11.6 **Brand perception map**

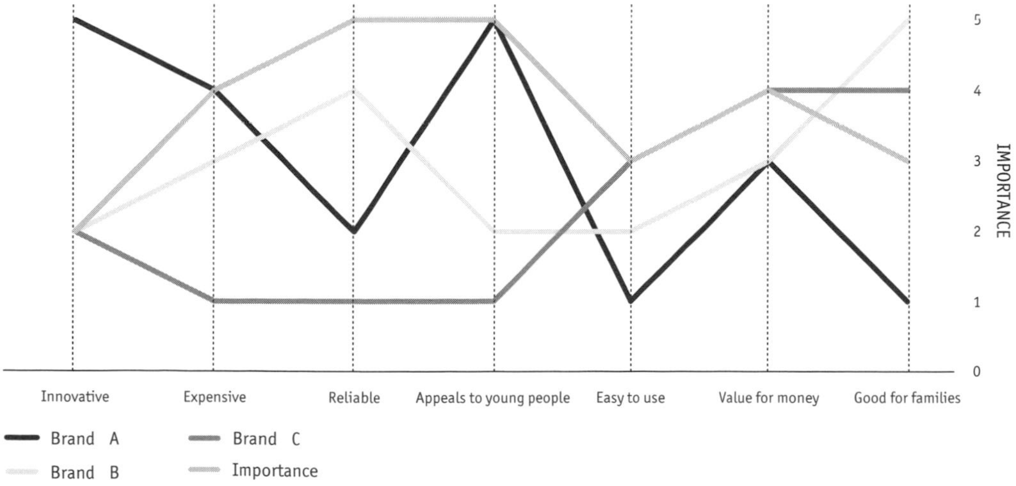

5
4
3
2
1
0
IMPORTANCE

Innovative
Expensive
Reliable
Appeals to young people
Easy to use
Value for money
Good for families

Brand A
Brand B
Brand C
Importance

Your marketing plan should state clearly what makes your product different from others and how it addresses identified customer needs. This is summarised in the value proposition. For example, a value proposition for a car could be "a reliable, safe car which families can afford". The concept of the value proposition includes tangible and intangible benefits that should be addressed consistently in all four aspects of the marketing mix. For example, if one element of the value proposition is "convenience", the convenience of using the product must be matched by the convenience of getting hold of the product in the first place, and the product design should make the product easy to use without consulting a lengthy manual.

THE MARKETING PLAN

The marketing analysis and resulting marketing strategy form part of the marketing plan. The marketing plan therefore contains a detailed description of the marketing mix and guidelines for the implementation of the business's marketing programmes. There should be a sufficient amount of detail to anchor the business plan in the real world:

- The product positioning against competitors should be explained.
- The target market segments should be identified and sized.
- Product specifications should be included and features should be described in terms of customer needs and benefits.
- If distribution involves wholesalers and retailers they should be named, and, if possible, there should be confirmation from key wholesalers and retailers that they are willing to carry the product. Retail and wholesale margins and incentives should be detailed.
- The advertising and promotions budget must be broken down into programmes, and possibly a rudimentary media plan should be included.
- Customer service, guarantees, order fulfilment and after-sales service must be addressed.

The quantitative aspects of the marketing plan – the demand and marketing forecast – are discussed in the next chapter.

12 Market forecasting

OBJECTIVES

You are convinced there is a profitable market for your product or service. Your business plan must be persuasive that there is. This chapter is primarily concerned with the revenue side of the business plan and concentrates on the potential market, total market volumes, prices, market values and market share. The result is a market forecast which flows into the marketing plan. The marketing plan contains a marketing planning model, which includes detailed forecasts of revenue and cost of sales.

Chart 12.1 **Market forecasting and planning for the business plan**

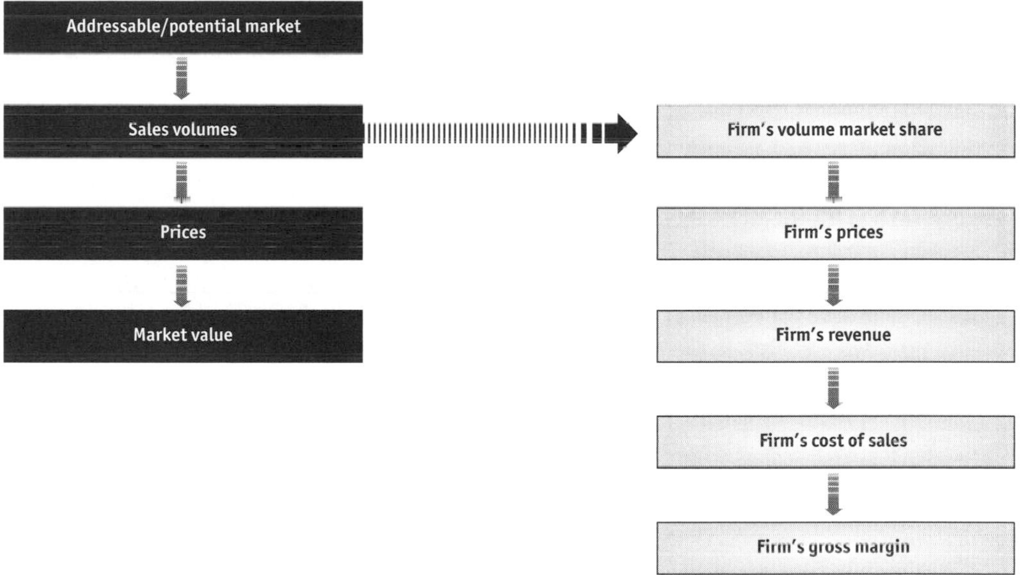

For medium-sized and large firms, the forecasts in a business plan are primarily concerned with the medium to long term. Smaller businesses normally have a shorter time horizon. In the case of an existing business, often the near-term forecast or budget is also part of a regular business planning exercise. A forecast of market demand usually spans a period of not less than three and not more than ten years. The time horizon should be appropriate in the context of the planned investment: for example, up to the point that the business no longer requires any funding (revenue covers operational expenditure and interest payments) or to payback. Highly capital-intensive businesses, such as large civil engineering projects, may have business plans in excess of 25 years.

At the time of making a forecast, you cannot know how accurate it will turn out to be, but a forecast of market demand should have the following characteristics:

- All assumptions and the way in which they affect the results are fully documented.
- There is supporting market research.

- The forecast is credible and stands up to reasonableness checks.
- There are no obvious contradictions with generally accepted models of market behaviour.
- The forecast supports the objective to be achieved.

Business planning is carried out for a purpose. Often being right is not the main issue. There may be overwhelming reasons why certain outcomes are deemed to be more credible than others are. It is no good presenting a forecast that is extremely well researched, well documented and well founded if nobody else believes in it. Therefore a forecaster should be aware of the organisational and external constraints in which the business has to fit. For example, if there is a consensus view that annual demand for a product will not exceed $100m, but your primary market research shows that it in fact reaches $300m, the figure is so far from what people expect that the research findings are likely to be rejected.

This chapter introduces some statistical and mathematical concepts relevant for forecasting. A more detailed step-by-step explanation of forecast modelling can be found in the *The Economist Guide to Business Modelling*.

THE MARKET FORECASTING PROCESS

Market demand is a crucial variable upon which an investment decision rests. If it cannot be demonstrated that sufficient demand exists, other forecasting or planning activities are largely pointless. Therefore the activities related to market forecasting should be scheduled early in the business planning process, the stages of which are as follows:

1. Define the market in which the business is to operate, both geographically and in the context of the competition. The market boundaries should be drawn sufficiently wide to include products that the new product may provide a substitute for or be complementary to.
2. Define the forecast intervals and forecast horizon. For funding and operational planning issues, quarterly or monthly time intervals may be required at least for the first one or two years, with annual data sufficient after that.
3. Decide the time and resources available to make the market forecast. This will narrow down the techniques that can be employed. For example, it is common for there not to be sufficient resources to carry out detailed primary market research.
4. Decide the appropriate forecasting technique. This will depend on the resources available and any forecasting problems. For example, with new products there is seldom relevant, historic data available.
5. Define what data has to be gathered to carry out the forecasting technique that has been decided upon.
6. Analyse the data and make the forecast; that is, develop a time series of demand, prices, market share and revenue. This will produce a sales forecast. The assumptions and rationale should be fully documented to allow others to validate the forecast.
7. Subject the forecasts to extensive reasonableness checks and benchmarking. For example, if you forecast an increase in air traffic of x, but there are not enough airports to handle the traffic, the forecast demand cannot be realised. Benchmarking

should include external data and internal metrics, macroeconomic and microeconomic data and common-sense checks.

8 In many cases iteration is required; that is, you have to revisit the forecast after it has been through the business planning model. Forecasts are in theory objective, but forecasting in the context of the business planning process is frequently driven by the objective of the business plan. Forecasting can be an elaborate way of substantiating preconceived ideas. In this case, you will be asked to review and adjust the forecast until it produces business plan figures that people believe in. In other cases, iteration becomes necessary because the forecast does not pass the reasonableness test. For example, if long-term profitability is extremely high, with margins well above the industry norm, it is likely that a parameter such as market share or prices may have to be adjusted downwards. In other words, while you may not see anything wrong with any single parameter, the outcome may not be believable and assumptions have to be adjusted to produce a credible outcome.
9 Present the forecast convincingly. However much effort goes into producing a forecast, it will be wasted if not enough is put into presenting the results and getting the message across. The presentation tells a plausible story and leads to the conclusion step by step, generally using well-organised tables and charts derived from spreadsheets, together with flow charts to demonstrate how variables interact. If the methodology behind the forecast is clear, it should be easy to communicate the assumptions and rationale.

Chart 12.2 **Stages in making a market forecast**

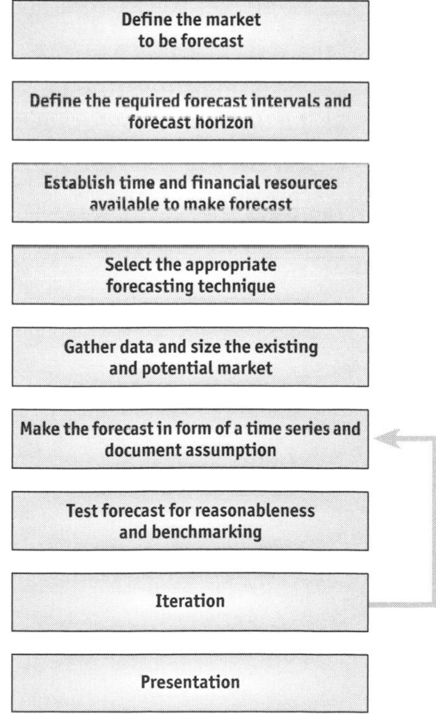

ESTABLISHING THE SIZE OF THE POTENTIAL MARKET

To gauge the market for a product or service, you should start by defining the addressable market: the consumers or businesses that have a conceivable need for and can afford to buy it. This will provide:

- a broad picture within which potential demand can be estimated. For example, in poorer areas only a small percentage of the population may be able to afford the product or service. Therefore penetration should not be measured as a percentage of the total population but as a percentage of the population who can afford the product;
- an initial reality check that will help keep your feet firmly on the forecasting ground;
- a sampling universe for a market survey. Market research interviews should be carried out only with individuals who are within the addressable market.

Recognising important differences

Depending on the type of business, the addressable market can be defined in different ways. For example, a sandwich bar might define it as people who work within a certain distance from the shop. For products such as cars or mobile phones, it would be defined in a much broader way. Easily obtainable data such as income distribution and the age structure of a population can show a significant difference in the addressable market. For example, assuming only individuals aged 18 and above can use the product and a minimum income threshold is required, the addressable market in Sweden and Mexico is very different. In Sweden, 79% of the population is aged 18 or over, compared with only 64% in Mexico. Income data may reveal that basically every Swede could afford the product, whereas only 30% of Mexicans could afford it. Therefore an initial appraisal indicates that the addressable market in Sweden is 79% of the population compared with 19.2% (64% × 30%) in Mexico (see Chart 12.3).

Chart 12.3 **Identifying the addressable market**

Sufficient income 30% of population	Total population 100%
Addressable market 19.2% of population	Aged 18+ 64% of population

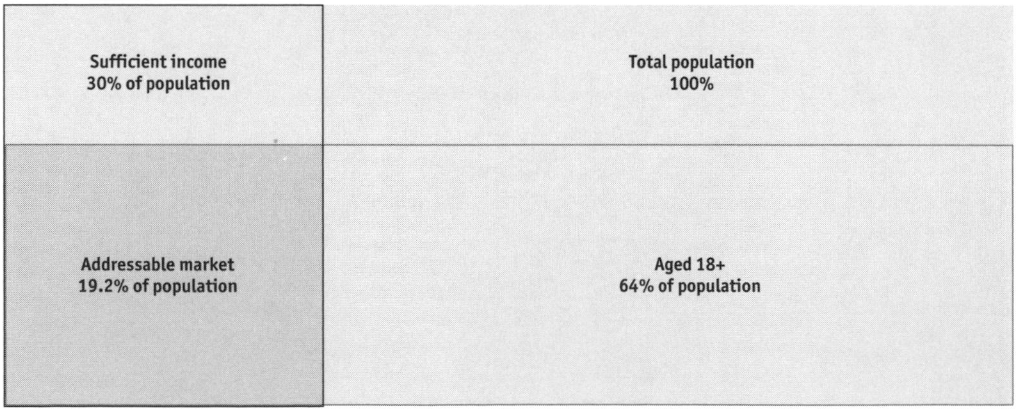

Adopting the right terms

It is important to define the addressable market in the right terms. For example, landline telephony is measured in terms of penetration of population, but the addressable market is households and businesses rather than people. Looking at an emerging market which might have a fixed-line penetration of 10% compared with 60% in a developed market, a first glance suggests that the teledensity in the emerging market is only 17% of that in the developed country. Closer analysis may reveal that the average household size in the emerging market is 7.0 compared with 2.4 in the developed country. Assuming that generally only one phone line per household is required, then a 20% penetration level in the emerging market is roughly equivalent to 60% penetration in the developed country. The conclusion is that the emerging market is much less underserved by telephony compared with more developed countries than might be thought.

Market research

Market research can be carried out using secondary sources or by conducting primary research. The former should always precede the latter, because primary research can be time-consuming and expensive, especially when it involves highly detailed customised surveys.

Secondary sources

Secondary data sources are extremely diverse and include freely available published statistics as well as high-priced published market research reports and industry surveys. Internet searches generate an enormous amount of data in a short time, and statistics for every country in the world are available on CD and online, including the World Development Indicators, published by the World Bank, Eurostat and national statistical offices.

Market research based on published sources quickly produces a broad understanding of the market in question, identifies existing forecasts or market size estimates and generates useful benchmarks. Benchmarks such as GDP per head, the number of people with tertiary education, the number of people with credit cards and similar indicators can be used to help make an initial estimate of a relative market potential between countries.

Primary market research

A common approach to determine existing and potential demand is to carry out a formal market research survey with potential buyers. This requires a questionnaire to be devised, tested and put to a sample of the population who fall into the addressable market.

Depending on whether face-to-face or telephone interviews are used, the set-up and interviewing phase may take two or three months. Computer-assisted telephone interviews are cheaper and take less time. The interviewer types in the responses, and a tabular analysis is available immediately after completion of the last questionnaire.

A good method of testing an idea before commissioning a custom-made survey is to pay for questions to be included in one of the omnibus surveys regularly carried out by market research agencies.

A market research survey provides data that help you arrive at a forecast; it is not a forecast in itself. If 50% of respondents express interest in a new product, it does not mean that they will buy the product immediately. Answering a question on what you might buy is a long way removed from making the real decision to purchase something, and the actual form of the product may not be the same as the respondent imagined it when answering the survey question. Stated purchase intentions such as "I would buy in the first six months of launch" tend to be unreliable, and judgment has to be exercised in interpreting them. Market research surveys in combination with other qualitative methods and market behaviour models can produce more reliable forecasts.

TOP-DOWN OR BOTTOM-UP FORECASTING

A top-down forecast uses a broad indicator to produce a forecast. For example, you could forecast the mobile telecommunication services market as a function of the total market for telecoms services, which, in turn, could be forecast as a percentage of GDP. This broad-brush approach quickly produces results, although they may not be as reliable as a bottom-up forecast.

To forecast the mobile telecommunications market from the bottom up involves making a penetration forecast, possibly by segment, and forecasting the average revenue by user. Thinking through the elements of the forecast helps to explore the components of the revenue stream, to identify the drivers for each component and the dynamics that drive the different values. The average spend per customer is driven by different revenue streams, such as voice telephony, messaging and mobile internet access, each with a different price, demand and price elasticity of demand.

Bottom-up forecasting requires the identification of the correct drivers of demand. This is a crucial exercise in preparing a forecast. Using the earlier example of fixed telephone lines, although forecasts are expressed as a penetration of population, total population is not the driver. The drivers are the numbers of households and businesses. Therefore a forecast linked to growth rates of businesses and households will not only be more accurate, but will also produce a segmentation in the business and consumer markets. This distinction enables more sophisticated forecasting, involving the use of, for example, different price elasticities for the segments.

The bottom-up method offers a much higher level of detail than the top-down method. It is more time consuming but it produces much more credible results. Nevertheless, the top-down method is useful as a reasonableness check. If the bottom-up forecast implies that the total market for a product will grow to an unreasonably high percentage of GDP, this should lead to a review of the values in the bottom-up forecast.

MARKET SEGMENTATION

Whenever possible, you should break a forecast down into market segments. These are parts of the total market that have different demand characteristics and require a different marketing approach. Market segmentation is discussed in detail in Chapter 11. Segmentation for marketing purposes may not always be the same as that used for forecasting purposes. Although in theory market segments should be quantifiable, in practice detailed quantitative data, particularly a historic time series, for different segments may not available.

Taking air travel as an extreme example, two obvious segments are leisure and business. They have totally different needs, trends, seasonal demand fluctuations and price elasticity of demand coefficients. Trend, seasonality and price elasticity are an integral part of many forecasts. To base a forecast of demand for air travel on the average for the two segments would be highly misleading. Even for less extreme cases, a segmented forecast adds more detail and therefore helps to tell the story.

REAL OR NOMINAL

It is important to consider whether prices and other monetary values should be forecast and expressed in real or nominal terms. A nominal forecast includes the impact of projected inflation on prices and costs, and a real forecast uses today's prices for everything. In a low-inflation environment, a year-on-year change of prices of, say, 2.5% is well within any forecasting error, but in the longer term inflation becomes much more significant. In year ten of the forecast the nominal figure is 28% higher than the real figure.

Financial statements and valuations are made in nominal terms, that is, after taking account of inflation. This is important because funding does not automatically increase in line with inflation. However, market forecasts are best made in real terms, that is, ignoring inflation. There are two reasons for this. First, if prices and wages increase equally as a result of inflation there should be no effect on volumes demanded. Second, a figure of x in nominal terms in ten years' time has no meaning unless the year ten inflation index is known. Put simply, if the price of a product is 100 in the current year and 120 in nominal terms in year ten, it is not apparent whether the price has increased or decreased in real terms.

Historic data is usually presented in nominal terms, but time series analysis, such as sales over the past ten years, should be based on real rather than nominal values. This is because sales may appear to be rising year on year, but the trend could be flat once inflation is taken out. Therefore before using historic sales data, for example to fit a trend line, nominal figures should be converted to real-term figures using the last year as the base.

MARKET FORECASTING TECHNIQUES

Forecasting techniques are grouped into two categories:

- quantitative methods such as regression analysis;
- qualitative or technological methods such as diffusion of innovation models.

Quantitative methods include time series methods and explanatory methods, both of which rely on the availability of sufficient quantitative information in the form of data sets. Mathematical analysis is applied to these data sets to generate formulae that can be used in forecasts. You can apply statistical methods to quantify the statistical error in the forecast. There is a fundamental difference between time series forecasting and explanatory forecasting:

- Time series forecasting does not involve finding out why things change over time; it simply relates change to time. Therefore the methods can be used even if systems that affect demand are not understood.
- Explanatory (or causal) methods involve an understanding of the way in which demand reacts to variables and recognise that many variables that affect demand have nothing to do with time but are a result of deliberate actions, such as the decision to reduce prices in order to increase sales volumes.

Qualitative or technological methods are employed where little or no data are available. The term qualitative does not imply that there are no quantitative outputs or inputs; it merely indicates that judgment is involved in the forecasting process. Generally, it is not possible to apply statistical methods to provide a quantification of error. However, techniques such as Monte Carlo analysis can be applied to generate a probability distribution of the forecast.

To make a forecast, quantitative and qualitative methods can be combined. For example, to forecast sales for the next 12 months you can extrapolate a trend, and to produce values for the longer term you can create an s-shaped product life cycle growth curve.

Time series methods

Time series methods rely on ample historical quantitative time series data being available so that you can detect and extrapolate an existing trend or pattern in the data. The assumption is made that patterns detected can be applied to the future, that is, there is an assumption of continuity. Essentially three types of patterns are detected and analysed by time series methods: seasonality, trend and cycle.

- Seasonality is the regular fluctuation of demand depending on the month or quarter of the year. If a business plan is based simply on annual averages, it will not allow for often crucial variations in demand during the year. Seasonality needs to be taken into account in short-term demand forecasts (a year or two) to help with detailed stock, capacity, resources and cash flow planning. It may be relevant on a monthly, weekly or even daily basis. For example, for many retailers peak periods include the months leading up to Christmas, the weeks they have sales, and Saturdays and other days when shops are open but most people do not have to go to work.
- The trend is the direction of the time series, irrespective of seasons or cycle. Some trends hold true for long time periods; for example, GDP is generally increasing. But many are more short term. The longer the forecast horizon, the less likely it is that the assumption of continuity will be valid. For example, under the product life cycle theory trends not only change, they also reverse.
- Identification of the business cycle helps give insights into the longer-term fluctuation in demand. This is relevant when a medium- to long-term forecast is required for an existing, relatively stable business. Some mature industries such as chemicals are often cyclical.

The main aim of analysing time series data is to detect a pattern in the data set. This means error or random effects have to be filtered out. When this has been done, the pattern can be described as a function and used in forecasting.

The random factor is also referred to as "error". Error is the difference between the actual data and the data predicted by the function. The function that best describes the pattern is the function that has the least amount of error. The least squares method is commonly used to measure and minimise error. This consists of minimising the sums of the squared error. The squared error is used so that negative and positive values do not cancel each other out. From the sum of squared errors (SSE) the mean squared error (MSE) is calculated.

In general terms, a time series can be written as:

$$Y = T \times S \times C \times E$$

Where:

Y = the data in the time series
T = the trend
S = seasonal factors
C = cyclical factors
E = error

The notation describes the multiplicative model, used in most forecasting situations. In this case, a seasonality factor is applied to the trend. Another way of writing a time series is the additive form. The additive form Y = T + S + C + E assumes that seasonal variations remain constant in absolute terms, regardless of the trend.

Estimating the trend

The description that follows relates to short-term forecasting. The trend is a line of good fit with the moving average of a quarterly or monthly time series. First the moving average has to be calculated (see Chart 12.4 on the next page). The easiest way is to use the moving average function built into spreadsheets, such as Microsoft Excel. The data has to be plotted on a chart. Using the built-in ADD TRENDLINE function and selecting MOVING AVERAGE, the trendline can be displayed. Depending on whether quarterly or monthly data are used, a 4- or 12-period moving average should be selected. To obtain the numerical values use the MOVING AVERAGE function, which is an add-in from Excel's Analysis Toolpack.

The four-quarter moving averages are found by averaging the quarters 1–4, then 2–5, and so on. Each calculation is placed in the mid-point of the dates used to calculate the average. The next step is to centre or synchronise the averages with the timing of the observed data. To do this, the 2-period moving average of the 4-period moving average is taken. Since the 4-period moving averages refer to mid-points between the quarter dates, taking the averages of the mid-point brings the data back to the end of quarter dates.

Chart 12.4 **Forecasting using trend and seasonality**

Year	*Quarter*	*Period*	*Actual sales*	*4-period moving average*	*Centred 4-period moving average*	*Ratio actual to moving average*	*Trend forecast*	*Final sales*
2003	1	1	24					
	2	2	44	52				
	3	3	61	58	55	111%		
	4	4	79	64	61	130%		
2004	1	5	48	71	67	71%		
	2	6	66	78	74	89%		
	3	7	91	83	80	114%		
	4	8	105	87	85	124%		
2005	1	9	68	90	88	77%		
	2	10	85	95	92	92%		
	3	11	100	104	99	101%		
	4	12	125	114	109	114%		
2006	1	13	107	124	119	90%		
	2	14	125	132	128	98%		
	3	15	138	139	136	102%		
	4	16	159	147	143	111%		
2007	1	17	135	156	151	89%		
	2	18	155	164	160	97%		
	3	19	175					
	4	20	192					
2008	1	21					176	143
	2	22					183	171
	3	23					190	201
	4	24					197	234

Calculation of seasonal indices

Year		*Q1*	*Q2*	*Q3*	*Q4*
2003				111%	130%
2004		71%	89%	114%	124%
2005		77%	92%	101%	114%
2006		90%	98%	102%	111%
2007		89%	97%		
Average	100.6%	81.9%	93.9%	106.7%	119.8%
Seasonal index	100.0%	81.4%	93.4%	106.1%	119.1%

To make a forecast based on the trend, Excel's TREND function can be applied to the moving average. The calculation of the trend is carried out by means of regression analysis, where time is the explanatory variable and the 4-period centred moving average is the dependent variable. Regression analysis is discussed in more detail below. While this produces a forecast for each quarter, the forecast is not seasonally adjusted, that is, the effects of seasonality are eliminated. This is fine if only the annual total is required, but if a quarter-by-quarter forecast is required the forecast has to be adjusted by seasonal indices.

Calculating seasonal indices
First the ratio of actual data to the corresponding moving average data has to be calculated, producing seasonal indices for each observation. From the function shown above, the actual data (Y) divided by the trend (T) is equal to the seasonal factor (S) times the random factors or error (E). Because error is random, the average of all errors is assumed to be zero. Therefore averaging the indices for each season produces the average seasonal factor for each season.

One further adjustment has to be made. Ideally, the average of the 4 seasonal indices is 1. But because the elimination of non-seasonal factors is not precise it may not be, in which case the factors should be adjusted proportionally so that the average is 1. The resulting seasonal indices are then multiplied with data generated by the TREND function to produce a quarterly forecast that takes account of both trend and seasonality.

Chart 12.5 **Quarterly sales forecast based on trend and seasonality**

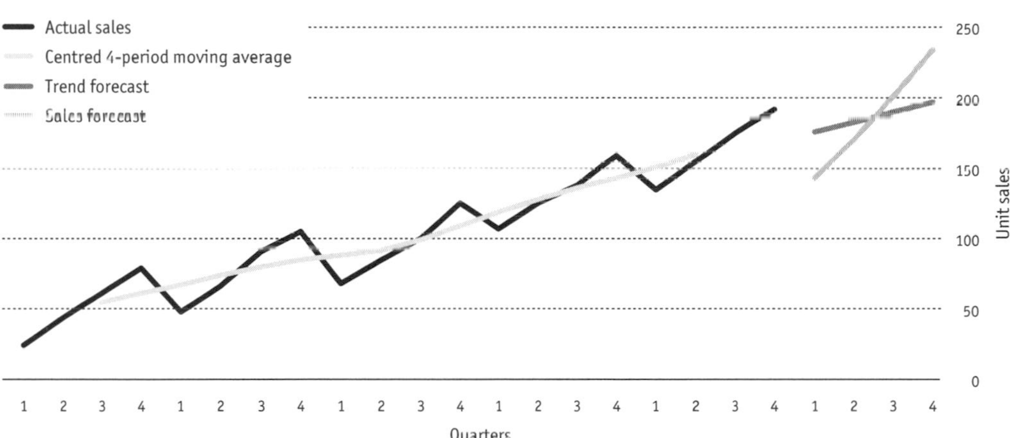

Measuring the cycle
Long-term fluctuations around the trend are referred to as the cycle. Basic mature industries and the economy as a whole tend to be cyclical. Because of its long-term nature, the cycle is generally ignored for the purposes of business planning. The effect of the cycle is more relevant for mature markets than for new products. In the case of new products, the effect of diffusion of innovation (see below) is far stronger than the cycle, and cyclical fluctuations can be treated as noise, that is, a minor fluctuation. Chart 12.6 on the next page shows the mobile telephony penetration curve against changes in GDP in Sweden, and Chart 12.7 shows the incremental change in mobile telephony penetration against changes in GDP. Recessions slightly delay growth but only marginally affect the basic s-shaped growth curve.

The cycle can be calculated from a time series using the moving average and the trend. The moving average values from a time series contain trend and cycle. To identify the cycle the moving average should be expressed as a percentage of the trend. The fluctuation around the 100% level may reveal a cyclical pattern.

Chart 12.6 **S-shaped mobile penetration curve and changes in GDP in Sweden**

Source: Coleago Consulting Ltd

Chart 12.7 **Effect of GDP on incremental mobile penetration in Sweden**

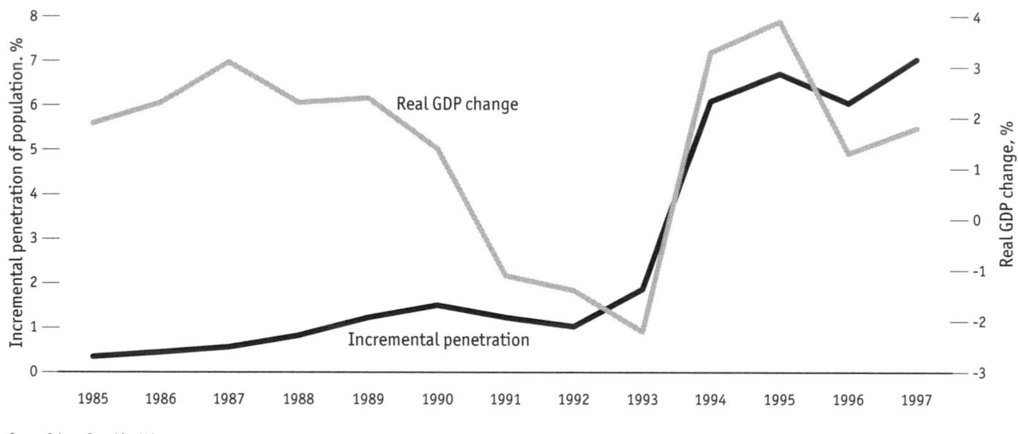

Source: Coleago Consulting Ltd

Explanatory methods

Explanatory or causal methods rely on observations that a change in one variable, for example price, has an effect on the change in another variable, typically demand. There are some practical applications for explanatory methods, especially for short-term forecasts; for example, supermarkets vary their shelf stocks on a daily basis according to the weather forecast. Causal relationships are also used to provide information that will help decision-making, for example to predict the effect an increase in advertising spend will have on sales.

Explanatory methods require that there is a sufficiently large amount of data that can be analysed using regression. Regression is used to determine how explanatory variables relate to the variable to be forecast. The objective is to arrive at a function of the type y = f (a, b, c, ...) which can be used in forecasts.

Generally, the relationship between a causal variable and the variable to be forecast is not directly proportional. The most common way of describing the relationships is through elasticities. Fundamental observations, such as price elasticity of demand, play an important part in business planning.

The scope for a strict mathematical application of explanatory methods is often limited. For example, to forecast demand as a function of price you would have to forecast prices. In many cases, prices relate to unit costs, and unit costs are a function of the total quantity demanded, so the argument is circular. A further limitation is that the way in which one variable affects another may not be constant over time or may hold true only within certain limits. Even if prices for some items fall substantially, demand generally does not increase beyond a saturation level. Despite these limitations, causal methods are an important element is making medium- to long-term forecasts.

Regression analysis

The objective of regression analysis is to find the function that best describes the relationship between causal variables and a dependent variable. The calculations involved in regression analysis are extensive, but in practice spreadsheet functions make them easy to do. The information required for regression analysis is as follows:

- A definition of the dependent variable, that is the variable to be forecast, for example demand.
- One or more explanatory variables, for example the number of people in a particular age group and disposable incomes.
- Sufficient data points to make statistical analysis meaningful. For example, if there are only five or six observations, statistical analysis is useless. With several hundred or even thousands of observations, such as past purchase data, statistical analysis is appropriate.
- The nature of the relationship between the variables – linear, exponential, polynomial and so on. This helps to eliminate spurious results. For example, by chance a polynomial function that waves about might fit the data, but in reality the relationship is linear.

There are two main outputs from a regression analysis:

- A function that describes the relationships between the explanatory variables and the dependent variable. This means the function can be readily used in spreadsheets for the purposes of forecasting.
- A measure of goodness of fit, how well the function fits the observed data. As with time series analysis, some of the variation in the observed data will be caused by random events, that is, error. Producing a good fit means minimising error.

Single variable linear regression is the simplest form of regression analysis. It is also referred to as simple regression and can be performed easily using a spreadsheet such as Excel:

- Plot the correlated data pairs in an xy chart.
- Highlight the data points, select ADD TRENDLINE from the menu and select LINEAR.
- Under OPTION, click to display the equation and the R^2 value.

The equation in the form of y = ax + b and the R^2 value will be displayed on the chart. The equation can easily be used to make a forecast, with x being the explanatory variable and y the dependent variable. R^2 is called the coefficient of determination. Discussion of the detailed mathematics to calculate R^2 is beyond the scope of this book, but its interpretation is important. The value of R^2 ranges from 0 to 1; 1 means that all of the variation in the data is explained by the explanatory variable, and 0 means the variable does not explain anything.

Chart 12.8 **Simple regression using Excel**

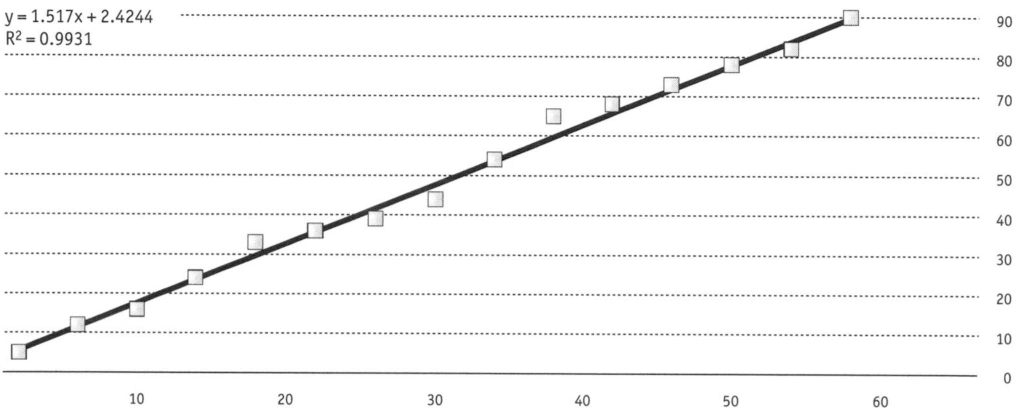

The linear function that best describes the relationship between the causal variable and the dependent variable is the one with the best "goodness of fit". The method commonly used to measure goodness of fit is the mean squared error (MSE) method. This examines the sum of the square of differences between the actual data and the values produced by the function. The function that produces the lowest MSE has the best goodness of fit.

An alternative to the graphical method is to use the TREND function. This is particularly useful for a speedy analysis, but it does not produce the coefficients necessary to write the function in the form y = ax + b. To generate values for a and b (the slope and the intercept of a linear function), the LINEST function can be used. The LINEST function also produces statistics such as the R^2 value. Use of the LINEST function is discussed in more detail in *The Economist Guide to Business Modelling.*

Non-linear regression

In many cases, relationships are non-linear but can be transformed into linear function so that simple regression using MSE can be applied. For example, the logarithmic function $y = a \times b^x$ can be transformed into a linear function by taking the logs on both sides to $\log(y) = \log(a) + \log(b) \times x$.

In practice, the graphical method in Excel can be used to identify the best function. Once the data is plotted in an xy chart, multiple trend lines can be fitted, showing the R^2 for each. Selecting the function with the R^2 value closest to 1 indicates that the best fitting function has been selected. However, care should be taken not to "over fit" data. For example, given that the number of data points is limited, a particular function might by chance produce the best R^2 value, but it does not have explanatory powers. From the study of market behaviour, it may be known that the type of function should have a particular form. For example, demand for a product may be high in high-income groups and disproportionately lower in lower-income groups, but there is limited demand even in very low-income groups. This suggests a logarithmic curve. In this case, it is best to use this type of curve, although it does not produce the R^2 value closest to 1. In some cases, the function with the R^2 value closest to 1 may produce negative demand for some values, which is obviously nonsense and this function should be ignored.

Multiple regression analysis

The dependent variable may depend on more than one variable. There may be multiple linear relationships or multiple non-linear relationships. In Excel the LINEST function can be used for multiple linear regression analysis. Similarly, the LOGEST function can be used for exponential relationships. Specialist statistical packages can be used for more complex regression analysis, but in practice these are rarely necessary in the context of writing a business plan.

Econometric modelling

Econometric modelling adds another layer of complexity to regression analysis, but because of its complexity it is seldom used in business planning. Econometrics deals with situations where multiple regression equations are interdependent in terms of the causal variable.

Qualitative and technological methods

Qualitative and technological methods involve judgment. They are also referred to as judgmental methods. They are used if there is insufficient data available for formal mathematical analysis, such as in the case of new products. The assumption of continuity, which is required for quantitative methods, is less likely to apply in medium- to long-term forecasts and in rapidly changing markets. Qualitative methods are therefore well suited for forecasts with a 5–10 year time horizon.

Expert opinion

The simplest and probably the most subjective approach is to rely on expert opinion. Several experts may have a discussion and arrive at an opinion. Another approach is to ask sales staff and managers to provide estimates. Using experts or sales staff to make a forecast is a highly unreliable method that generally does not stand up to external scrutiny. For example, sales people may have a vested interest in providing a low estimate so that the targets set as a result of the forecast will be easily achievable.

Delphi technique

A commonly used form of accessing expert opinion is the Delphi technique, originally developed by the Rand Corporation. It is a systematic approach to asking experts without the drawback of committee or group effects. Experts, who should work independently of each other, are asked to submit written responses to a central team. The central team then categorises these and filters out extremes. This has the effect of homing in on a consensus. The results are sent back to the experts, without identifying the individuals who gave the different opinions, to give each expert the opportunity to revise their forecast. This can be repeated several times until a consensus is reached.

Curve fitting and using s-shaped curves

Curve fitting is a form of extrapolation. It is based on the observation that technological and market developments generally follow an s-shaped pattern. It is related to the product life cycle and diffusion of innovation theories that are discussed in more detail below. It is applicable to medium- to long-term forecasts. Curve fitting generally relies on a small number of historic data points, for example sales or penetration rates during the past five years. Because of the limited number of data points quantitative methods are not suitable.

The basis of curve fitting is to select the parameters in an s-shaped curve function that produce a good fit with the historic data. If the selected function had been good at "predicting" what happened in the past, it can be assumed it will be good at predicting the future. To fit a curve to an existing data set, the least squares method could be used, but in practice there may be too few data points. Furthermore, more recent data should weigh more heavily. There may also be reasons why demand in the past grew more slowly in some years; for example, a recession may have occurred. Although the market will develop in an s-shaped pattern, events such as a recession or price or competitor changes will cause fluctuations around the basic s-shaped curve. For example, there may have been a sharp price cut two years ago, leading to a surge in demand. In the following year, demand did not increase as fast, suggesting that growth is slowing down. However, without the price cut, there would have been a very good s-shaped growth curve.

Curve fitting requires an estimate for the upper asymptote of the curve, that is, the line that describes maturity of demand, or maximum potential demand. This can be obtained through market research. The upper asymptote may itself move over time. If the demand forecast is made as a percentage of people above a certain income, then increases in wealth widen the addressable market. This results in a gentle upward slope of the upper asymptote.

A variety of different functions produce s-shaped curves. In Chart 12.9, y denotes the penetration expressed as a percentage of the maximum potential, or saturation, and t denotes time, usually years; a and b are constants that can be manipulated to fit the curve to the existing data. One constant elongates the curve; the other changes the shape.

Chart 12.9 **Formulae for s-shaped curves**

$y = (1 - ae^{-bt})^3$ (Von Baertalanffy's curve)
$y = Le^{(-ae)-bt}$ (Gompertz's equation)
$y = 1 / (1 + ae^{-bt})$ (Pearl's equation logistic curve)

Except in terms of practicality, no curve is inherently better than another. Pearl's equation logistic curve can be used in the following way:

$$y_t = m \times (1 \div (1 + a \times e^{(-b \times t)}))$$

Where:

y_t = the penetration in year t
m = the penetration ceiling, or maximum potential
a = a factor giving more or less growth later or earlier; the neutral value is 99
b = a factor shortening or lengthening the time to maturity
t = number of years after launch

Chart 12.10 shows an assumption set for a demand forecast using Pearl's equation logistic curve. The number of people using the product since launch is known as an annual time series. This gives the beginning of an s-shaped curve. The maximum potential penetration is estimated through market research. The historic values are used to fit a curve using Pearl's equation logistic curve by varying the factors a and b to produce a good fit. Rather than using an abstract value for b, which determines the time to maturity, it is better to input the number of years to maturity. b can be approximately calculated using the following formula:

$$b = 1 \div (t_m \times \ln (a \div (1 \div 0.99 - 1)))$$

Where:

t_m = the total number of years from launch to maturity
a = a factor giving more or less growth later or earlier; the neutral value is 99

Chart 12.10 **Assumption set for s-shaped demand forecast**

Product launch year	1995
Maximum potential penetration of population	17%
Population '000 end 2007	10,035
Annual population growth rate	0.03%
Total years to maturity	24
a	135
b (calculated)	0.39585

Chart 12.11 **Curve fitting**

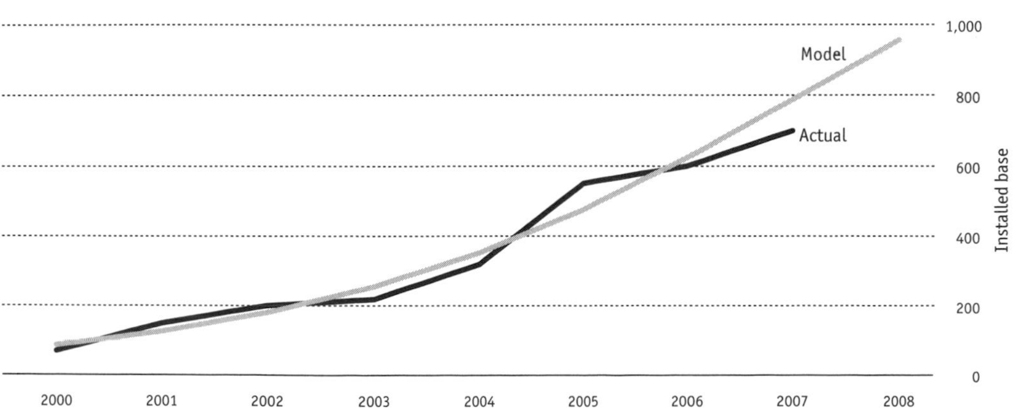

Chart 12.12 **Forecast using Pearl's equation logistic curve**

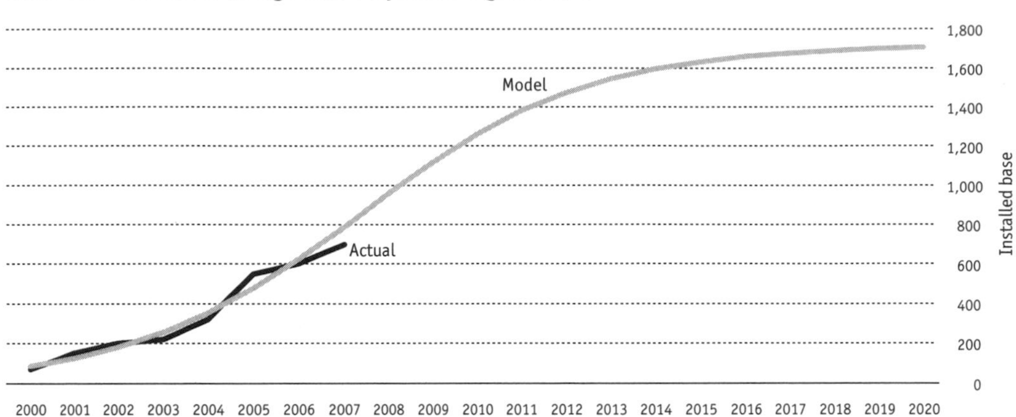

MARKET BEHAVIOUR MODELS

Economics and business studies provide a wealth of empirical data. From the study of how markets, competitors and prices behave, a number of generally accepted models have emerged. These models are similar to the laws of natural science and provide a useful toolbox for the forecaster. Market behaviour models fall into the category of qualitative forecast methods. They also share similarities with time series and causal models, because they explain what happens over time and how different factors are related. For example, price elasticity is an observation that describes how demand reacts to price, and it may be possible to determine the price elasticity coefficient using regression analysis.

The product life cycle

It has been observed that markets for products grow in an s-shaped manner and eventually decline to be replaced by new products. The product and industry life cycle and its use in strategic analysis are discussed in Chapters 7 and 8. For the purposes of market forecasting, the product life cycle is best analysed in five phases:

- Introduction phase. Sales volumes are low and increase in a near linear fashion. There are few competitors, the product may suffer from quality problems and there is little variety between different versions of the product. Unit costs and prices are high.
- Accelerating growth phase. Buyer groups widen and sales increase rapidly. More suppliers enter the market and prices start to fall. A greater variety of product forms start to appear.
- Decelerating growth phase. Penetration is still increasing, but at a declining rate. Prices are falling more quickly and become a significant issue. Variety increases further and there is an increased focus on product quality. Late adopters buy the product.
- Maturity. Penetration is no longer increasing. There may be consolidation. Prices are declining further, but at a slower rate.
- Declining phase. Prices are low, but no longer declining. Some competitors may exit the market.

Chart 12.13 **The product life cycle curve**

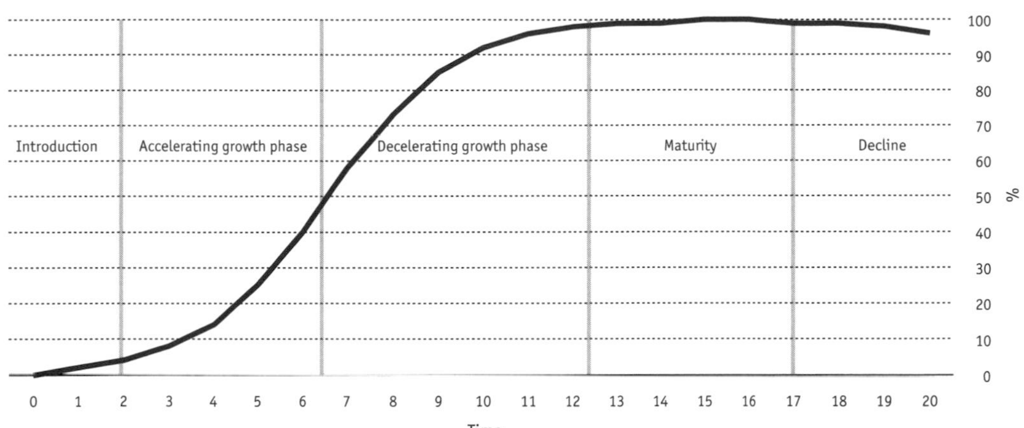

These observations provide inputs with regard to forecasting sales volumes, prices and market share: the essential elements of the demand forecast. This is extremely useful, because it means that by using an s-curve to forecast penetration, it is possible to forecast price. It may be argued that lower prices increase demand. Therefore you have to forecast price to establish demand. However, prices relate in some ways to costs, and costs are a function of volumes (see the experience effect below). Although in specific cases cause and effect can be clearly identified, medium- to long-term forecasts are subject to many influences in a complex system. The product life cycle model encapsulates these effects and is therefore an appropriate model for medium- to long-term demand forecasts.

Diffusion of innovation

Everett Rogers[1] and Frank Bass[2] proposed models that describe how a new product or service is adopted by a population. Because of its better predictive power, the Bass model is commonly used. It is based on the observation that there are some innovators who adopt products early and imitators who adopt the products as a result of having seen other people using them. The Bass curve can be written as follows:

$$n_t = n_{t-1} + p\,(m - n_{t-1}) + q\,(n_{t-1} \div m)\,(m - n_{t-1})$$

Where:

- n_t = the number of users in year t
- m = the maximum penetration or market potential, which is the total number of people who will eventually use the product or service
- p = the coefficient of external influence or coefficient of innovation, which is the probability that an individual will start using the product or service because of advertising or other external factors
- q = the coefficient of internal influence or imitation, which is the probability that individuals buy the product because of word-of-mouth or other influences from those who already have the product

Estimates for p and q can be obtained by looking at similar products or through market research. An estimate for m, the maximum potential penetration, can also be obtained through market research. The Bass model explains well how innovation diffuses, but because of uncertainty in establishing the values for p and q, it does not solve the forecasting problem. Academic arguments aside, the Bass model is another useful way of producing and using an s-curve.

Chart 12.14 **Bass curves**

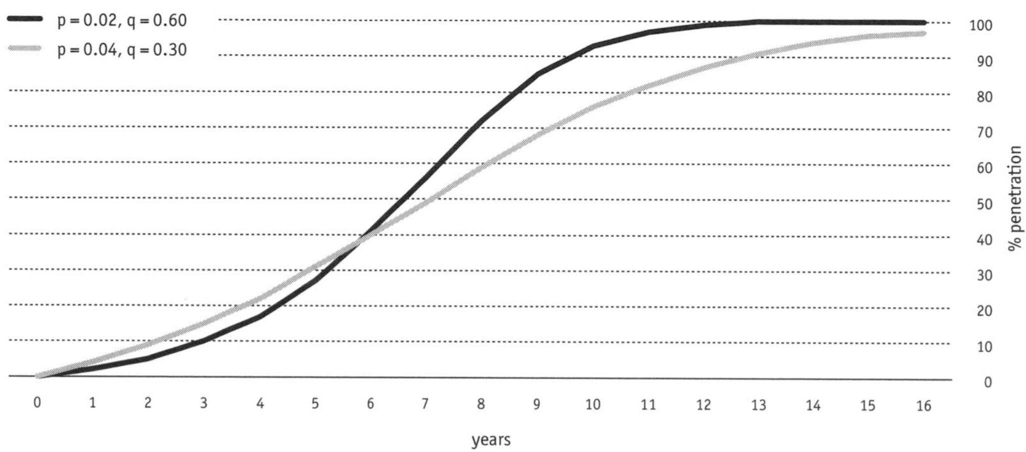

The experience curve

At the heart of the experience curve is the observation that unit costs decline in a predictable manner as the total quantity produced over time increases. Research carried out by the Boston Consulting Group showed that each time cumulative production volume doubled, unit costs declined by 20–30%. The experience curve can be written as follows:

$$C_n = C_1 \times V^{-E}$$

Where:

C_n = price of the nth unit
C_1 = price of the first unit
V = cumulative production/sales volume
E = the experience effect, which is the % by which costs fall each time cumulative production volume doubles

Chart 12.15 **Experience curves**

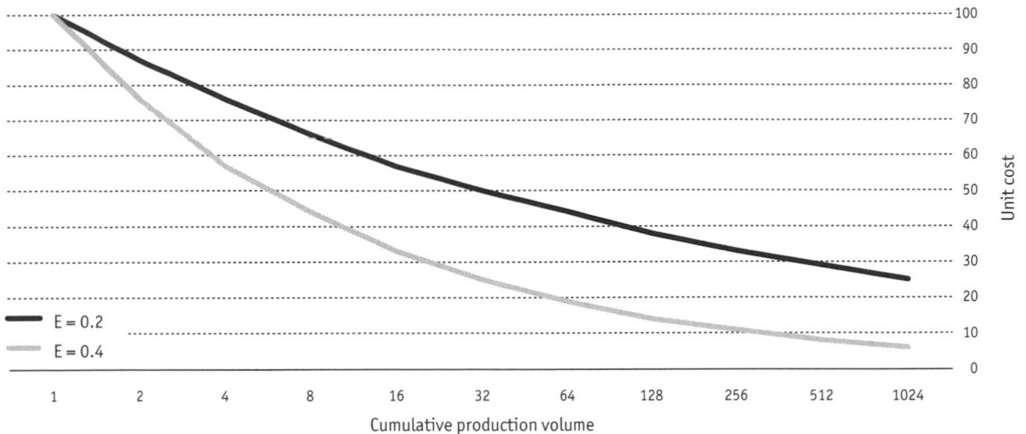

The experience curve, which forecasts costs, can be used in the context of a demand forecast as an input into the price forecast. Although costs are only one aspect in pricing, it provides an indication of how far and how fast prices may decline. If a penetration forecast is made for a consumer durable product and replacement sales are calculated (see below), the cumulative production volume can be easily calculated.

Price elasticity of demand and other elasticities

Elasticities are a measure of how a change in a variable affects demand. There are many different types of elasticities, such as price elasticity of demand, cross-price elasticity of demand, elasticity to advertising expenditure, income elasticity, and so on. Elasticities occur where causal relationships exist. If elasticities are known and remain constant, forecasting becomes a mathematical exercise (see Regression analysis on page 119).

In practice, elasticities have to be estimated. Furthermore, they are generally not constant. The law of diminishing returns applies. For example, if prices fall to zero demand would have to be infinite. Clearly this is not the case.

In the context of market forecasting, the most important elasticity is price elasticity of demand. The price elasticity coefficient is the ratio of percentage demand growth of a product to percentage drop in the unit price of the product. In other words, the price elasticity coefficient indicates the proportional effect of a change in price on demand. A price elasticity coefficient of –1 means demand is completely price elastic; that is, a percentage drop in price is offset by an equal percentage increase in demand, so that the market value is constant. 0 means demand is totally price inelastic; that is, it remains the same whatever you do to the price. If the price elasticity is greater than –1, price reductions yield revenue growth. In many cases, price elasticity coefficients are between 0 and –1. This means as prices fall, revenue falls, but not as fast. The price elasticity of demand formula can be written as follows:

$$E = ((Q_2 - Q_1) \div ((Q_1 + Q_2) \div 2)) \div ((P_2 - P_1) \div ((P_1 + P_2) \div 2))$$

Where:

E = the price elasticity coefficient
Q = the quantity demanded
P = the price

Or:

$$Q_2 = (Q_1 \times (1 + E \times (P_2-P_1) \div (P_1+P_2)) \div (1 - (E \times (P_2-P_1) \div (P_1+P_2))$$

Chart 12.16 **Price elasticity of demand**

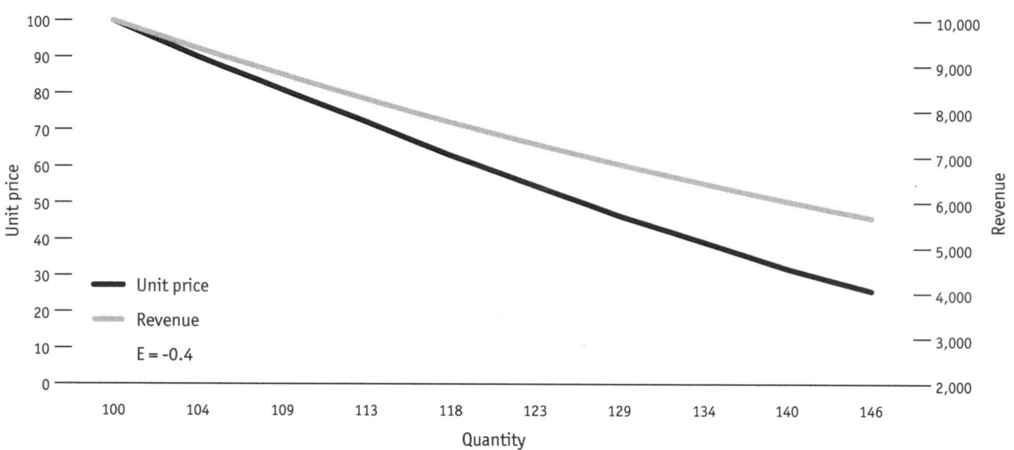

An alternative definition of the price elasticity coefficient is simply the change in quantity demanded divided by the change in price:

$$E = \Delta Q \div \Delta P = ((Q_1 - Q_2) \div Q_1) \div ((P_1 - P_2) \div P_1)$$

Where:
E = the price elasticity coefficient
Q = the quantity demanded
P = the price

The result differs from the previous definition: with a price elasticity coefficient of −1, the percentage decrease in price is equal to the percentage increase in the quantity demanded. Total revenue declines, rather than remaining constant.

Although the price elasticity coefficient may not be known, in any forecast an assumption should be made that a change in prices has some effect on demand. The forecast may simply assume that if prices drop by 10%, revenue will decline by 10%, that is, the quantity demanded remains constant and so the price elasticity coefficient is 0. It is much better to use price elasticity explicitly. Even if the price elasticity coefficient is not an explicit input, it should be calculated as an output.

In some cases, there are difficulties in establishing the quantities demanded. For example, in the case of a mobile phone, the monthly bill consists of the subscription or line rental charge (which may include some minutes of usage), the per minute charge for voice calls and an amount for data services. Different rates may apply for different types of minutes and data services. With a great deal of effort the elasticities for each could be established. A way around this difficulty is to apply the price elasticity coefficient directly to the monthly bill:

$$B_2 = B_1 \times (1 + (P_1 - P_2) \div P_1 \times (1 - E))$$

Where:

B = the average monthly bill
E = the price elasticity coefficient
P = the price index

This demonstrates that the general principle of price elasticity of demand and other elasticities can be used imaginatively to develop a forecast that is still based on accepted models of market behaviour.

Using price elasticity as an explanatory variable to forecast demand has limitations. As is apparent from diffusion of innovation theories, demand increases regardless of changes in price. However, a combination of different methods may yield appropriate results. The example below illustrates how the problem of forecasting revenue from mobile internet services can be tackled.

- Empirical evidence shows that average monthly bills are decreasing (see Chart 12.17 on the next page). This is used as supporting evidence. On average, later adopters are willing to spend less than earlier adopters are.
- Existing mobile phone users react to changes in tariffs in an elastic manner (see Chart 12.18 on the next page). As tariffs decrease, they spend less but also use the handset more. The increase in usage partially offsets the decrease in prices. Price elasticity coefficients can be used to forecast the average monthly bill for existing customers as a function of changes in tariffs.
- Market research into how much potential users of mobile internet services are prepared to pay reveals a classic price elasticity of demand curve (see Chart 12.19 on page 131).
- Based on market research, an s-shaped penetration curve is used to make a forecast for the penetration of mobile internet services among the population.
- An assumption is made that prices for mobile internet services decrease following an s-shaped curve.

The average monthly spend for mobile internet services is calculated in two steps (see Chart 12.20 on page 131). First, the formula from the price elasticity chart is used to calculate how much marginal users will spend per month, that is, what the monthly bill of marginal customers will be. Second, the average monthly bill is calculated as the sum of the marginal bills, adjusted by how existing users react to price decreases. In the example, a price elasticity coefficient of −0.3 is used in the formula that applies price elasticity directly to the monthly bill.

Chart 12.17 **Empirical evidence of declining monthly bill in the US mobile telephony market**

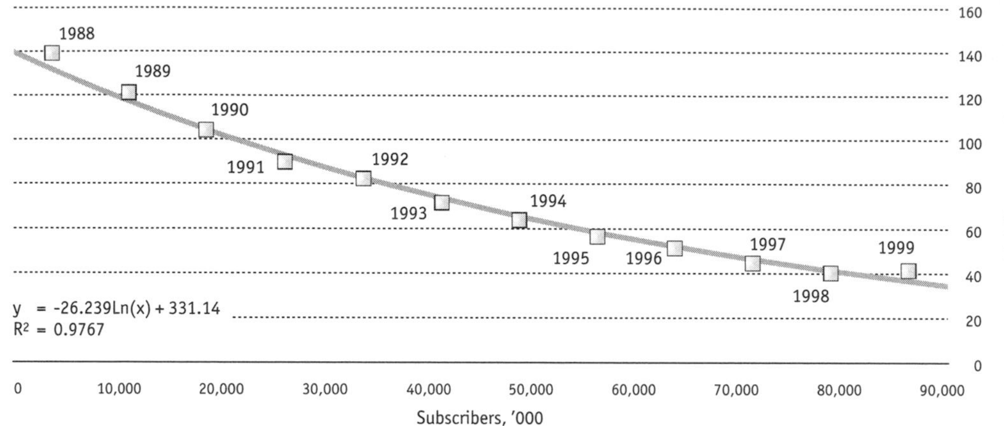

*Excluding long distance and roaming.
Source: CTIA

Chart 12.18 **Empirical evidence of price elasticity of demand in the UK telephony market**

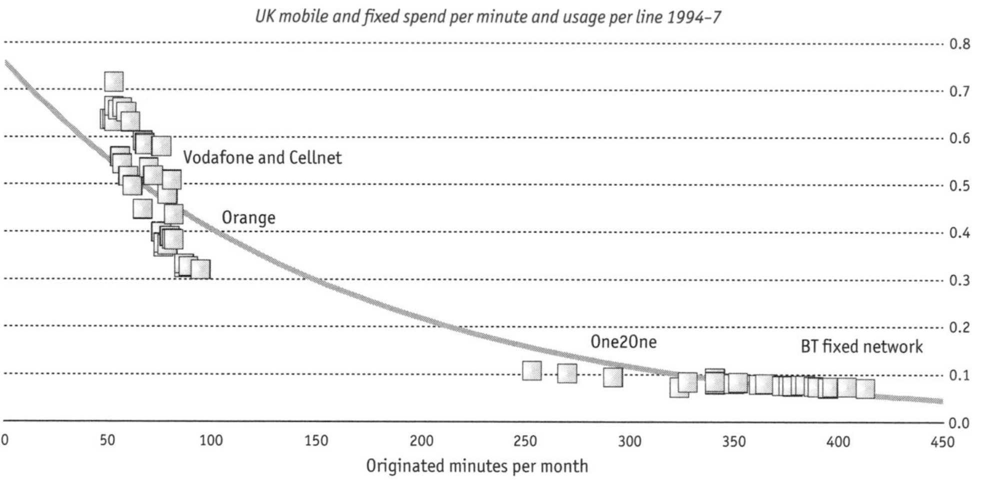

Source: Oftel Quarterly Data 1994-97

Chart 12.19 **Mobile internet demand survey**

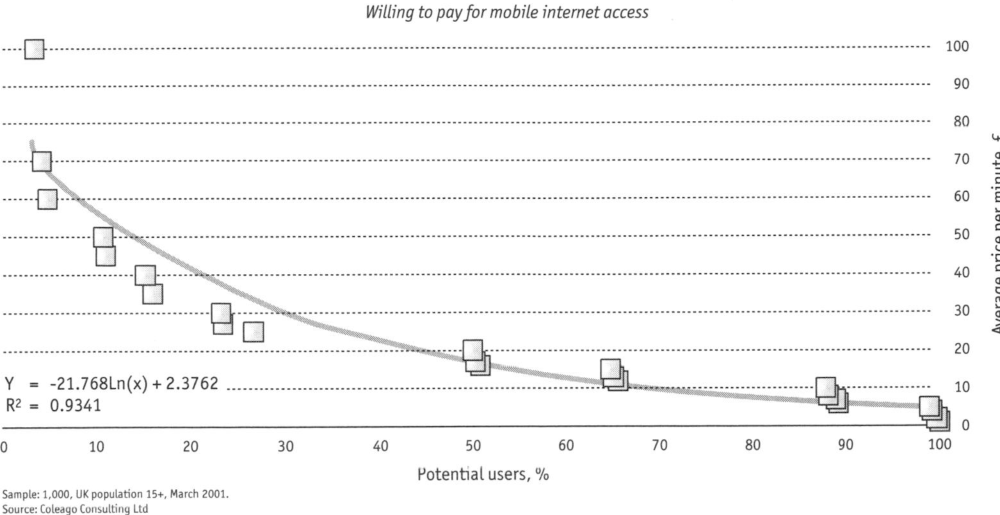

Sample: 1,000, UK population 15+, March 2001.
Source: Coleago Consulting Ltd

Chart 12.20 **Average monthly bill forecast**

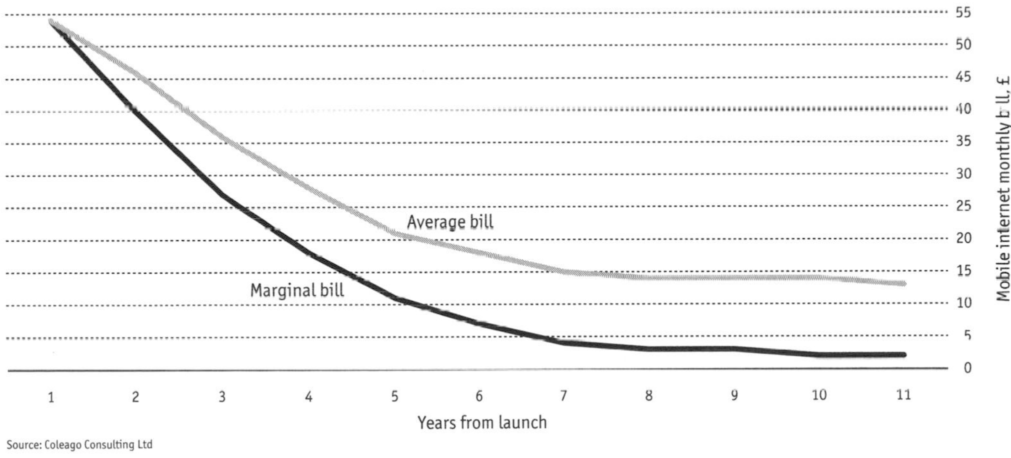

Source: Coleago Consulting Ltd

Repeat and replacement sales

In the case of non-durable products or services, the sales volume is a function of how many customers are using the product and how often they make a repeat purchase. For consumer durable products, sales volumes are a function of first-adoption and replacement sales. In both cases, it is advisable first to forecast the number of first-time users (which can be done based on the diffusion of innovation theory) and second to make an assumption for the frequency of repeat sales. This two-step approach makes the forecasting process easier and also provides a breakdown of sales. In marketing terms, there is a big difference between the number of people using a product and repeat sales.

In the case of consumer durable goods, the annual sales volume is a function of the increase in the installed base, or first-time sales, and replacement sales to those who are already using the product. Replacement sales are a function of product failure, obsolescence, or upgrades. The average useful life of a product may change over time.

The calculation of replacement sales could be very complex. This is because, for every period, the number of replacement sales is not a function of the installed base, but a function of the number of new sales n years before the current year, where n is the average product life before replacement. Given that n is an estimated average and the precise age distribution of the existing base is normally not known, a simpler approach, such as expressing replacement sales as a percentage of the installed base at the end of the previous period, is just as good.

Chart 12.21 **Replacement sales forecast for a consumer durable**

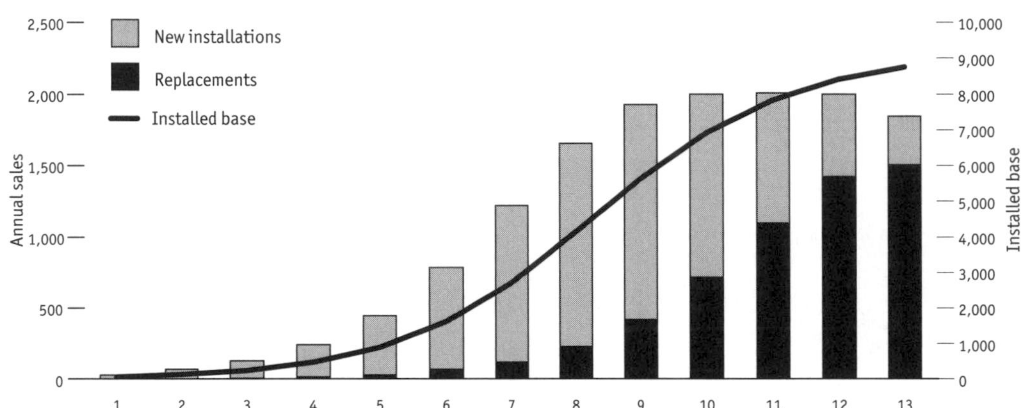

Combining market behaviour models to make a forecast

As indicated above, an s-shaped product life cycle in combination with the experience effect and a repeat or replacement sales calculation can be used to construct a forecast where all variables are dependent on the product life cycle curve. Chart 12.22 shows a simple sales projection for the total market. The market share assumption has to be added to this in order to calculate the firm's sales.

The penetration of potential demand is forecast using the formula on page 123. Sales prices have been forecast using the observation of how prices decrease over the product life cycle. The assumption has been made that the decrease is inversely proportional to the rate of market growth. When the market grows fastest, prices are also falling rapidly.

Chart 12.22 **Marketing forecast model**

Product life cycle model inputs	
Maximum potential penetration	10%
Years to maturity	10
PLC curve skew value a	99
Product launched in year	1
Experience factor	0.4
Cost of first unit	1,000
Sales price in year 1	600
Margin in year 10	60%
Replacement %	40%

Year	*1*	*2*	*3*	*4*	*5*	*6*	*7*	*8*	*9*	*10*	*11*
Population	10,000	10,030	10,060	10,090	10,121	10,151	10,181	10,212	10,243	10,273	10,304
Potential installed base '000	1,000	1,003	1,006	1,009	1,012	1,015	1,018	1,021	1,024	1,027	1,030
Value b	0.988842										
Penetration of potential	1%	3%	7%	16%	35%	59%	79%	91%	96%	99%	100%
Years product on market	0	1	2	3	4	5	6	7	8	9	10
Installed base	10	27	68	166	349	595	807	930	988	1,014	1,025
New sales	10	17	42	97	184	246	211	124	58	25	12
Replacements	0	2	19	47	103	189	280	347	384	400	408
Total unit sales	10	19	61	144	287	435	492	471	442	426	419
Cumulative sales	10	29	89	233	520	955	1,447	1,918	2,360	2,785	3,205
Average unit cost	525	306	196	131	93	71	59	51	47	43	41
Sales price	600	587	566	518	428	308	205	146	119	108	102
Margin	12%	48%	65%	75%	78%	77%	71%	65%	61%	60%	60%
Implied price elasticity		-26.9	-29.7	-9.2	-3.5	-1.3	-0.3	0.1	0.3	0.4	0.2
Market value	6,000	10,865	34,481	74,557	122,800	133,811	100,922	68,814	52,644	46,124	42,659
Costs	5,253	5,671	11,924	18,829	26,754	30,980	28,830	24,148	20,564	18,405	17,064
Profits	747	5,194	22,556	55,728	96,046	102,831	72,092	44,665	32,080	27,719	25,596

Chart 12.23 **Installed base, unit sales, costs, prices**

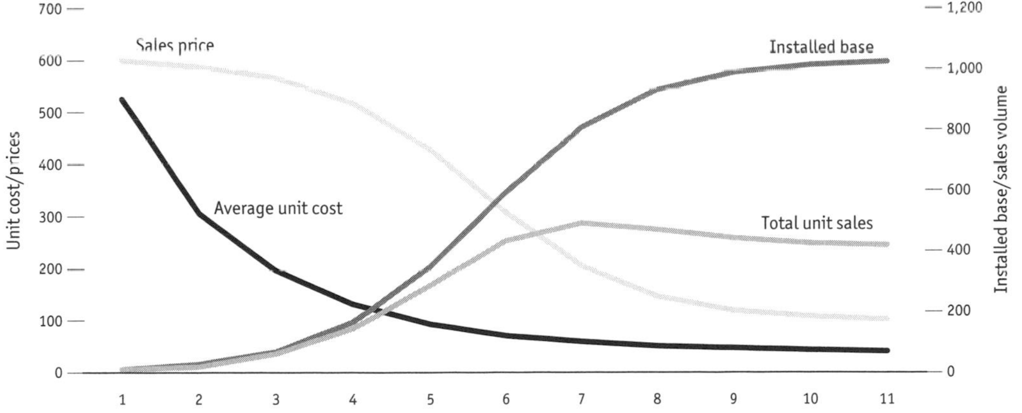

Chart 12.24 **Total unit sales and market value**

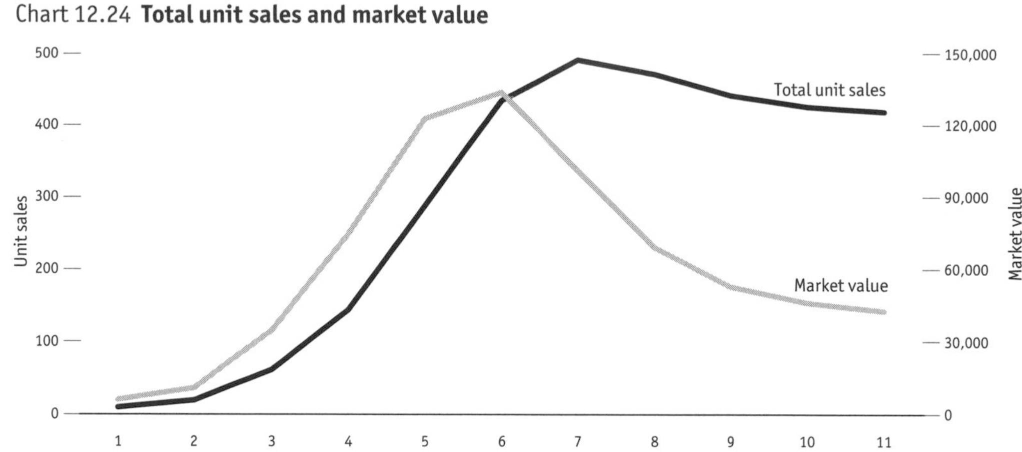

REASONABLENESS CHECKS

Even if a forecast is based on detailed quantitative techniques and careful use of market behaviour models, it is advisable to carry out several reasonableness checks. These can be both external (using a top-down approach) and internal.

- The forecast market value can be compared with GDP. Does the market forecast imply that the total market value will grow to an unrealistically high proportion of GDP?
- If the business is limited by the number of retail outlets it can establish, this may become the limiting factor in the forecast. It may not be possible to establish the required number of retail outlets in the time available owing to practical issues such as obtaining planning permission.

Ideally, these reasonableness checks should be built into the forecast. In practical terms, this means that several ratios should be tracked for each forecast period. The choice of ratios will depend on the business in question. These ratios should be relatively simple so that a judgment as to whether the ratios trend in a reasonable manner can easily be made.

LIMITATIONS OF FORECASTING METHODS AND TECHNIQUES

Economics and business studies are social sciences. In contrast to natural science, there is a lack of exactitude. Rather than the laws of natural science, the business planner has to rely on data that is obscured by random effects and use descriptive models. In a scientific experiment the outcome can be exactly predicted, but with demand forecasts the future is not known. Observations and models such as price elasticity of demand are helpful in explaining what may happen and why. However, the limitation in the context of forecasting is that in order to forecast demand as a function of price changes, you would have to make a forecast of both price changes and the price elasticity coefficient.

Models are by their nature reductionist. Therefore, while statistical analysis and models are the forecaster's tools of trade, the forecaster has to stand back and take a broader view. If a forecast seems implausible, this is generally because it is implausible. Markets are not closed systems. For example, if a forecast results in an extremely high return on investment, it is likely that the forecast underpinning the business plan is unrealistic. If an industry is very profitable, more competitors are likely to enter the market, leading to a loss in market share and increased price competition. This would change the firm's demand and revenue forecast.

Despite these limitations, the application of available techniques and models will produce a forecast that stands up to scrutiny. The application of a well-researched and clearly structured methodology, based on accepted economic theory and market models, instils confidence in decision-makers, investors and lenders.

THE MARKETING PLANNING MODEL

The marketing plan is the description of how the marketing strategy is to be implemented: the segmentation and the tactics to be employed. This is covered in Chapter 11. Crucially, the marketing plan also includes the marketing forecast. This means the marketing plan is not just a word document, but also normally includes a detailed spreadsheet model, the marketing planning model. The marketing model contains the marketing forecast, including potential demand, total market and market share, all of which are discussed above.

The marketing plan should also include the costs of sales, advertising and promotions. A cost of sale is a cost that would not have occurred had a particular unit sale not taken place. For example, if a business buys in goods for resale the buy in cost is a cost of sale, and if sales people receive a commission per sale this is also a cost of sale. However, the salary of a salesperson is not a cost of sale because it has to be paid independently of the volume of sales. Net revenue minus cost of sales is defined as the gross margin. This means the marketing plan (see Chart 12.25 on the next page) includes a gross margin forecast and therefore has a strong financial component.

Often marketing management focuses on revenue. However, giving marketing management responsibility to produce a forecast to gross margin and to generate the forecast for marketing operational expenditure makes it become more profit focused. This leads to better financial discipline. Gross margin is an important measure because it shows the contribution from incremental sales.

Gross margin should be forecast for each product. For example, a mobile phone company may have segmented the market into prepaid customers, consumer contract customers, small and medium-sized enterprise contract customers and large corporate customers. A specific offer will be made to each segment, and there will be a separate product manager in charge of each offer; for example, the prepaid product manager will be responsible for prepaid tariffs. It is the responsibility of the prepaid product manager to deliver gross margin from prepaid customers. Therefore the profit and loss account (income statement) has to identify the prepaid gross margin, and this must be reflected in the marketing planning model.

Chart 12.25 **The marketing planning model**

Marketing plan		*Period 1*	*Period 2*	*Period 3*	*Period 4*
Unit sales	'000	1,000	1,100	1,210	1,331
Unit price		10	9	8	7
Gross revenue	'000	10,000	9,900	9,680	9,317
Revenue discounts	'000	(300)	(297)	(290)	(280)
Net revenue	'000	9,700	9,603	9,390	9,037
Cost of goods for resale	'000	(2,000)	(2,079)	(2,130)	(2,096)
Direct sales commission	'000	(388)	(384)	(376)	(361)
Other costs of sales	'000	0	0	0	0
Bad debt	'000	(146)	(144)	(141)	(136)
Total costs of sales	'000	(2,534)	(2,607)	(2,647)	(2,593)
Gross margin	'000	7,166	6,996	6,743	6,444
Gross margin	%	74	73	72	71
Advertising costs	'000	(200)	(220)	(242)	(266)
Promotions costs	'000	(30)	(30)	(160)	(30)
Other marketing costs	'000	(40)	(42)	(44)	(46)
Total marketing costs	'000	(270)	(292)	(446)	(342)
Marketing costs/sales	%	3	3	5	4

Next to the financial statements and valuation, the marketing plan is probably the part of a business plan that will be most scrutinised by decision-makers. It provides the basis for the sales forecast, which more or less drives all other business plan assumptions. The marketing plan is part of demonstrating that unmet demand exists and can be served profitably.

USES OF OUTCOMES IN THE BUSINESS PLAN

The demand forecast, and with it the sales forecast, is the most important aspect of a business plan. The sales forecast drives the marketing planning model, which in turn drives almost all other variables of the business planning model. So considerable attention must be paid to the demand and sales forecast. If there is insufficient demand the business will fail, regardless of how well it is organised.

Investors and decision-makers will examine the demand and sales forecast in some detail. It should also be subjected to extensive sensitivity testing. For example, you should find out by how much you could undershoot your sales forecast before the investment is no longer viable; the margin should be relatively wide. Investigating the impact of lower sales on the business will also reveal how scalable your business is – whether, if sales are lower than expected, the scale and investment can be reduced. In such a case, the business will be simply on a smaller scale but still profitable. Some businesses may not be scalable and the risk of demand being lower than forecast is therefore greater.

References

1 Rogers, E.M., *Diffusion of Innovations*, 4th edition, The Free Press, 1995.

2 Bass, F.M, "A new product growth model for consumer durables", *Management Science*, Vol. 15, No. 5, 1969.

13 The operational plan

OBJECTIVES

To explain how the business will actually carry out its activity, an operational plan is required. The operational plan is central to the allocation of resources. It uses inputs from the marketing plan to scale operations in order to deliver what is set out in the marketing plan, and it includes information about all stages of primary value chain activities as well as support activities.

The operational plan should contain a description of the organisational structure, including an organisation chart. Human resources are one of the most important resources of a business, and payroll and related costs account for a large part of operational expenditure.

In the context of business modelling, the operational plan is a spreadsheet model which includes most operational and capital expenditure items and the quantification of physical items, such as office space, plant and machinery. The operational plan is the main cost driver, whereas the marketing plan (see Chapter 11) is the revenue driver. It includes the cost of sales and some marketing costs.

LEGAL FORM OF BUSINESS AND OTHER FORMALITIES

One of the first steps is to decide the legal form of the business: sole trader, partnership, limited liability partnership, limited company, or another corporate form that may be available in different jurisdictions. The legal form should be appropriate to the business in question, its future expansion and capital structure.

The legal form of the business is also important in terms of control and corporate governance. The relationships between investors can be further refined by means of shareholder agreements or specific clauses in the articles of association.

Among the formalities that should be addressed are the following:

- Company formation
- Location of registered office
- Appointment of accountant and auditor
- Appointment of company secretary
- Registration of business in commercial register or chamber of commerce
- Membership of industry associations
- Registration with the tax authorities
- VAT registration
- Registration of internet domain name
- Establishment of company bank account and payment facilities
- Registration of trade marks

It is important to be aware that in some countries, such as the UK and the United States, a business can be set up quickly (often in one day) and cheaply, but in others the process can take up to two months and may involve a great deal of form filling, authorisations, certified translations, notarised documents, fees, and so on.

ORGANISATIONAL STRUCTURE

The organisational structure itself should be consistent with the vision and objectives of the business and can be a source of competitive advantage. The organisation chart should reflect responsibilities for delivering margin and take account of the elements of the value chain. It identifies the departments, lines of reporting, span of control and staff numbers. Departments reflect the specialist skills that are necessary to deliver value to the customer. Reporting lines identify responsibilities, power and information flow. The number of subordinates directly controlled by a manager or supervisor is referred to as span of control. Particularly in larger organisations, management layers are an important cost factor. There should be a balance between what managers can achieve without being overburdened and the desire for a lean organisational structure.

Types of organisational structures

The structure of an organisation will depend on size, geographic scope and type of industry.

Functional structure

A functional organisational structure divides the business along the main value chain activities, with each function reporting to the top management. This type of structure is simple and provides clear reporting lines. It is suitable for small companies because people can communicate easily and are usually aware of what other departments are doing. In very small firms, one individual may carry out several functions, but the functional positions should be identified. For example, an inventor who founded a business may be the chief executive officer and the chief technical officer.

Divisional structure

A divisional structure is suitable for larger companies. The divisions may be strategic business units (SBUs), which can be extremely diverse with very different products and markets. The structure must be tailored to meet the needs of each SBU. Some functions, notably support functions of the value chain such as finance, human resources, and research and development, may be located at head-office level.

Decisions on whether to locate particular support functions at head-office or divisional level depend on the diversity of the SBUs and the benefits of centralisation compared with decentralisation. The more decentralised an organisation is, the easier it is to apply a product-portfolio approach to strategy development. However, decentralisation may also imply duplication and the inability to exploit cross-divisional synergies.

A divisional structure may be particularly appropriate where the SBUs are also physically separate, for example located at different sites or even in different countries. It may be necessary for legal reasons to operate an SBU in another country as a subsidiary rather than as a branch office. Where businesses are located on different continents, differences in time zone, language and culture may necessitate a division along geographic lines, but some functions, such as R&D, may still be centralised.

Holding company structure

A holding company is a small unit controlling a collection of independent companies which may not even be wholly owned subsidiaries. The holding-company functions are reduced to a few support functions such as finance and overall strategic planning.

Matrix structure

The matrix structure combines elements of the functional and divisional structure. The value chain and the marketing view of business (see Chapter 11, Chart 11.1, on page 99) both require a product-oriented structure. If a product manager is responsible for delivering margin, he or she must have some influence across all primary activities. The manager has to ensure that the value chain is optimally configured and resourced to support the chosen product strategy.

However, primary and support functions are a shared resource among several products. For example, a telephony company may have a consumer and business telephony product because the needs of the segments are very different. But the network over which services are delivered (switches, transmission and so on) is the same, and there has to be one person responsible for network operations.

The dichotomy of the product-management approach and functional organisation is resolved by adopting a matrix organisational structure. A matrix structure is more complex and requires more management interaction. Conflicts can arise if reporting structures or responsibilities are not clear. In the case of the telephony company, the quality of service the business product manager requires may be different from what the consumer product manager requires, but this cannot be provided because the network is the same. There has to be a final arbiter who is hierarchically above the product managers, but the responsibility of delivering margin for a product always stays with the product managers.

Chart 13.1 **Functional structure**

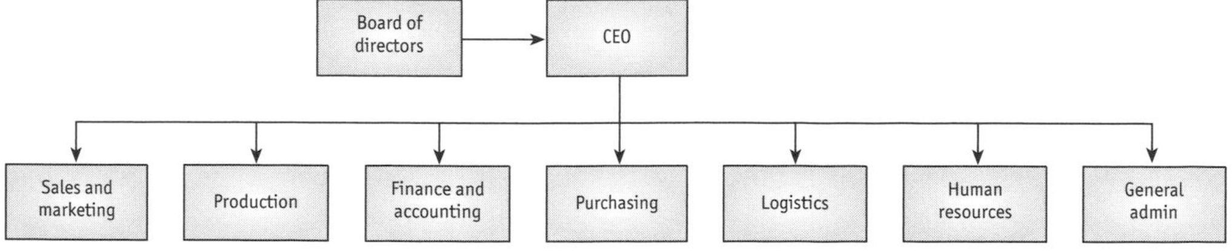

Chart 13.2 **Divisional structure**

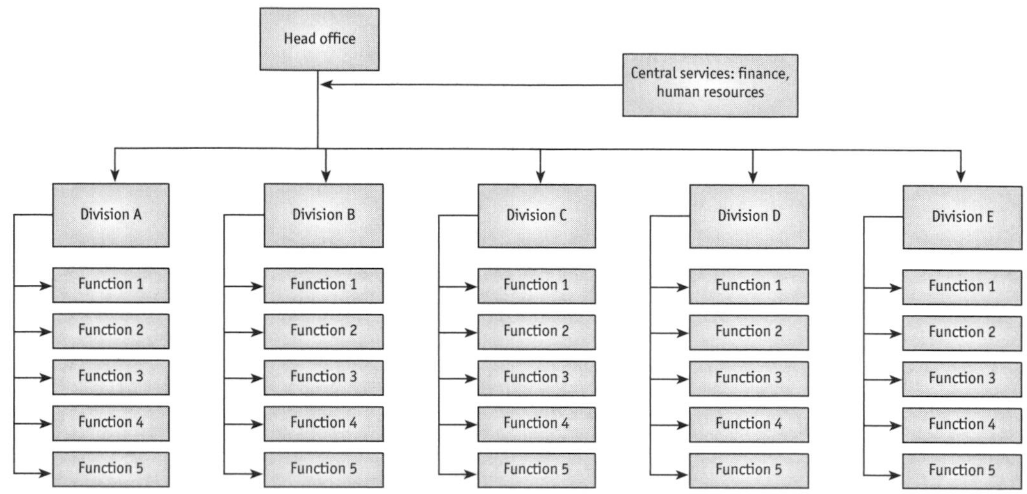

Chart 13.3 **Matrix structure**

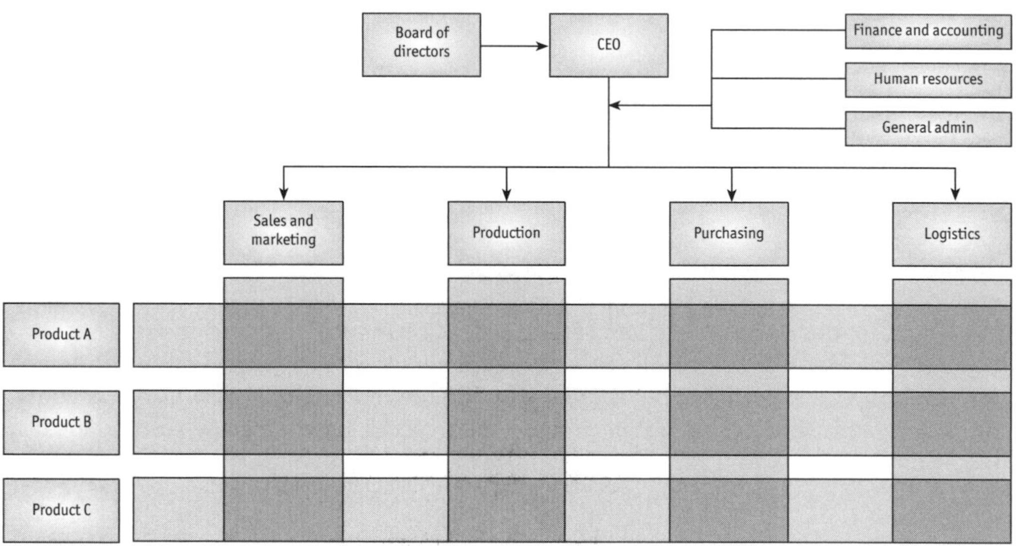

The management team and corporate governance

It is important, particularly for new businesses, to demonstrate that a management team with the right skills is in place. A new investment is a bet on the future where the odds are substantially improved if the business is run by managers who can not only execute the plan but also respond flexibly to changes in the environment as they arise. Board directors (including non-executive directors), top management and key functional managers must be identified by name. Their CVs should be in the appendix to the business plan.

The functioning of the board should be described and the role of the chairman compared with the managing director or CEO should be explained. If appropriate, make reference to guidelines of corporate governance and explain how shareholders exercise control of the board.

HUMAN RESOURCE MANAGEMENT

Having identified and described the management team, the next step is to address staffing. This includes staff numbers, recruitment, retention, training and redundancy. These factors will be a major driver of operational costs. The costs are not just salary and related costs such as employer's contribution to insurance, pensions and training, but also office space, workstations and other items.

Human resource issues to be addressed in the business plan include:

- Appropriate staffing to cover shifts, holidays, illness.
- Span of control, that is, how many managers per staff.
- Salary levels.
- Are trained staff available or do staff have to be trained.
- Continuing training.
- Recruitment costs.
- Staff turnover.
- Employment legislation (working hours, work environment, health and safety, pensions, redundancy).

PHYSICAL INFRASTRUCTURE

Investors want to know what their money is being spent on, so the business plan must identify and describe the physical infrastructure of the firm. The infrastructure comprises all major assets, new assets that have to be acquired, and their function and physical location. Such assets include office space, production facilities, IT and support systems, vehicles and any other facility used by the organisation.

If factories are to be built, the sites should be identified. The reasons for location at a particular site should be explained, for example the price of land, the availability of transport links, nearby qualified staff, or government grants.

Facilities can be bought (capital expenditure) or rented (operational expenditure). Either way, the physical infrastructure is a major cost driver and deserves appropriate attention. Rent or buy decisions should be based on careful analysis of the financial implications, looking at funding, profitability, tax and liability issues. For example, long leases create a liability to pay future rents, whereas loans can be secured against a building that is owned outright.

In some cases, the business plan must include a detailed technical description of the facilities. For example, if a new telecommunications network investment is considered there must be a network plan with all relevant elements identified and costed. For a manufacturing business, the processes and required machinery should be described. Depending on the relative capital intensity of a firm, the description of fixed assets and how they are financed will be more or less detailed.

CAPITAL AND OPERATIONAL EXPENDITURE

The operational plan drives capital expenditure (capex) and operational expenditure (opex). The business plan modelling of these is discussed in Chapter 14. The manner in which opex and capex are modelled should reflect the organisational structure. This will make it easier to understand the link between the financials and operations. In practical terms, this could mean organising the spreadsheet business planning model along departmental lines. There could be one worksheet per department, showing clearly that the budgetary responsibility lies with the relevant departmental manager, who is also identified on the organisation chart.

The linkage between organisational structure and financials makes it possible to identify the cost of particular activities. As a result, the profitability of SBUs or products can be ascertained not just at gross margin level (see Chapter 11) but also at EBIT (earnings before interest and tax) level.

You may even go further and identify the cost of value chain activities. An understanding of costs is as important as understanding revenue, for without knowing costs it is impossible to identify where value is added. In mature markets, an understanding of costs and how to trim them is of pre-eminent importance.

USES OF OUTCOMES IN THE BUSINESS PLAN

The operational plan explains how the business is structured, what resources are required and how these resources are employed to achieve the strategic objectives. It explains how investors' money is spent. In financial terms, it provides most operational expenditure items and all capital expenditure items as inputs into the business planning model.

14 Modelling the business

OBJECTIVES

The main reason for developing a business model is to generate the financial forecasts that are a fundamental element of any business plan. But a business model also allows you to understand better the economics and drivers of the business and helps in the assessment of risk. It enables you to evaluate quantitatively alternative strategic options as well as assess the funding requirement. If sufficiently detailed, it can provide a tool for the day-to-day management of the business.

APPROACHES TO BUSINESS MODELLING

The most commonly used tool for business modelling is a spreadsheet package such as Microsoft's Excel. The examples in Chapters 15–19 and the business planning model that accompanies them (see page 145) have been built in Excel, although the principles apply to any spreadsheet package. A basic knowledge of spreadsheets is assumed in the following chapters, but if detailed help with business modelling is required see *The Economist Guide to Business Modelling*, which explains in full many of the techniques used.

CHARACTERISTICS OF A GOOD BUSINESS MODEL

A good business model should be:

- free of computational and technical errors;
- consistent with the assumptions made about the market and the strategy and tactics to be executed;
- capable of generating the results necessary to evaluate alternative strategic options;
- complete in terms of capturing all the relevant revenues, operating costs and capital expenditure items as well as any financing cash flows, including interest and principal repayments on debt or dividends on equity;
- cover the appropriate business planning time horizon and also the time period each year is broken down into, be it weekly, monthly, quarterly or annually;
- capable of easily running sensitivities and scenarios to test how robust the plan is in terms of unexpected changes in the environment;
- constructed to the appropriate level of detail.

The length of the forecast

The number of years to include in the business model and the number of periods each year is broken down into will vary between business planning projects. A small business should forecast a few years beyond the year in which it expects to start generating cash. As most small businesses will hope to begin generating cash within 1–3 years at most and often within a few months, a business model covering up to 3–5 years is usually sufficient. For large companies considering major investments the payback period may extend many years, and in such cases a ten-year forecast is usually developed. In uncertain markets, even forecasting three or five years is difficult and extending the forecast much beyond this point provides little additional benefit.

Bankers and equity investors providing finance to small businesses will be interested to know when their money is required and for how long. In these cases it may be necessary to develop the model on a monthly or quarterly basis, especially if the forecast is for only a few years. If the business plan is intended to form the basis of the operational budget, a monthly-based forecast will probably be required. Otherwise a quarterly or annual forecast is usually sufficient.

THE BUSINESS PLANNING MODEL

The business planning model that accompanies this book has been designed primarily to help the reader understand basic accounting principles. The model can be downloaded from www.guidetobusinessplanning.com. Readers with good spreadsheet skills will be able to modify the model for use in their own business. The model covers a ten-year period on an annual basis and generates a complete set of financial statements, including profit and loss account (income statement), balance sheet and cash flow statements, as well as various valuation measures and a comprehensive set of financial ratios. The model incorporates two product items and two items of stock as well as two customer segments, although only one product and stock item is used in the worked example. The model also contains the following:

- Staff cost calculations.
- Bad debt assumptions.
- Nine other operating cost categories that can be labelled by the user.
- Inputs for expenditure on physical capital, such as vehicles, as well as expenditure on intangible items such as patents and licences.
- Depreciation and amortisation workings for tangible and intangible assets based on the straight line method of depreciation, a concept addressed in more detail in the following chapters.
- Working capital calculations for debtors, stock, trade creditors and taxation creditors.
- Simple financing that includes a mixture of debt, equity or bank overdraft.
- Computations for interest charges, principal repayments and the interest earned on short-term cash deposits at banks.

USING THE MODEL

The model has been designed to be easy to use, even for those with little or no experience of Excel. To explore the model, select the version of the model entitled "Blank Model". On opening it, click ENABLE in relation to macros. A warning may also be encountered in relation to circular references. If a warning appears, follow these steps: click OK on the warning, close down any help messages that might appear, select TOOLS from the menu bar and OPTIONS, select the CALCULATION tab, check the iteration box and enter 100 for the maximum number of iterations, then click OK.

The model is menu-based and you can navigate between sheets by simply clicking on the appropriate button. Chart 14.1 shows the opening menu screen for the model.

Chart 14.1 **Main menu screen**

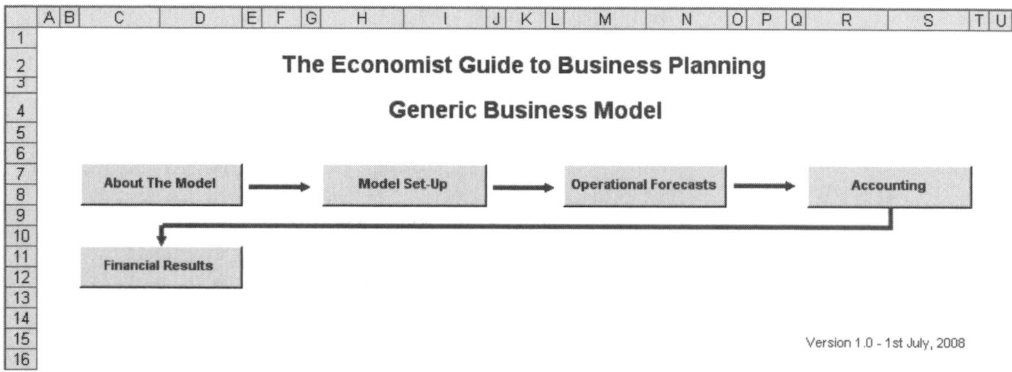

By clicking on a button, for example OPERATIONAL FORECASTS, the user is taken to the appropriate section menu. The operational forecasts section menu is shown in Chart 14.2.

Chart 14.2 **Section menu**

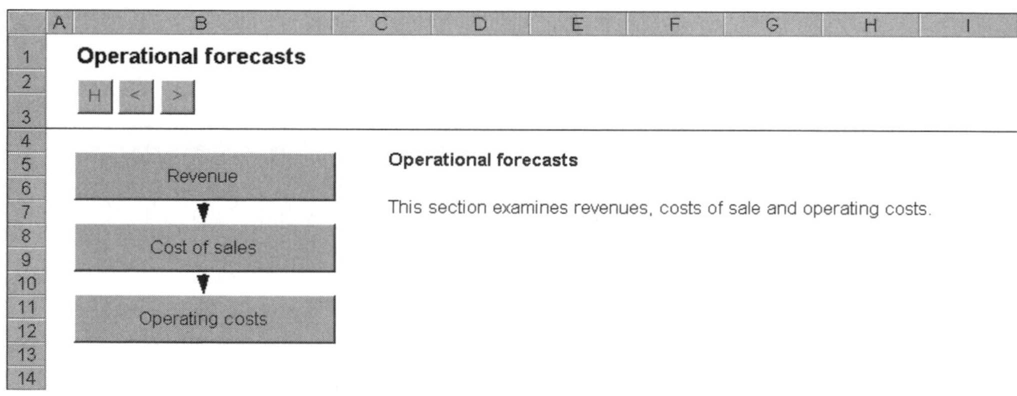

The H button returns you to the main menu, and the arrows move you to the previous or next section – the back arrow to the model set-up section and the forward arrow to the accounting section – in accordance with the flow chart of the main menu.

Within a particular subsection or sheet there are up to four buttons (a typical example is shown in Chart 14.3). The revenue sheet can be selected by clicking on the REVENUE button in the operational forecast section menu. Within a sheet, the H button will return you to the main menu, the C button to the section menu and the arrows move you through the subsections.

Chart 14.3 **Subsection structure**

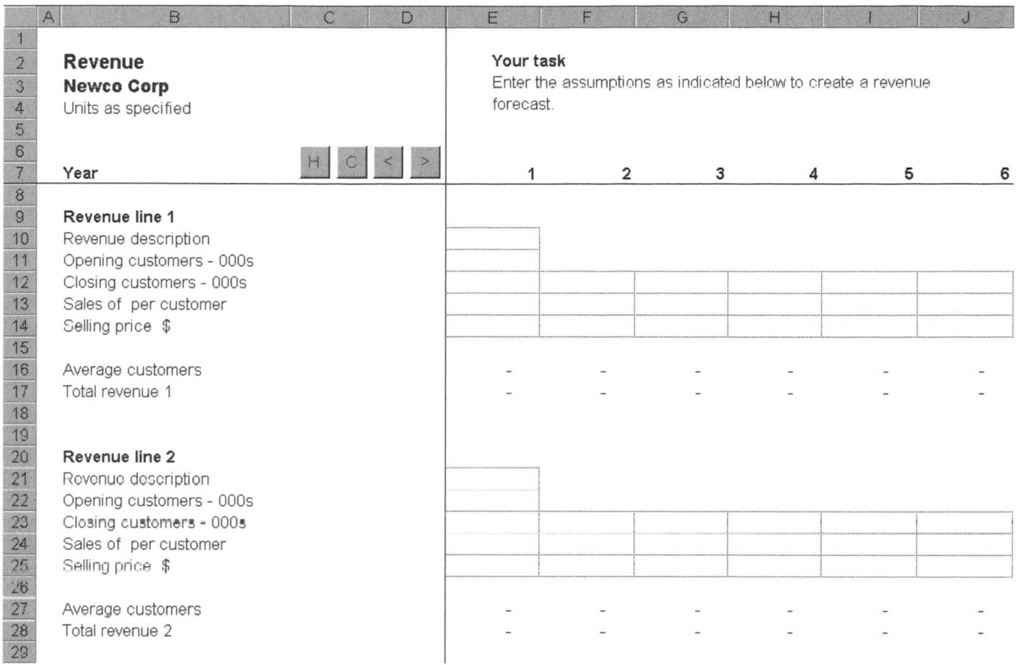

Inputs for the model are entered in the appropriate sheets or subsections to provide context and for users to see immediately the results of their actions. User inputs are required in the boxes surrounded by a dotted line and all user inputs appear in blue. The model has been protected so that entries are possible only in the input cells. An example of user inputs can be seen in Chart 14.4. To access the model set-up page from the main menu, select model set-up. The book uses (MAIN MENU → MODEL SET-UP) as a standard notation for guiding you in the use of the menu structure.

Chart 14.4 **User inputs**

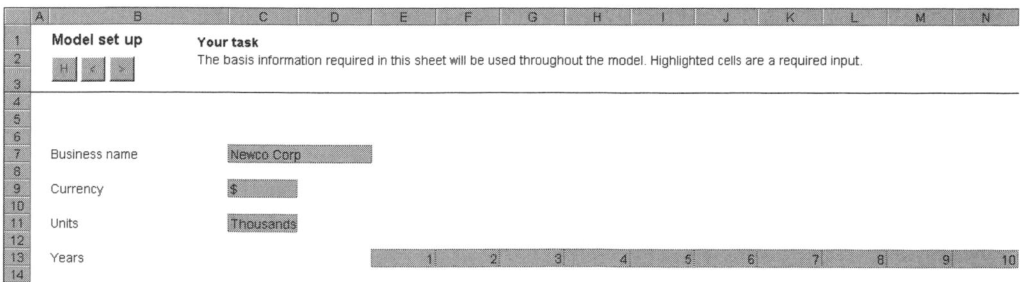

An overview of the structure of the model and sheets within each section is presented in Chart 14.5 on the next page. The subsection or sheets in italics require user inputs.

Chart 14.5 **Model structure**

About the model	Model set-up	Operational forecasts	Accounting	Financial results
About the model	*Model set-up*	*Revenue*	*Depreciation*	Profit and loss
		Cost of sales	*Amortisation*	*Balance sheet*
		Operating costs	*Working capital*	Cash flow statement
			Financing	Ratios
			Taxation	*Valuation*

If you wish to turn off the protection to allow for further development, select TOOLS on the main menu bar and then PROTECTION and finally UNPROTECT SHEET. No password has been used to protect the model.

Within a particular subsection the sheet has been divided into two or four sections. Use the standard Excel scroll bars to ensure that the relevant columns are visible when reviewing results in the model.

THE WORKED EXAMPLE

As well as the blank version of the model, there is a fully completed version (Complete Model) of the worked example developed in the following chapters. The Appendix also contains all the sections of the model, representing the results of completing all stages of the worked example. Intermediate results arising from the initial stages of the worked example will not necessarily correspond to the results in the completed model. All stages of the worked example must be completed before the results will agree.

A set of business planning assumptions is used for a fictitious company to illustrate the basic principles of accounting. You can enter the suggested inputs from the worked examples into the blank version to see how they flow through the workings of the model to the financial statements. Alternatively, you can simply follow the examples in the book and review the completed model in the Appendix.

A scenario-style commentary on the worked example is provided to give some context. The fictitious company is Newco Corp, the first company to introduce the widget into the market of Newberg. Newco is a start-up company with no existing operations, staff, revenues or costs. As a result, the balance sheet at the start of the forecast period is blank. The widget is a mass-market product and revenues are expected to be in multiples of millions.

The business intends to spend aggressively on advertising to raise awareness of the value of widgets among the population of Newberg. There is only one customer segment, but they can buy any number of widgets in the year. The one stock item that enters the widget manufacturing process is the zapper. A certain amount of manufacturing equipment is required to produce the widget, so a factory and workers are required. Some pieces of equipment are purchased and others are leased. The premises are rented.

The widget is produced under licence from the inventor, so it is necessary to purchase a licence to manufacture it. The business is financed through a combination of equity, bank loans and an overdraft facility.

Inflation and interest rates are stable as Newberg is part of a trading union, and its currency is the dollar. The stability of the dollar allows the forecast to be generated in nominal terms. Nominal forecasts include the effects of inflation such that the price of the widget in year 9 is the price the customer will actually pay in year 9. In contrast, in a real forecast all future figures are quoted in today's prices and the impact of inflation is excluded.

USING THE MODEL IN YOUR OWN BUSINESS

Although the business model that accompanies this book lacks the detail and complexity of more comprehensive models, it is more than adequate to generate an initial financial forecast for most small businesses. In the examples that follow, a number of rows that are not used in the example have been hidden. To view the full model including these rows, select the entire sheet, unprotect it, then select FORMAT → ROW → UNHIDE. Hidden rows can be found in the working capital and profit and loss sheets. Readers who do not already have a business model but are skilled in business modelling can develop the model to meet the needs of their own business. For those with limited experience of business modelling and accounting, the remainder of this chapter may be best read once the next two chapters have been completed. Some of the more advanced developments that could be performed are described below.

- The model could be changed to a quarterly or monthly version. If the length of the periods is altered from an annual basis you must either adapt the calculations for interest, working capital and discount rates and so on to reflect the altered length of period or alter the inputs to accommodate this change in duration.
- A further change may be to enhance the revenue forecasting elements to incorporate the techniques covered in Chapter 12. Simple development options include increasing the number of customer segments and increasing the range of products sold.
- Additional stock items can be introduced.
- More sophisticated stock valuation techniques can also be employed, such as last in first out (LIFO) or first in first out (FIFO), which are discussed in the next chapter.
- Prepayments and accruals can be included.
- The model could be extended to include a dividend debtor account.
- The model could be extended to include different types of capital expenditure items and the number of depreciation and amortisation workings could be expanded to reflect assets with varying asset lives.
- The sophistication of the capital expenditure workings could be expanded to introduce the disposal of fixed assets and the profit or loss on the disposal.
- The taxation workings can be enhanced by limiting the length of time that losses can be carried forward.

15 Accounting principles

THE FIVE FUNDAMENTAL ACCOUNTING PRINCIPLES

Accountants have developed five fundamental accounting principles that provide the basis for all accounting policies. These ensure that the most prudent and objective presentation of the financial results is achieved.

Matching

The principle of matching implies that, when calculating profits for an accounting period, the revenues must be matched against all the costs incurred in generating that revenue, although the money relating to those revenues and costs may not have been received or paid in that accounting period.

Going concern

This principle assumes that the business will continue in operation and that there is no immediate possibility that it is about to be put into liquidation. If the business is not a going concern, it must be accounted for on a break-up basis.

Consistency

The consistency principle requires that similar items within the same set of accounts should receive the same accounting treatment, and that the same accounting treatment should be applied from one accounting period to the next.

Prudence

Prudence implies that when a number of different treatments or valuations are possible the procedure that provides the most cautious view of the financial statements should be employed. The most pessimistic view of revenues (low) and costs and liabilities (high) ensures profits and the assets of the firm will not be overstated.

Cost

The last fundamental principle states that assets or resources are presented in the accounts at the lower of cost or their net realisable value: the amount that could be achieved were the assets to be disposed of.

THE FINANCIAL STATEMENTS

Double-entry book-keeping

Accountants have developed the technique of double-entry book-keeping for the preparation of financial statements. As the name implies, this requires that for every transaction there are two entries: a debit entry and a credit entry. In accounting, the transactions of interest relate to sales, costs or capital expenditure. This is best illustrated with an example.

A business purchases a machine and pays a cash sum of $5,000. The transaction can be recorded in ledger or t-accounts. They are called t-accounts because their shape makes the letter T. Debit entries are always placed on the left and credit entries on the right. For the purchase of the machine:

- debit: fixed assets account with $5,000
- credit: cash account with $5,000

Fixed assets account

Debit	$	Credit	$
Machine	5,000		

Cash account

Debit	$	Credit	$
		Purchase of machine	5,000

Suppose that the business in the example also made a sale to a customer for cash. For the sale of goods:

- debit: cash account with $10,000
- credit: sales account with $10,000

Cash account

Debit	$	Credit	$
Sale of goods	10,000	Purchase of machine	5,000
		Balancing figure	5,000
	10,000		10,000

Sales account

Debit	$	Credit	$
		Sales for cash	10,000

When all the ledger accounts have been completed, all the debits and all the credits within each account are totalled, and the difference between the totals is calculated to yield a debit or credit balance for the account. If the total debits are greater than the total credits, the account is said to have a debit balance; if credits exceed debits, the account has a credit balance. In the case of the cash account, a balancing figure has been computed representing a debit balance of $5,000.

At the end of an accounting period a trial balance can be prepared. This combines all the ledger accounts that have been completed during the period and represents a list of all the debit and credit balances. In reality there would be many more ledger accounts, but for this simple example the trial balance would appear as follows.

Chart 15.1 **Trial balance**

	Debit ($)	*Credit ($)*
Cash	5,000	
Fixed assets	5,000	
Sales		10,000
Total	10,000	10,000

As a result of double-entry book-keeping, the sum of all the debits and credits must be equal. This is a useful check to ensure that the accounts have been completed accurately. If a difference arises, the entries in the ledger should be reviewed for errors of omission or incorrectly posting entries to the wrong side. To help ensure entries are posted to the appropriate side in the case of a cash transaction, it is useful to start with the cash account. Cash moves through the cash ledger account from left to right: cash received is always a debit entry and cash paid out is always a credit entry. This may appear counter-intuitive to some people, who compare company accounts with their own personal accounts where a credit entry represents a cash inflow into their account. This apparent contradiction can be reconciled by recognising that a personal bank statement is actually a T account in the bank's books and a credit entry in its books is cash that would be paid out should you decide to withdraw the amount of your credit balance. Once the cash side of a transaction has been posted, there is less chance of making an error with the other side.

If double-entry book-keeping is used for all transactions that take place during the year, all the ledger accounts will contain enough information with which to prepare the financial statements.

What are they and what do they look like?

The following three sections comprise a review of the layout and content of the financial statements followed by an examination of the individual transactions that make up the actual content of the statements. Initially, the financial statements will be examined at a high level. Some of the ideas may be difficult to grasp at this stage, but they will become clearer as you progress through the worked examples. Note that the figures are for illustration only and do not represent a legitimate set of accounts. This means you will not be able to reconcile the accounts completely.

The profit and loss account or income statement

The profit and loss account (P&L account) or income statement captures, for a specific period, all the sales and the costs associated with achieving either a profit or a loss for the period, even if the associated cash flows did not take place during that time. The P&L account meets the fundamental accounting principle of matching. Chart 15.2 shows the format for a typical profit and loss account.

Chart 15.2 **Profit and loss account for the 12 months ended March 31st**

	$
Sales revenue	236,000
Cost of sales	(60,000)
Gross profit	176,000
Staff salaries	(45,000)
Rent, light and heat	(7,000)
Advertising	(15,000)
General administration	(26,000)
Total operating costs	(93,000)
Operating profit	83,000
Depreciation	(22,000)
Amortisation	(13,000)
Interest income	2,250
Interest charges	(9,500)
Profit before tax	40,750
Tax	(12,250)
Profit after tax	28,500
Dividends	(19,950)
Retained profit for the year	8,550

Calculating gross profit

Sales revenue is recorded net of any sales tax, such as value-added tax in the UK, and relates to all the sales achieved in a specific accounting period, which could be a year, a quarter, a month or even a week. The costs of sales are the direct costs associated with achieving the sales revenue. A direct cost is one that is directly related to the volume of sales, such that, if an additional unit of a product is sold, the cost of sales increases by the cost of that additional unit. Sales revenue, less the cost of sales, gives the gross profit for the business. The business must generate sufficient gross profit to cover all the other indirect costs associated with achieving the sales.

Calculating operating profit

If the cost of sales relates only to direct costs that vary directly with sales volume, operating costs such as salaries, premises rentals and advertising expenditure are indirect costs. The levels of these cost items do not vary with the level of sales. They are interchangeably referred to as indirect, fixed or overhead costs. The difference between gross profit and total operating costs gives the operating profit for the business. This is the profit generated from normal operating activities. However, there are additional costs and potential revenues that must be accounted for.

Depreciation and amortisation

Many businesses are required to buy capital items, such as plant or machinery, which they use for a number of years. The principle of matching requires that these costs be matched against the revenues to which they have contributed. If the full cost of a machine, which is used for three years, is charged as an operating cost in year one, the business may well appear to make a significant loss in the first year followed by two years of large profits. To ensure that the profitability of a business in any year is representative, the business must spread the cost of the machine over the period during which it contributes to sales. In the case of a machine that is used for three years, one-third of the cost of the machine would be charged in the profit and loss account each year. The spreading of the cost of a capital item is called depreciation, which is dealt with in more detail later in this chapter. Depreciation charges relate to the spreading of the cost of physical capital items. Non-tangible items, such as licences and patents that exist for a number of years, are treated exactly the same way but the charge to the P&L account is described as amortisation.

Interest income and charges

To finance its operations a business may have borrowed money from the bank. As a result, the interest charges relating to the debts of the business must also be included in the P&L account. The interest charges reflect the cost of financing the assets necessary to support the generation of the revenues. A successful business will generate cash and build up cash reserves at a bank, on which it will earn interest income. This non-operating income must also be included in the P&L account.

Calculating profit before tax

The profit before tax (PBT) figure is calculated by deducting non-operating costs, such as depreciation, amortisation, interest, foreign exchange losses and others, from operating profits and adding non-operating income.

Corporation tax, profit after tax and dividends

Businesses that generate profits are required to pay corporation tax on their profits, so a taxation charge is deducted from profits before tax to give profit after tax. Because profit after tax has been calculated after paying interest on loans from providers of debt finance, any profit remaining is available to be paid to shareholders as dividends or to be retained in the business. The amount retained within the business is added to the profit and loss reserve recorded in the balance sheet. The retained profits still belong to the shareholders – they have simply been retained within the business.

Balance sheet

The P&L account examines a specific accounting period. The balance sheet represents a snapshot of the business's position at a particular point in time – the end of the accounting period covered by the P&L account so far as the published annual accounts are concerned – but reflects transactions that have taken place throughout the history of the business. It lists all the business's assets and liabilities as well as the shareholders' funds. Assets are the things owned by the business that support the transactions recorded in the P&L account, as well as all the money owed to the business by its customers. Assets can be thought of as anything that can be used to generate cash (fixed assets) soon will be cash (e.g. debtors or stock) or hard cash (notes and coins). Liabilities represent all the money owed to others by the business; they are claims against the business that will have to be settled in cash. Shareholders' funds represent the equity share capital placed in the business and any profits, or losses, retained by the business. Chart 15.3 shows the format of a typical balance sheet.

Chart 15.3 **Balance sheet as at March 31st**

	$
Tangible fixed assets	51,500
Intangible fixed assets	9,000
Total fixed assets	60,500
Debtors	500
Stock	750
Cash at bank	50
Total current assets	1,300
Creditors	(8,000)
Overdraft	(6,000)
Total current liabilities	(14,000)
Net current assets	(12,700)
Total assets less current liabilities	**47,800**
Equity	30,000
Retained profits	12,000
Debt	5,800
Total capital employed	**47,800**

Fixed assets

Tangible fixed assets represent the total cost of all physical assets such as machinery, vehicles and buildings that have been purchased to support the business, less the total depreciation that has ever been charged in the P&L account. However, the cost of any assets that have been sold and the corresponding depreciation that was charged are eliminated from this total. The tangible fixed asset figure therefore represents the cost of all physical assets that have been bought by the business but have not yet been charged as depreciation to the P&L account. The difference between the total cost of the assets and the total depreciation is the net book value of the assets. Capital items are said to be presented in the balance sheet at their net book value. Intangible fixed assets are directly comparable to tangible fixed assets, the only difference being that they do not reflect physical assets. A brand is an example of an intangible asset. Tangible and intangible fixed assets combined represent the total fixed assets of the business.

Current assets

Sales to customers may be paid for in cash, but many customers are given credit, for example 30 days. The value of the goods received but not yet paid for is the debtors' figure in the balance sheet. As debts are money owed to the business, they are treated as an asset.

A business that manufactures and sells a product will, at any point in time, have items of stock that it has not yet sold. Their value will appear as an asset in the balance sheet entitled "stock". As stocks can be sold to generate sales, they are also treated as an asset.

If the business has performed well, or has just received a loan from the bank, it may have positive cash balances at the bank. As these can be used to purchase stock or to pay salaries that support sales activity, cash balances are defined as an asset.

Debtors, stock and cash combined are described as the total current assets of the business. They are called "current" because they are assets that are currently being used by the business.

Current liabilities and working capital

Creditors are the opposite of debtors, representing those to whom the business owes money. These are described as liabilities: items that represent a future cash outflow for the business. An overdraft at the bank also represents a liability, as it must be repaid at some stage in the future. The difference between total current assets and total liabilities is called the net current assets or liabilities, sometimes referred to as working capital.

Total net assets

If the business's net current assets or liabilities are combined with the total fixed assets, they represent the total net assets of the business. This is the net financial value of the components that make up the business and support the sales activity. The total assets less current liabilities of the business must be financed through different sources of capital, which are described in the bottom half of the balance sheet.

Shareholders' funds

Equity is the money that shareholders have provided to the business in return for shares that entitle them to a future dividend stream from the business. If the business decides not to pay out all the profits generated in the year they are retained in the business, but the shareholders still retain the right to those profits. They are described as retained profits or shareholders' reserves. Dividends cannot be paid until the business has eliminated all previous retained losses.

Debt

Debt represents the funding of the assets of the business that has come from banks and the holders of bonds.

Fundamental accounting identity

In accounting, there is a fundamental accounting identity or relationship that states that the total assets of the business must equal the total liabilities. This relationship must always hold true because of the equal and opposite entries of double-entry book-keeping. This also ensures that the balance sheet balances.

Cash flow statement

The cash flow statement examines the actual cash flows that take place during an accounting period and underlie the P&L account and the balance sheet. The P&L account can suggest that the business is making strong profits, but the cash flow statement provides a view of the harsh realities. Profits can be flattered by careful accounting treatments, but the cash flow statement demonstrates whether the business is generating more cash than it is spending, which is the ultimate test of its success. As a result, the cash flow statement is one of the most important of all the financial statements. Chart 15.4 shows a typical cash flow statement. Note that this example does not relate to the earlier examples.

Chart 15.4 **Cash flow statement for the year ending March 31st**

	$
Operating profit/(loss)	94,000
Movement in working capital	(30,000)
Cash flow from operating activities	64,000
Capital expenditure	(56,000)
Tax paid	(15,000)
Cash flow before financial cash flows	(7,000)
Interest paid	(2,000)
Interest received	0
Cash flow before financing	(9,000)
Equity issued	5,500
Debt raised	4,000
Cash flow after financing	500
Dividends paid	0
Cash flow for the period	500

Cash flow from operating activities

The starting point for the cash flow statement is the operating profit or loss. This figure represents the sales and associated supporting costs for the accounting period but does not take into account when the monies were actually received or paid. Before proceeding, it is necessary to convert the operating profit or loss into a corresponding cash flow. This is achieved by adjusting the profit or loss from operating activities to take account of the movement in working capital or net current assets. This idea is best demonstrated by a simple example.

A business makes two sales for $100 each, giving total sales of $200, and the total cost of sales is $100. The profit from operating activities is therefore $100.

Sales	$200
Less: cost of sales	($100)
Profit from operating activities	$100

One of the sales was for cash and the other on credit. As a result of the sale, debtors have increased by $100 and cash has increased by $100.

The cost of the materials was $50 each and three items of stock were purchased. The first two purchases were for cash and the remaining purchase was on credit with the supplier. As a result, the cash balance has fallen by $100; creditors have increased by $50 and stocks have increased by $50, as only two items of stock were sold. Intuitively, it is apparent that the combination of the cash sale ($100 increase in cash) and the cash purchase ($100 fall in cash) has resulted in a zero net movement in cash. The same result can be obtained by adjusting operating profits to take account of movements in working capital.

Movements in working capital

An increase in debtors represents money that has not yet been received by the business despite the sale, so it should be deducted from operating profits to calculate the actual cash flows. An increase in creditors represents money that has not yet left the business despite a purchase being recorded in the P&L account, so an increase in creditors should be added to operating profits. An increase in stock represents money that has left the business but does not support a transaction that featured in the profit or loss of the business for that period, so an increase in stock should be deducted from operating profits. The combination of these three calculations represents the movement in working capital for the period.

	$
Operating profit	100
Less: increase in debtors	(100)
Less: increase in stock	(50)
Add: increase in creditors	50
Cash flow from operating activities	0

Despite a profit of $100 reported in the P&L account, the business has not generated any actual cash. This is consistent with the intuitive result obtained above.

Cash flow before financing activities

Once the cash flow from operating activities has been computed, the actual amount of money spent on capital items is deducted as well as any actual tax paid. With all these transactions the emphasis is on the flow of actual cash.

Cash flows associated with financing activities

With all the operational cash flows accounted for, the statement examines the cash flows associated with financing activities. Any interest paid or received is included to give a cash flow for the period. If the business actually consumes more cash than it generates, there will be a financing requirement. The inflow of cash from shareholders or lenders is then included to give a cash flow after financing. Lastly, if any dividends have been paid, the amount is deducted to give the final movement in cash or cash equivalents during the period. In the example above (Chart 15.4 on page 157), there is a cash inflow of $500 for the period which will be reflected as an increase in the business's cash balances at the bank.

Interaction of the financial statements

All three financial statements are closely interlinked. For example, the retained profits for the year in the P&L account are added to profit and loss reserves in the balance sheet, and the tax paid in the cash flow statement reduces the tax creditor in the balance sheet. Accountants describe this interaction as articulation. When the business model is used to examine the individual transactions, this will become apparent.

BUILDING UP THE FINANCIAL STATEMENTS

The following sections begin to build up a full financial forecast for Newco Corp, using the blank version of the business planning model. Open the file entitled "Blank Model" and enable macros. If a warning appears in relation to circular references, select TOOLS → OPTIONS → CALCULATION TAB, check the iteration box and enter 100 for maximum iterations, then click OK. The full forecast in the completed version of the model can be examined at any time, and the outputs from the model can be found in the spreadsheets in the Appendix. The same results can be achieved manually by entering all the transactions into a series of ledger or t-accounts. A list of the required ledger accounts is provided in Chart 15.5.

Chart 15.5 **Ledger accounts**

Cash	Advertising
Equity	Legal and professional
Debt	Telephone, fax and IT
Stock	Stationery
Stock creditors	Travel and subsistence
Tangible fixed assets	Other operating cost creditors
Intangible fixed assets	Sales
Depreciation	Debtors
Amortisation	Bad debt
Capital expenditure creditor	Profit and loss
Staff	Leasing equipment
Rent	Light and heat

Injecting capital into the business

Before Newco can begin commercial activities, it will require financing to fund the purchase of machinery and stock and to commence manufacturing and sales activities. Finance has been agreed with shareholders and a bank. All figures are in thousands unless stated otherwise. In the first year, the business will raise $38,490 from its shareholders and $19,245 from a bank. The accounting entries are detailed below.

For the injection of shareholder capital:

- debit: cash account $38,490 with equity share capital
- credit: share capital with $38,490 equity share capital issued

For the debt raised:

- debit: cash account $19,245 with debt raised
- credit: long-term debtors with $19,245 monies owed

These entries can be made in the appropriate ledger accounts or in the business planning model.

To model the equity injection, move to the financing sheet and enter the equity issued of $38,490 in cell E10 (MAIN MENU → ACCOUNTING → FINANCING → cell E10 → enter 38,490) as shown in Chart 15.6.

Chart 15.6 **Raising equity**

	A	B	C	D	E	F	G	H	I	J
1										
2		**Financing**			**Your task**					
3		**Newco Corp**			Enter assumptions relating to the financing of the business.					
4		$ Thousands								
5										
6										
7		**Year**	H C	< >	1	2	3	4	5	6
8										
9		**Financing assumptions**								
10		Equity issued			38,490					
11		Debt raised								
12		Debt repaid								
13		Interest rate on debt								
14		Interest rate on overdraft								
15		Interest on cash deposits								
16		Dividend proportion								
17										

To study the results in the model, click on the H button to return to the main menu, select FINANCIAL RESULTS and then CASH FLOW STATEMENT. In cell E33, the model reports a cash inflow of $38,490 as seen in Chart 15.7.

Chart 15.7 **Equity cash inflow**

	A	B	C	D	E	F	G	H	I	J
1										
2		**Cash flow statement**			**Information only**					
3		**Newco Corp**			No inputs are required in this section.					
4		$ Thousands								
5										
6										
7		**Year**	H C	< >	1	2	3	4	5	6
31		Cash flow before financing								
32										
33		Equity issued			38,490	0	0	0	0	0
34		Debt issued			0	0	0	0	0	0
35		Debt repaid			0	0	0	0	0	0
36										
37		Cash flow for the period before dividends			38,490	0	0	0	0	0
38										
39		Dividends paid			0	0	0	0	0	0
40										
41		Cash flow for the period			38,490	0	0	0	0	0
42										

It is now possible to examine how the financial statements articulate. In the balance sheet (MAIN MENU → FINANCIAL RESULTS → BALANCE SHEET), there is now cash at bank of $38,490, reported in cell E17, and equity, in the bottom half of the balance sheet in cell E32, which matches the cash at the bank, as seen in Chart 15.8. These two results represent the first of the double entries described above.

Chart 15.8 **Balance sheet and equity**

	B	D	E	F	G	H	I	J
1								
2	**Balance sheet**		**Information only**					
3	Newco Corp		No inputs are required in this section.					
4	$ Thousands							
5								
6								
7	**Year**	H C < >	1	2	3	4	5	6
12								
13	Debtors widgets	0	0	0	0	0	0	0
14	Debtors	0	0	0	0	0	0	0
15	Stock zapper	0	0	0	0	0	0	0
16	Stock	0	0	0	0	0	0	0
17	Cash at bank	0	38,490	38,490	38,490	38,490	38,490	38,490
18	Total current assets	0	38,490	38,490	38,490	38,490	38,490	38,490
19								
20	Creditors zapper	0	0	0	0	0	0	0
21	Creditors	0	0	0	0	0	0	0
22	Capital expenditure creditor	0	0	0	0	0	0	0
23	Intangible expenditure creditor	0	0	0	0	0	0	0
24	Taxation creditor	0	0	0	0	0	0	0
25	Overdraft	0	0	0	0	0	0	0
26	Total current liabilities	0	0	0	0	0	0	0
27								
28	Net current assets	0	38,490	38,490	38,490	38,490	38,490	38,490
29								
30	**Total assets less current liabilities**	**0**	**38,490**	**38,490**	**38,490**	**38,490**	**38,490**	**38,490**
31								
32	Equity	0	38,490	38,490	38,490	38,490	38,490	38,490
33	Retained profits	0	0	0	0	0	0	0
34	Debt	0	0	0	0	0	0	0
35								
36	**Total capital employed**	**0**	**38,490**	**38,490**	**38,490**	**38,490**	**38,490**	**38,490**
37								

The $19,245 raised from the banks can now be entered in cell E11 on the financing sheet (MAIN MENU → ACCOUNTING → FINANCING → cell E11 → enter 19,245). The transaction can be traced through the cash flow statement (MAIN MENU → FINANCIAL RESULTS → CASH FLOW STATEMENT → cell E34) and the changes observed in the balance sheet. Total cash now stands at $57,735 (MAIN MENU → FINANCIAL RESULTS → BALANCE SHEET → cell E17), which is matched by the total capital employed comprising both amounts for equity and debt (BALANCE SHEET → cell E36) as seen in Chart 15.9 on the next page.

Chart 15.9 **Balance sheet cash raised**

	A	B	C	D	E	F	G	H	I	J
1										
2		**Balance sheet**			**Information only**					
3		**Newco Corp**			No inputs are required in this section.					
4		$ Thousands								
5										
6				H C < >						
7		**Year**			**1**	**2**	**3**	**4**	**5**	**6**
12										
13		Debtors widgets		0	0	0	0	0	0	0
14		Debtors		0	0	0	0	0	0	0
15		Stock zapper		0	0	0	0	0	0	0
16		Stock		0	0	0	0	0	0	0
17		Cash at bank		0	57,735	57,735	57,735	57,735	57,735	57,735
18		Total current assets		0	57,735	57,735	57,735	57,735	57,735	57,735
19										
20		Creditors zapper		0	0	0	0	0	0	0
21		Creditors		0	0	0	0	0	0	0
22		Capital expenditure creditor		0	0	0	0	0	0	0
23		Intangible expenditure creditor		0	0	0	0	0	0	0
24		Taxation creditor		0	0	0	0	0	0	0
25		Overdraft		0	0	0	0	0	0	0
26		Total current liabilities		0	0	0	0	0	0	0
27										
28		Net current assets		0	57,735	57,735	57,735	57,735	57,735	57,735
29										
30		**Total assets less current liabilities**		**0**	**57,735**	**57,735**	**57,735**	**57,735**	**57,735**	**57,735**
31										
32		Equity		0	38,490	38,490	38,490	38,490	38,490	38,490
33		Retained profits		0	0	0	0	0	0	0
34		Debt		0	19,245	19,245	19,245	19,245	19,245	19,245
35										
36		**Total capital employed**		**0**	**57,735**	**57,735**	**57,735**	**57,735**	**57,735**	**57,735**
37										

With cash now available in the bank the business can purchase some stock.

Buying stock

The only component required to manufacture a widget is a zapper. The managers have decided to make an initial purchase of 55,000 zappers, which cost $15 each (figures as indicated).

The accounting entries for this transaction are:

- debit: stock with $825,000 (55,000 × $15)
- credit: purchase of stock $825,000 to the cash account

To enter this transaction in the model, type the word "zapper" in cell E10 on the cost of sales sheet (MAIN MENU → OPERATIONAL FORECASTS → COST OF SALES → cell E10 → enter zapper). The quantity and price assumptions above should be entered in cells E11 and E12 respectively on the same sheet (COST OF SALES → cell E11 → enter 55, cell E12 → enter 15).

Chart 15.10 **Basic stock data**

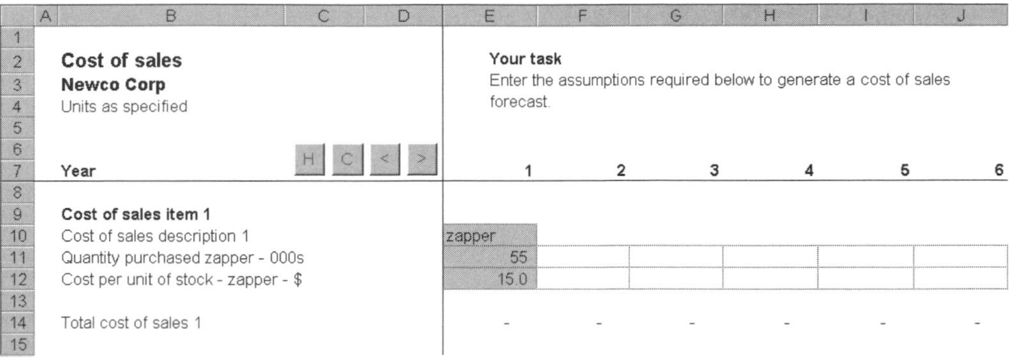

Cost of sales
Newco Corp
Units as specified

Your task
Enter the assumptions required below to generate a cost of sales forecast.

	Year 1	2	3	4	5	6
Cost of sales item 1						
Cost of sales description 1	zapper					
Quantity purchased zapper - 000s	55					
Cost per unit of stock - zapper - $	15.0					
Total cost of sales 1	-	-	-	-	-	-

As no sales have taken place, there have been no entries so far in the profit and loss account. However, in the balance sheet stock has increased by $825 (all figures are in thousands) (MAIN MENU → FINANCIAL RESULTS → BALANCE SHEET → cell E15). From the double entry above, the cash account would be expected to fall by $825. Moving to the cash flow statement sheet (MAIN MENU → FINANCIAL RESULTS → CASH FLOW STATEMENT → cell E13), note that there is now an outflow of cash of $825 representing the increase in stock. As discussed earlier, an increase in stock represents an outflow of cash, and the cash flow from operating activities in row 19 also captures this outflow.

Chart 15.11 **Cash reduction resulting from the purchase of stock**

Cash flow statement
Newco Corp
$ Thousands

Information only
No inputs are required in this section.

Year	1	2	3	4	5	6
Operating profit / (loss)	0	0	0	0	0	0
Debtors widgets	0	0	0	0	0	0
Debtors	0	0	0	0	0	0
Stock zapper	(825)	0	0	0	0	0
Stock	0	0	0	0	0	0
Creditors zapper	0	0	0	0	0	0
Creditors	0	0	0	0	0	0
Movement in working capital	(825)	0	0	0	0	0
Cash flow from operating activities	(825)	0	0	0	0	0

The cash in the balance sheet in Chart 15.12 (on the next page) or the model (MAIN MENU → FINANCIAL RESULTS → BALANCE SHEET → cell E17) has fallen from $57,735 to $56,910, a decrease of $825 reflecting the credit entry of the double entry. The total value of the capital employed in the business remains unchanged at $57,735 (BALANCE SHEET → cell E36), but it is now represented by both cash and stock.

Chart 15.12 **Stock and cash in the balance sheet**

	A	B	C	D	E	F	G	H	I	J
1										
2		**Balance sheet**			**Information only**					
3		**Newco Corp**			No inputs are required in this section.					
4		$ Thousands								
5										
6										
7		**Year**	H C	< >	**1**	**2**	**3**	**4**	**5**	**6**
12										
13		Debtors widgets		0	0	0	0	0	0	0
14		Debtors		0	0	0	0	0	0	0
15		Stock zapper		0	825	825	825	825	825	825
16		Stock		0	0	0	0	0	0	0
17		Cash at bank		0	56,910	56,910	56,910	56,910	56,910	56,910
18		Total current assets		0	57,735	57,735	57,735	57,735	57,735	57,735
19										
20		Creditors zapper		0	0	0	0	0	0	0
21		Creditors		0	0	0	0	0	0	0
22		Capital expenditure creditor		0	0	0	0	0	0	0
23		Intangible expenditure creditor		0	0	0	0	0	0	0
24		Taxation creditor		0	0	0	0	0	0	0
25		Overdraft		0	0	0	0	0	0	0
26		Total current liabilities		0	0	0	0	0	0	0
27										
28		Net current assets		0	57,735	57,735	57,735	57,735	57,735	57,735
29										
30		**Total assets less current liabilities**		**0**	**57,735**	**57,735**	**57,735**	**57,735**	**57,735**	**57,735**
31										
32		Equity		0	38,490	38,490	38,490	38,490	38,490	38,490
33		Retained profits		0	0	0	0	0	0	0
34		Debt		0	19,245	19,245	19,245	19,245	19,245	19,245
35										
36		**Total capital employed**		**0**	**57,735**	**57,735**	**57,735**	**57,735**	**57,735**	**57,735**
37										

Newco has negotiated a credit term of 30 days with the supplier of zappers. This implies that at the end of an accounting period there will be 30 days' worth of stock value owing to the supplier, which will appear as a creditor in the accounts. The following calculation is made to identify the value of the creditor:

$$\text{Creditor} = \text{Total cost of goods purchased} \times \frac{\text{creditor days}}{365}$$

$$\text{Creditor} = \$825 \times 30 \div 365 = \$68$$

Therefore the actual cash paid to the supplier is $757 = $825 – $68 (the amount owing at the end of the period).

The accounting entries for the purchase of stock must now be amended slightly (figures as indicated):

- debit: stock with $825,000 (55,000 × $15)
- credit: purchase of stock $757,000 to the cash account
- credit: creditors with money owed $68,000

Note that the debit and the sum of the two credit entries are equal, as they must be in double-entry book-keeping.

To see these results in the model, the 30 days can be entered in cell E30 on the working capital sheet (MAIN MENU → ACCOUNTING → WORKING CAPITAL → cell E30 → enter 30) as seen in Chart 15.13.

Chart 15.13 **Creditor day assumptions**

	A	B	C	D	E	F	G	H	I	J
1										
2		**Working capital**			**Your task**					
3		**Newco Corp**			Enter assumptions relating to debtor and creditor days.					
4		$ Thousands								
5										
6										
7		**Year**	H C	< >	1	2	3	4	5	6
28										
29		**Creditors account zapper**								
30		Creditor days zapper			30					
31		Opening balance			0	68	0	0	0	0
32		Costs in the period			825	0	0	0	0	0
33		Cash paid			(757)	(68)	0	0	0	0
34		Closing balance			68	0	0	0	0	0
35										

It is now possible to study the impact on the financial statements. In the balance sheet (MAIN MENU → FINANCIAL RESULTS → BALANCE SHEET) there is now a creditor in cell E20 of $68 (figures in thousands), representing the monies owed to the supplier as at the end of the accounting period. The cash at the bank in cell E17 has increased from $56,910 (see Chart 15.12) to $56,978, reflecting the increase in creditors. An increase in creditors implies an increase in cash.

Chart 15.14 **The impact of creditor days**

	A	B	C	D	E	F	G	H	I	J
1										
2		**Balance sheet**			**Information only**					
3		**Newco Corp**			No inputs are required in this section.					
4		$ Thousands								
5										
6										
7		**Year**		H C < >	**1**	**2**	**3**	**4**	**5**	**6**
12										
13		Debtors widgets		0	0	0	0	0	0	0
14		Debtors		0	0	0	0	0	0	0
15		Stock zapper		0	825	825	825	825	825	825
16		Stock		0	0	0	0	0	0	0
17		Cash at bank		0	56,978	56,910	56,910	56,910	56,910	56,910
18		Total current assets		0	57,803	57,735	57,735	57,735	57,735	57,735
19										
20		Creditors zapper		0	(68)	0	0	0	0	0
21		Creditors		0	0	0	0	0	0	0
22		Capital expenditure creditor		0	0	0	0	0	0	0
23		Intangible expenditure creditor		0	0	0	0	0	0	0
24		Taxation creditor		0	0	0	0	0	0	0
25		Overdraft		0	0	0	0	0	0	0
26		Total current liabilities		0	(68)	0	0	0	0	0
27										
28		Net current assets		0	57,735	57,735	57,735	57,735	57,735	57,735
29										
30		**Total assets less current liabilities**		**0**	**57,735**	**57,735**	**57,735**	**57,735**	**57,735**	**57,735**
31										
32		Equity		0	38,490	38,490	38,490	38,490	38,490	38,490
33		Retained profits		0	0	0	0	0	0	0
34		Debt		0	19,245	19,245	19,245	19,245	19,245	19,245
35										
36		**Total capital employed**		**0**	**57,735**	**57,735**	**57,735**	**57,735**	**57,735**	**57,735**
37										

The cash flow statement (MAIN MENU → FINANCIAL RESULTS → CASH FLOW STATEMENT) shows an increase in creditors of $68 in cell E15, representing the increase in the cash balance. As noted earlier, an increase in creditors represents an increase in cash for the business. The model assumes that the creditor is paid in the following year, hence the reduction in creditors in year 2.

Chart 15.15 **Increasing creditors increases the cash balance**

	A	B	C	D	E	F	G	H	I	J
1										
2		**Cash flow statement**			**Information only**					
3		**Newco Corp**			No inputs are required in this section.					
4		$ Thousands								
5										
6										
7		**Year**		H C < >	**1**	**2**	**3**	**4**	**5**	**6**
8										
9		Operating profit / (loss)			0	0	0	0	0	0
10										
11		Debtors widgets			0	0	0	0	0	0
12		Debtors			0	0	0	0	0	0
13		Stock zapper			(825)	0	0	0	0	0
14		Stock			0	0	0	0	0	0
15		Creditors zapper			68	(68)	0	0	0	0
16		Creditors			0	0	0	0	0	0
17		Movement in working capital			(757)	(68)	0	0	0	0
18										
19		Cash flow from operating activities			(757)	(68)	0	0	0	0
20										

This is a basic description of how to account for stock. It can be much more complicated, especially when some stock items are manufactured by the business and the cost of manufacture must be included in the value of the stock. Further complications arise when items of the same stock are bought at different times and at different prices.

When stock has been purchased at different prices a number of valuation approaches can be applied. A stock valuation based on last in first out (LIFO) means that it is assumed that the last item of stock in is the first item of stock out, so the weighted average of the value of stock is calculated accordingly. The first in first out (FIFO) system assumes that the first item of stock into the warehouse is the first item of stock to leave. A detailed exposition of the various accounting treatments for stock is beyond the scope of this book; a dedicated accounting text is recommended for this. However, the fundamental principle of stock valuations is that stock should be presented in the balance sheet at the lower of cost or net realisable value. If the stock was purchased for $100, but because of a change in market conditions is now worth only $50, then it must be presented in the accounts at $50. The reduction in value will be a cost to the P&L account.

Purchasing equipment

With cash in the bank and stock purchased, Newco requires some plant and machinery to manufacture the widgets. It begins by purchasing $55,000 worth of machinery. The terms it negotiates with the supplier are 20 days, so at the end of the accounting period the business has spent $51,986 cash on fixed assets and owes a further $3,014 to the supplier.

Creditor = $55,000 × 20 ÷ 365 = $3,014

Actual cash paid = $55,000 – $3,014 = $51,986

The accounting entries are as follows:

- debit: fixed assets with the cost of the machinery $55,000
- credit: cash with the cash spent on the machinery $51,986
- credit: capital expenditure creditors $3,014 with the money owed

Note that the debit and two credit entries balance, as should always be the case.

To make these entries in the model:

- MAIN MENU → ACCOUNTING → DEPRECIATION → cell E10 → enter 55,000
- MAIN MENU → ACCOUNTING → WORKING CAPITAL → cell E50 → enter 20

There are now fixed assets of $55,000 in the balance sheet (MAIN MENU → FINANCIAL RESULTS → BALANCE SHEET → cell E9). The cash at the bank has fallen by $51,986 (the amount paid to the supplier) to $4,992 in cell E17, and a capital expenditure creditor has appeared in the balance sheet at cell E22.

Chart 15.16 **The impact of buying plant and machinery**

Balance sheet Newco Corp $ Thousands		**Information only** No inputs are required in this section.					
Year		**1**	**2**	**3**	**4**	**5**	**6**
Tangible fixed assets	0	55,000	55,000	55,000	55,000	55,000	55,000
Intangible fixed assets	0	0	0	0	0	0	0
Total fixed assets	0	55,000	55,000	55,000	55,000	55,000	55,000
Debtors widgets	0	0	0	0	0	0	0
Debtors	0	0	0	0	0	0	0
Stock zapper	0	825	825	825	825	825	825
Stock	0	0	0	0	0	0	0
Cash at bank	0	4,992	1,910	1,910	1,910	1,910	1,910
Total current assets	0	5,817	2,735	2,735	2,735	2,735	2,735
Creditors zapper	0	(68)	0	0	0	0	0
Creditors	0	0	0	0	0	0	0
Capital expenditure creditor	0	(3,014)	0	0	0	0	0
Intangible expenditure creditor	0	0	0	0	0	0	0
Taxation creditor	0	0	0	0	0	0	0
Overdraft	0	0	0	0	0	0	0
Total current liabilities	0	(3,082)	0	0	0	0	0
Net current assets	0	2,735	2,735	2,735	2,735	2,735	2,735
Total assets less current liabilities	**0**	**57,735**	**57,735**	**57,735**	**57,735**	**57,735**	**57,735**

Depreciation

Newco knows for certain that it will make sales this year and these transactions will be discussed shortly. However, the fundamental accounting principle of matching requires that the cost of a machine is spread over the accounting periods for which it supports sales. Accountants use the term useful economic life (UEL) to describe the number of years during which an asset will support sales activity and for which it will be providing economic service to the business. In this example, the machine has a UEL of eight years, and this is the period over which its cost will be depreciated. To enter the depreciation period, select MAIN MENU → ACCOUNTING → DEPRECIATION → cell E11 → enter 8, as seen in Chart 15.17.

Chart 15.17 **Depreciation**

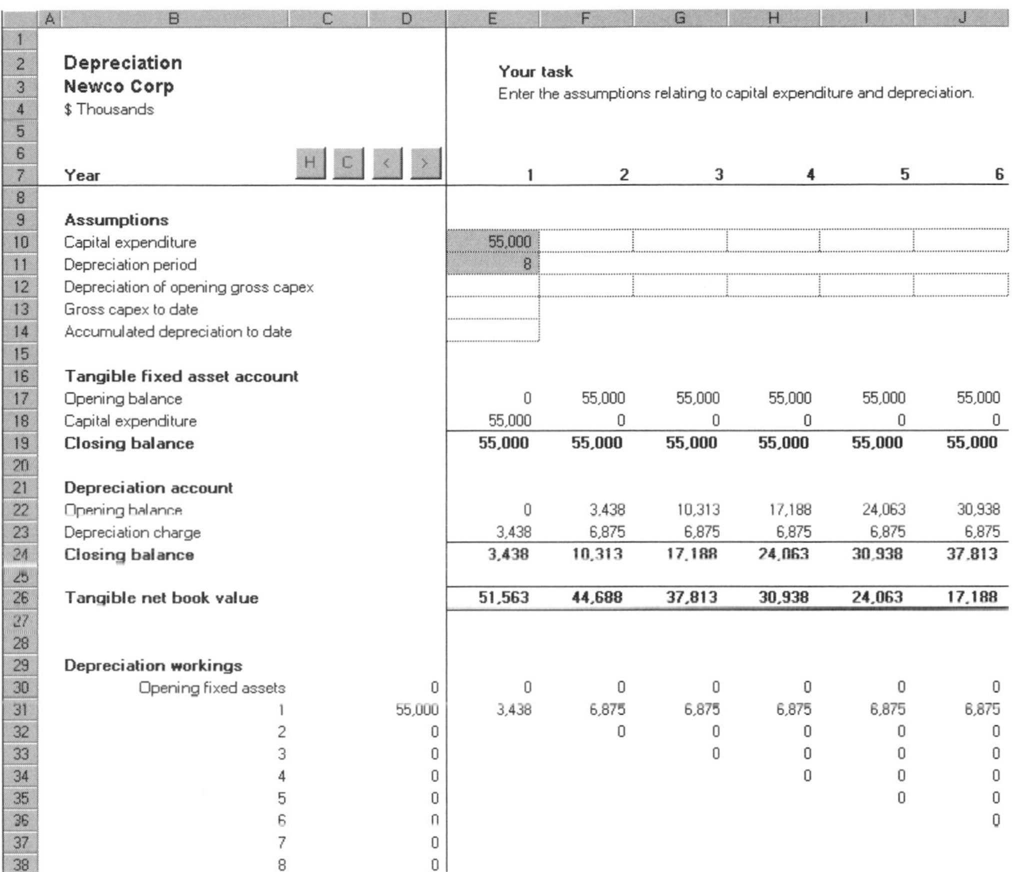

Depreciation
Newco Corp
$ Thousands

Your task
Enter the assumptions relating to capital expenditure and depreciation.

	A/B	C	D	E	F	G	H	I	J
7	**Year**			1	2	3	4	5	6
9	**Assumptions**								
10	Capital expenditure			55,000					
11	Depreciation period			8					
12	Depreciation of opening gross capex								
13	Gross capex to date								
14	Accumulated depreciation to date								
16	**Tangible fixed asset account**								
17	Opening balance			0	55,000	55,000	55,000	55,000	55,000
18	Capital expenditure			55,000	0	0	0	0	0
19	**Closing balance**			**55,000**	**55,000**	**55,000**	**55,000**	**55,000**	**55,000**
21	**Depreciation account**								
22	Opening balance			0	3,438	10,313	17,188	24,063	30,938
23	Depreciation charge			3,438	6,875	6,875	6,875	6,875	6,875
24	**Closing balance**			**3,438**	**10,313**	**17,188**	**24,063**	**30,938**	**37,813**
26	**Tangible net book value**			**51,563**	**44,688**	**37,813**	**30,938**	**24,063**	**17,188**
29	**Depreciation workings**								
30	Opening fixed assets		0	0	0	0	0	0	0
31	1		55,000	3,438	6,875	6,875	6,875	6,875	6,875
32	2		0		0	0	0	0	0
33	3		0			0	0	0	0
34	4		0				0	0	0
35	5		0					0	0
36	6		0						0
37	7		0						
38	8		0						

Row 19 shows the total historic cost of all capital expenditure and remains at $55,000 for the entire forecast period. The depreciation account begins at row 21. Row 23 indicates the depreciation that will be included in the profit and loss account each year for the machine's support of sales activity. The model assumes that the machine was bought halfway through the year, so only six months of depreciation is charged in the first year in cell E23 ($55,000 ÷ 8 ÷ 2 = $3,438). Thereafter a full year's depreciation is charged (for example, cell F23 $6,875), apart from year 9 when only six months is charged again. Row 24 calculates the cumulative total of all depreciation charged. Row 26 gives the net book value (NBV) of the machine: the difference between the total capital expenditure to date and the total accumulated depreciation to date ($55,000 – $3,438 = $51,563). By year 9 the machine has been fully depreciated and has an NBV of zero. The value of the machine is presented in the balance sheet at the end of each year at its NBV. The accounting entries for the first year's depreciation charge are as follows:

- debit: profit and loss account with depreciation $3,438
- credit: depreciation account with depreciation $3,438

The entries for the entire ten-year period can be traced through the model or in the profit and loss account and balance sheet in the Appendix (see row 31 on the depreciation sheet, page 254). As there was no cash associated with these accounting entries, the cash flow statement and the cash at bank in the balance sheet remain unchanged.

The accounting treatment above has implicitly assumed that there was no residual value for the machine. This means that, at the end of the machine's UEL, it had no scrap value. If the machine could have been sold for scrap for, say, $5,000 then this would have had to have been included in the depreciation calculation. The annual depreciation charge would have been ($55,000 – $5,000) ÷ 8 = $6,250.

Purchasing an intangible asset

Newco must also obtain a licence to manufacture the widgets. This must be purchased at the outset, then after three and then four years, at a cost of $10,000 for each renewal. A term of 180 days has been agreed with the licence owner.

The purchase of the licence would be as follows:

- debit: intangible fixed assets with the cost of the licence $10,000
- credit: cash with the cash spent on the licence $5,068
- credit: intangible creditors $4,932 with the money owed

The calculation of the creditor is identical to the capital expenditure creditor calculation.

To make these entries in the model:

- MAIN MENU → ACCOUNTING → AMORTISATION → cell E10 → enter 10,000
- MAIN MENU → ACCOUNTING → WORKING CAPITAL → cell E57 → enter 180

The costs of the licence are amortised over a four-year period. The accounting treatment and the workings are identical to those for depreciation. For the first period (six months), amortisation would be:

Amortisation charge = $10,000 ÷ 4 ÷ 2 = $1,250 for six months ($2,500 for a full year)

The accounting entries are shown below.

- debit: profit and loss account with amortisation $1,250
- credit: amortisation account with amortisation $1,250

To enter this information into the model:

- MAIN MENU → ACCOUNTING → AMORTISATION → cell E11 → enter 4

The transactions can be traced through the model in the profit and loss account (MAIN MENU → FINANCIAL RESULTS → PROFIT AND LOSS → cell E34) as well as the balance sheet (MAIN MENU → FINANCIAL RESULTS → BALANCE SHEET → cell E10). These transactions can be studied in the Appendix (see row 31 on the amortisation sheet, page 255). The value of the licence in the balance sheet is the original $10,000 spent to purchase it minus six months' amortisation of $1,250, which gives an NBV for intangible assets of $8,750. An intangible creditor has also appeared in the balance sheet of $4,932 in cell E23.

Chart 15.18 **Balance sheet**

Balance sheet
Newco Corp
$ Thousands

Information only
No inputs are required in this section.

Year		**1**	**2**	**3**	**4**	**5**	**6**
Tangible fixed assets	0	51,563	63,438	58,750	53,438	61,563	55,938
Intangible fixed assets	0	8,750	6,250	3,750	10,000	6,250	3,750
Total fixed assets	0	60,313	69,688	62,500	63,438	67,813	59,688
Debtors widgets	0	152	533	1,174	2,727	5,504	9,027
Debtors	0	0	0	0	0	0	0
Stock zapper	0	75	367	963	2,675	5,517	11,356
Stock	0	0	0	0	0	0	0
Cash at bank	0	0	0	0	0	0	0
Total current assets	0	227	900	2,137	5,402	11,021	20,383
Creditors zapper	0	(60)	(240)	(525)	(1,248)	(2,590)	(4,482)
Creditors	0	0	0	0	0	0	0
Capital expenditure creditor	0	(3,014)	(1,096)	(274)	(274)	(1,096)	(438)
Intangible expenditure creditor	0	(4,932)	0	0	(4,932)	0	0
Taxation creditor	0	0	0	0	0	0	0
Overdraft	0	(7,109)	(14,495)	(13,420)	(19,218)	(23,275)	(10,244)
Total current liabilities	0	(15,122)	(15,831)	(14,219)	(25,671)	(26,961)	(15,165)
Net current assets	0	(14,895)	(14,931)	(12,082)	(20,269)	(15,940)	5,219
Total assets less current liabilities	**0**	**45,417**	**54,756**	**50,418**	**43,168**	**51,873**	**64,906**
Equity	0	38,490	56,940	65,590	67,850	71,910	71,910
Retained profits	0	(12,318)	(30,649)	(47,952)	(58,592)	(55,974)	(33,957)
Debt	0	19,245	28,465	32,780	33,910	35,937	26,953
Total capital employed	**0**	**45,417**	**54,756**	**50,418**	**43,168**	**51,873**	**64,906**

Operating leases

Rather than purchasing capital items outright, some businesses lease them through an agreement called an operating lease. Where a piece of machinery is used under an operating lease, the costs associated with its use are charged as a cost in the profit and loss account but the machinery does not appear as an asset in the business's balance sheet. Under an operating lease the business does not have legal title to the machine.

Newco leases equipment and the charge in the first year is $2,000. This appears in the profit and loss account as an operating cost and also as a reduction in cash through the cash flow statement (operating losses have increased by the amount of the lease payment). The accounting entries are as follows:

- debit: profit and loss account with lease payments $2,000
- credit: cash with payment to lease business $2,000

The modelling entry is MAIN MENU → OPERATIONAL FORECASTS → OPERATING COSTS → cell E34 → enter 2000.

This transaction can be seen in the profit and loss account (MAIN MENU → FINANCIAL RESULTS → PROFIT AND LOSS → cell E27) and the cash flow statement (MAIN MENU → FINANCIAL RESULTS → CASH FLOW STATEMENT → cell E9). To study these transactions refer to the Appendix.

Finance leases

Some machinery can be operated under a finance lease. This differs from an operating lease as the title of the machine transfers to the business. With finance leases the asset does appear in the business's balance sheet and a depreciation charge is made to the profit and loss account. An entry is also made in the balance sheet for the creditor to whom the monies for the machine are owed. Finance charges are then computed for the financing of the machine and these are charged to the profit and loss account. A detailed exposition of accounting for finance leases is beyond the scope of this book, and reference to an accounting text is recommended. Fortunately, Newco does not have any finance leases.

Employing staff

Newco has decided to recruit some staff, and by the end of the first accounting period 22 people are employed. It is assumed that staff join evenly throughout the year. This is a typical simplifying assumption used in financial modelling. At day one there are zero, by the middle of the year there are 11 and by the end of the year there are 22 (figures as indicated). To calculate the business's salary bill, an average number of employees for the year (0 + 22 ÷ 2 = 11) is calculated, as seen in row 18 of Chart 15.19. It is assumed that the opening salary level is $35,000 (figures as indicated), salaries increase by 3% per year and bonuses, training and so on total 30% of salary. So in the first year the salary bill is average staff (11) × average salary ($35,000) = $385,000 and additional salary costs are 30% × $385,000 = $116,000. Thus total employment costs for the year are $501,000.

The accounting entries are as follows:

- debit: profit and loss account with staff costs $501,000
- credit: cash with payment to staff $501,000

To enter these assumptions in the model:

- MAIN MENU → OPERATIONAL FORECASTS → OPERATING COSTS → cell E10 → enter 22
- MAIN MENU → OPERATIONAL FORECASTS → OPERATING COSTS → cell E11 → enter 35
- MAIN MENU → OPERATIONAL FORECASTS → OPERATING COSTS → cell E12 → enter 3%
- MAIN MENU → OPERATIONAL FORECASTS → OPERATING COSTS → cell E13 → enter 30%

These calculations can all be seen in Chart 15.19.

Chart 15.19 **Staff costs**

	B	C	D	E	F	G	H	I	J
1									
2	**Operating costs**			**Your task**					
3	**Newco Corp**			This section examines staff costs, other operating costs and bad debt.					
4	$ Thousands			Enter the assumptions as indicated below.					
5									
6									
7	**Year**	H C	< >	**1**	**2**	**3**	**4**	**5**	**6**
8									
9	**Staff cost assumptions**								
10	Headcount			22	22	22	22	22	22
11	Opening salary			35					
12	Salary growth			3%					
13	Additional salary costs			30%					
14									
15	**Staff numbers**								
16	Opening staff			-					
17	Closing number of staff			22	22	22	22	22	22
18	Average number of staff			11	22	22	22	22	22
19									
20	**Salary costs**								
21	Salary levels			35	36	37	38	39	41
22	Total salary costs			385	793	817	841	867	893
23	Additional employment costs			116	238	245	252	260	268
24	Total staff costs			501	1,031	1,062	1,094	1,127	1,160
25									

Other costs

All businesses will incur a vast array of additional costs that can be forecast at differing levels of detail. Before completing a business planning model, the planner should brainstorm all the different cost items that should be included in the operating cost base of the business. It is often useful to perform this exercise on a departmental basis. At the end of this chapter there is a list of potential cost items that you may wish to include in your own forecast. In selecting which cost items to include the business planner should focus only on the large, material items and avoid unnecessary detail that does not add to the overall understanding of the financial performance of the business.

In this simple model, ten operating cost items are included. The costs associated with leasing equipment and employing staff have been discussed, and bad debt is dealt with in a separate section. The remaining cost items in Chart 15.20 on the next page can be entered into column E of the operating cost sheet (MAIN MENU → OPERATIONAL FORECASTS → OPERATING COSTS), commencing at row 28 as shown in Chart 15.21.

Chart 15.20 **Operating costs**

	Column E ('000)
Rent	2,100
Light and heat	210
Advertising	1,500
Legal and professional	600
Telephone, fax and IT	550
Stationery	300
Leasing of equipment	Already entered
Travel and subsistence	220

The accounting entries for these are very similar:

- debit: profit and loss account with cost item $X
- credit: cash with payment of cost item $X

Chart 15.21 **Other operating costs**

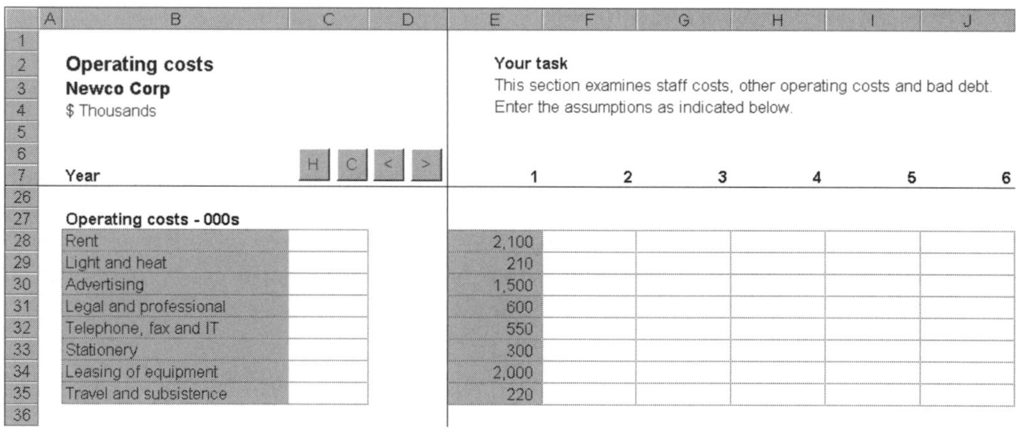

Operating costs
Newco Corp
$ Thousands

Your task
This section examines staff costs, other operating costs and bad debt.
Enter the assumptions as indicated below.

Year	**1**	**2**	**3**	**4**	**5**	**6**
Operating costs - 000s						
Rent	2,100					
Light and heat	210					
Advertising	1,500					
Legal and professional	600					
Telephone, fax and IT	550					
Stationery	300					
Leasing of equipment	2,000					
Travel and subsistence	220					

For simplicity, it is assumed that there are no creditors for other operating costs.

Making the first sales

Having raised financing, invested in plant and machinery, purchased stock, employed staff and met a series of operating costs, Newco has now made its first sale. At the end of the year the company is assumed to have 50,000 customers (figures as indicated). As customers at the start of the year were zero, the average number of customers during the year was 25,000. Each customer is assumed to purchase 2 widgets, and the selling price for each widget is $37. The business also offers 30 days' credit, and all customers take exactly 30 days to pay.

Average customers (25,000) × quantity per customer (2) × price per unit (37) = $1,850,000 total sales. At the end of the accounting period, the outstanding debtor balance will be

$1,850,000 × 30 ÷ 365 = $152,000, and the total cash received will be $1,850,000 – $152,000 = $1,698,000.

The accounting entries are (figures in thousands):

- debit: cash with proceeds received from sales $1,698
- debit: debtors with monies owed by customer at the year end $152
- credit: profit and loss with sales $1,850

The model entries are as follows:

- MAIN MENU → OPERATIONAL FORECASTS → REVENUE
  - cell E10 → widgets
  - Closing customers → cell E12 → enter 50
  - Sales per customer → cell E13 → enter 2
  - Sales price → cell E14 → enter 37
- MAIN MENU → ACCOUNTING → WORKING CAPITAL → cell E10 → enter 30

Chart 15.22 **Sales assumptions**

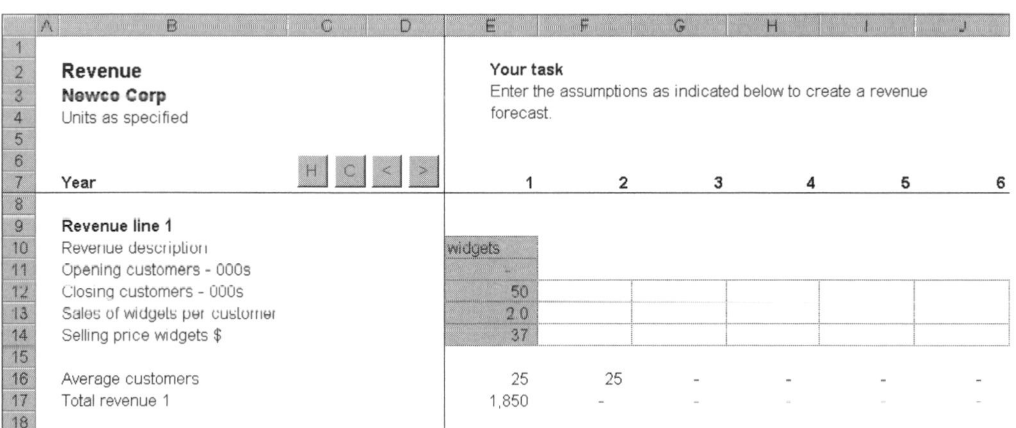

Revenue
Newco Corp
Units as specified

Your task
Enter the assumptions as indicated below to create a revenue forecast.

Year	1	2	3	4	5	6
Revenue line 1						
Revenue description	widgets					
Opening customers - 000s	-					
Closing customers - 000s	50					
Sales of widgets per customer	2.0					
Selling price widgets $	37					
Average customers	25	25	-	-	-	-
Total revenue 1	1,850	-	-	-	-	-

Total revenue is shown in row 17 of Chart 15.22 and the debtor calculations can be seen in Chart 15.23 on the next page.

Chart 15.23 **Debtor assumptions and workings**

Working capital
Newco Corp
$ Thousands

Your task
Enter assumptions relating to debtor and creditor days.

Year	1	2	3	4	5	6
Debtors account widgets						
Debtor days widgets	30					
Opening balance	0	152	0	0	0	0
Sales in the period	1,850	0	0	0	0	0
Cash received	(1,698)	(152)	0	0	0	0
Closing balance	152	0	0	0	0	0

The impact of the sales can be seen in the sales line of the profit and loss account (MAIN MENU → FINANCIAL RESULTS → PROFIT AND LOSS → cell E9), the debtors' balance in the balance sheet (MAIN MENU → FINANCIAL RESULTS → BALANCE SHEET → cell E13) and the movement in working capital in the cash flow statement (MAIN MENU → FINANCIAL RESULTS → CASH FLOW STATEMENT → cell E11). These entries can be studied in the Appendix.

Cost of sales

As a result of the recent sales, the stock account created earlier in this chapter and the profit and loss account must be updated to reflect the cost of the sales. The total cost of the sales is $750,000 (figures as indicated): 50,000 items of stock were sold at $15 per item.

The accounting entries are as follows:

- debit: cost of sales in the profit and loss account $750,000
- credit: stock with the cost of stock sold $750,000

This figure can be seen in the profit and loss account (MAIN MENU → FINANCIAL RESULTS → PROFIT AND LOSS → cell E13). The other side of this entry is to reduce the stock balance. This can be seen in the working capital sheet (MAIN MENU → ACCOUNTING → WORKING CAPITAL → cell E26) and in the balance sheet (MAIN MENU → FINANCIAL RESULTS → BALANCE SHEET → cell E15). The stock balance in the balance sheet has fallen from $825 to $75 representing the sale of $750 worth of stock (figures in thousands).

Bad debt

Unfortunately, a small proportion of customers who have purchased widgets will not pay the money they owe the business because of fraud or bankruptcy. As a result, the business will have to write off a certain amount of sales as bad debts. Experience suggests that on average 3% of widget sales will not be recovered. In detailed accounts, the business will make a provision for doubtful debts by making a debit to the profit and loss account and a credit to the provision for doubtful debts account. The debtors' figure in the balance sheet is presented net of this provision. This is an example of the application of the concept of prudence.

A simplified approach is used in the model: a charge is made to the profit and loss account and the cash flow is reduced as a result of bad debts. The cost of bad debt in the first year is $1,850 × 3% = $56.

The accounting entries are as follows:

- debit: profit and loss with bad debts $56
- credit: cash with reduction in sales receipts from debtors $56

The bad debt assumption should be entered in cell E39 of the operating costs sheet (MAIN MENU → OPERATIONAL FORECASTS → OPERATING COSTS → cell E39 → enter 3%). The impact can be seen in the profit and loss account (MAIN MENU → FINANCIAL RESULTS → PROFIT AND LOSS → cell E19). These entries can be studied in the Appendix.

Prepayments and accruals

There are two other basic accounting concepts that are not included in the model but are discussed in this chapter for completeness: prepayments and accruals. These reflect the accounting concept of matching.

Prepayments are best explained by an example of rent. Suppose Newco had to pay its annual rent at the start of the year in month 1 in cash and was forecasting its profit and loss account on a monthly basis. Month 1's profits would be much lower than those of the other 11 months of the year because it would include 12 months' worth of rent charges. To match the rents to the sales, the concept of prepayments is used. In month 1, a prepayment account is created.

If annual rents are $120,000, the accounting entries are as follows (figures as indicated):

- debit: prepaid rent $120,000
- credit: cash rent paid in advance $120,000

Rent is then charged to the profit and loss account on a monthly basis at $10,000 per month. A rent charge to the profit and loss account would be made in the first month and then the same entry would be made in subsequent months.

The accounting entry is as follows:

- debit: profit and loss account with rent for the month $10,000
- credit: prepaid rent with the charge to the profit and loss $10,000

Each month the value of the prepaid rent account would decrease by $10,000, and each month there would be a rent charge in the profit and loss account. The results of the accounting entries are as follows:

'000	1	2	3	4	5	6	7	8	9	10	11	12
Cash account	120	–	–	–	–	–	–	–	–	–	–	–
Balance sheet prepayment	110	100	90	80	70	60	50	40	30	20	10	0
Profit & loss	10	10	10	10	10	10	10	10	10	10	10	10

The concept of accruals is simply the reverse of prepayments. Costs are incurred, but the cash payment for those costs is not made until some time in the future.

Suppose Newco paid commission to its sales team for sales of widgets, but the payment of the commission did not take place until the end of the year when the annual sales performance of all sales staff could be reviewed. A charge should be made against the profit and loss account each month to reflect the commission relating to the sales in that month.

The accounting entries on a monthly basis are as follows, assuming an average commission of $15,000 per month:

- debit: profit and loss account with commission for the month $15,000
- credit: commission accruals account with commission for the month $15,000

The credit entry is to an accruals account where the commission to be eventually paid is accrued. At the end of the year, the commission is paid in cash to the sales staff.

The final accounting entry is:

- debit: commission accruals account $180,000
- credit: cash account with commission actually paid $180,000

The monthly movement on the accounts is as follows:

'000	1	2	3	4	5	6	7	8	9	10	11	12
Cash account	–	–	–	–	–	–	–	–	–	–	–	180
Balance sheet prepayment	15	30	45	60	75	90	105	120	135	150	165	–
Profit & loss	15	15	15	15	15	15	15	15	15	15	15	15

This chapter has covered the accounting entries associated with the main operational aspects of the business. The following chapter examines the techniques and accounting entries to complete the financial accounts.

Typical operating costs by department

Sales and marketing
Advertising
Public relations
Market research
Consultancy services
Direct mail
Exhibitions, seminars, etc
Commissions
Bonuses
Display materials, point-of-sales material
Brochures, printed materials
Journals and publications
Purchase of industry reports

Distribution
Rent of warehouses
Vehicles
Insurance
Fuel

Manufacturing
Stock
Depreciation
Rent of factories
Operating and finance leases
Repairs and maintenance

Accounting
Legal and professional fees
Audit fees
Subscriptions

Human resources
Recruitment costs
Staff costs
Pension contributions
National insurance
Employee insurance
Training

Information technology
Telephone lines
High bandwidth communication lines
Software licences
Maintenance

Customer relationship management
Telephone lines
Call centre costs
Customer database costs
Contact systems
Customer diagnostic software

Head office and administration
Telephone
Fax
Information services
Postage and couriers
Dues and subscriptions

Other cost items
Bad debt
Amortisation
Profit or loss on the disposal of fixed assets
Interest costs
Foreign exchange gains and losses

16 Completing the financial statements

OBJECTIVES

The previous chapter covered the elements of the financial statements relating to the operational aspects of the company. This chapter focuses on accounting for interest, corporate taxation, dividends and retained earnings, which completes the financial statements. Reference is made to the completed version of the model, which has been populated with data for every year of the forecast (Complete Model), but only year 8 is calculated in the worked examples. The results can be viewed in the completed version of the model or in the Appendix. The full financial statements for years 1–10 are presented below for easy reference (Charts 16.1, 16.2 and 16.3). No further modelling is required, but those who wish to develop the full ten-year forecast for themselves can continue using the model from the previous chapter, referring to the Appendix to obtain the remaining input assumptions.

The menu structure was described in detail in the previous chapter, so comprehensive navigation instructions are not given in this chapter. If guidance on navigating the model is required, return to Chapter 14. If assistance is required on the structure of the model, refer to Chart 14.5 on page 148.

Chart 16.1 **Profit and loss account/income statement**

Profit and loss
Newco Corp
$ Thousands

Information only
No inputs are required in this section.

Year	1	2	3	4	5	6	7	8	9	10
widgets	1,850	6,480	14,280	33,184	66,960	109,830	149,422	176,150	184,035	183,469
Total revenue	**1,850**	**6,480**	**14,280**	**33,184**	**66,960**	**109,830**	**149,422**	**176,150**	**184,035**	**183,469**
zapper	(750)	(2,628)	(5,794)	(13,469)	(28,667)	(48,691)	(69,908)	(81,734)	(85,616)	(85,063)
Total cost of sales	**(750)**	**(2,628)**	**(5,794)**	**(13,469)**	**(28,667)**	**(48,691)**	**(69,908)**	**(81,734)**	**(85,616)**	**(85,063)**
Gross profit	**1,100**	**3,852**	**8,486**	**19,715**	**38,293**	**61,139**	**79,514**	**94,416**	**98,418**	**98,406**
Bad debt	(56)	(194)	(428)	(996)	(2,009)	(3,295)	(4,483)	(5,285)	(5,521)	(5,504)
Staff dosts	(501)	(1,172)	(1,400)	(1,616)	(1,920)	(2,664)	(5,053)	(8,394)	(10,778)	(11,992)
Rent	(2,100)	(2,200)	(2,320)	(2,520)	(3,090)	(3,190)	(3,280)	(3,360)	(3,480)	(3,590)
Light and heat	(210)	(221)	(235)	(255)	(310)	(320)	(330)	(340)	(350)	(360)
Advertising	(1,500)	(1,800)	(2,400)	(3,200)	(3,930)	(4,370)	(4,520)	(4,630)	(4,740)	(4,800)
Legal and professional	(600)	(800)	(1,000)	(1,100)	(1,200)	(1,260)	(1,330)	(1,390)	(1,460)	(1,530)
Telephone, fax and IT	(550)	(700)	(750)	(875)	(920)	(1,220)	(1,500)	(1,750)	(1,990)	(2,050)
Stationery	(300)	(310)	(320)	(335)	(450)	(600)	(900)	(1,200)	(1,300)	(1,350)
Leasing of equipment	(2,000)	(2,040)	(2,080)	(2,400)	(2,600)	(2,700)	(2,800)	(2,850)	(2,900)	(2,970)
Travel and subsistence	(220)	(280)	(300)	(350)	(600)	(800)	(1,250)	(1,750)	(1,990)	(2,050)
Total operating costs	**(8,036)**	**(9,717)**	**(11,233)**	**(13,646)**	**(17,029)**	**(20,419)**	**(25,445)**	**(30,948)**	**(34,509)**	**(36,196)**
Operating profit	**(6,936)**	**(5,865)**	**(2,747)**	**6,069**	**21,264**	**40,720**	**54,069**	**63,468**	**63,909**	**62,210**
Depreciation	(3,438)	(8,125)	(9,688)	(10,313)	(11,875)	(13,625)	(14,625)	(15,625)	(13,188)	(9,500)
Amortisation	(1,250)	(2,500)	(2,500)	(3,750)	(3,750)	(2,500)	(2,500)	(2,500)	(2,500)	(2,500)
Profits before interest and tax	**(11,624)**	**(16,490)**	**(14,934)**	**(7,994)**	**5,639**	**24,595**	**36,944**	**45,343**	**48,222**	**50,210**
Interest paid on debt	(481)	(1,193)	(1,531)	(1,667)	(1,746)	(1,572)	(1,123)	(674)	(449)	(449)
Interest paid on overdrafts	(213)	(648)	(837)	(979)	(1,275)	(1,006)	(307)	0	0	0
Interest received on cash deposits	0	0	0	0	0	0	313	781	1,006	1,171
Profit before tax	**(12,318)**	**(18,331)**	**(17,303)**	**(10,640)**	**2,618**	**22,017**	**35,826**	**45,451**	**48,778**	**50,932**
Taxation	0	0	0	0	0	0	(561)	(13,635)	(14,633)	(15,279)
Profit after tax	**(12,318)**	**(18,331)**	**(17,303)**	**(10,640)**	**2,618**	**22,017**	**35,265**	**31,815**	**34,145**	**35,652**
Dividends declared	0	0	0	0	0	0	(1,308)	(23,862)	(25,609)	(26,739)
Retained profit for the year	**(12,318)**	**(18,331)**	**(17,303)**	**(10,640)**	**2,618**	**22,017**	**33,957**	**7,954**	**8,536**	**8,913**

Chart 16.2 **Balance sheet**

Balance sheet
Newco Corp
$ Thousands

Information only
No inputs are required in this section.

Year		1	2	3	4	5	6	7	8	9	10
Tangible fixed assets	0	51,563	63,438	58,750	53,438	61,563	55,938	49,313	41,688	36,500	35,000
Intangible fixed assets	0	8,750	6,250	3,750	10,000	6,250	3,750	1,250	8,750	6,250	3,750
Total fixed assets	0	60,313	69,688	62,500	63,438	67,813	59,688	50,563	50,438	42,750	38,750
Debtors widgets	0	152	533	1,174	2,727	5,504	9,027	12,281	14,478	15,126	15,080
Debtors	0	0	0	0	0	0	0	0	0	0	0
Stock zapper	0	75	367	963	2,675	5,517	11,356	18,738	26,904	35,448	44,225
Stock	0	0	0	0	0	0	0	0	0	0	0
Cash at bank	0	0	0	0	0	0	0	15,649	23,423	26,872	31,674
Total current assets	0	227	900	2,137	5,402	11,021	20,383	46,668	64,805	77,446	90,979
Creditors zapper	0	(68)	(240)	(525)	(1,248)	(2,590)	(4,482)	(6,353)	(7,389)	(7,739)	(7,713)
Creditors	0	0	0	0	0	0	0	0	0	0	0
Capital expenditure creditor	0	(3,014)	(1,096)	(274)	(274)	(1,096)	(438)	(438)	(438)	(438)	(438)
Intangible expenditure creditor	0	(4,932)	0	0	(4,932)	0	0	0	(4,932)	0	0
Taxation creditor	0	0	0	0	0	0	0	(561)	(13,635)	(14,633)	(15,279)
Overdraft	0	(7,109)	(14,495)	(13,420)	(19,218)	(23,275)	(10,244)	0	0	0	0
Total current liabilities	0	(15,122)	(15,831)	(14,219)	(25,671)	(26,961)	(15,165)	(7,352)	(26,394)	(22,811)	(23,431)
Net current assets	0	(14,895)	(14,931)	(12,082)	(20,269)	(15,940)	5,219	39,317	38,411	54,635	67,548
Total assets less current liabilities	**0**	**45,417**	**54,756**	**50,418**	**43,168**	**51,873**	**64,906**	**89,879**	**88,849**	**97,385**	**106,298**
Equity	0	38,490	56,940	65,590	67,850	71,910	71,910	71,910	71,910	71,910	71,910
Retained profits	0	(12,318)	(30,649)	(47,952)	(58,592)	(55,974)	(33,957)	0	7,954	16,490	25,403
Debt	0	19,245	28,465	32,780	33,910	35,937	26,953	17,969	8,985	8,985	8,985
Total capital employed	**0**	**45,417**	**54,756**	**50,418**	**43,168**	**51,873**	**64,906**	**89,879**	**88,849**	**97,385**	**106,298**

Chart 16.3 **Cash flow statement**

Cash flow statement
Newco Corp
$ Thousands

Information only
No inputs are required in this section.

Year	1	2	3	4	5	6	7	8	9	10
Operating profit / (loss)	(6,936)	(5,865)	(2,747)	6,069	21,264	40,720	54,069	63,468	63,909	62,210
Debtors widgets	(152)	(381)	(641)	(1,554)	(2,776)	(3,524)	(3,254)	(2,197)	(648)	46
Debtors	0	0	0	0	0	0	0	0	0	0
Stock zapper	(75)	(292)	(596)	(1,711)	(2,843)	(5,839)	(7,382)	(8,166)	(8,544)	(8,777)
Stock	0	0	0	0	0	0	0	0	0	0
Creditors zapper	68	172	285	722	1,342	1,892	1,871	1,036	350	(26)
Creditors	0	0	0	0	0	0	0	0	0	0
Movement in working capital	(159)	(500)	(952)	(2,542)	(4,277)	(7,470)	(8,765)	(9,327)	(8,842)	(8,757)
Cash flow from operating activities	(7,095)	(6,365)	(3,699)	3,526	16,987	33,250	45,303	54,141	55,067	53,453
Tangible capital expenditure	(51,986)	(21,918)	(5,822)	(5,000)	(19,178)	(8,658)	(8,000)	(8,000)	(8,000)	(8,000)
Intangible capital expenditure	(5,068)	(4,932)	0	(5,068)	(4,932)	0	0	(5,068)	(4,932)	0
Tax paid	0	0	0	0	0	0	0	(561)	(13,635)	(14,633)
Cash flow before financial cashflows	(64,150)	(33,215)	(9,521)	(6,542)	(7,123)	24,592	37,303	40,512	28,501	30,819
Interest paid on debt	(481)	(1,193)	(1,531)	(1,667)	(1,746)	(1,572)	(1,123)	(674)	(449)	(449)
Interest paid on overdrafts	(213)	(648)	(837)	(979)	(1,275)	(1,006)	(307)	0	0	0
Interest received on cash deposits	0	0	0	0	0	0	313	781	1,006	1,171
Cash flow before financing	(64,844)	(35,056)	(11,890)	(9,189)	(10,144)	22,015	36,186	40,620	29,057	31,541
Equity issued	38,490	18,450	8,650	2,260	4,060	0	0	0	0	0
Debt issued	19,245	9,220	4,315	1,130	2,027	0	0	0	0	0
Debt repaid	0	0	0	0	0	(8,984)	(8,984)	(8,984)	0	0
Cash flow for the period before dividends	(7,109)	(7,386)	1,075	(5,799)	(4,057)	13,031	27,202	31,636	29,057	31,541
Dividends paid	0	0	0	0	0	0	(1,308)	(23,862)	(25,609)	(26,739)
Cash flow for the period	(7,109)	(7,386)	1,075	(5,799)	(4,057)	13,031	25,893	7,774	3,449	4,802

DEVELOPING THE PROFIT AND LOSS ACCOUNT

Interest charges

A business that borrows money has to pay interest on the loan, and at some stage it will also have to repay the loan. To calculate interest, the average debt balance for the period is calculated and multiplied by the interest rate.

Chart 16.4 **Interest and income calculations**

Financing
Newco Corp
$ Thousands

Your task
Enter assumptions relating to the financing of the business.

Row	Year	1	2	3	4	5	6	7	8	9	10
9	**Financing assumptions**										
10	Equity issued	38,490	18,450	8,650	2,260	4,060					
11	Debt raised	19,245	9,220	4,315	1,130	2,027					
12	Debt repaid						8,984	8,984	8,984		
13	Interest rate on debt	5%	5%	5%	5%	5%	5%	5%	5%	5%	5%
14	Interest rate on overdraft	6%	6%	6%	6%	6%	6%	6%	6%	6%	6%
15	Interest on cash deposits	4%	4%	4%	4%	4%	4%	4%	4%	4%	4%
16	Dividend proportion	75%	75%	75%	75%	75%	75%	75%	75%	75%	75%
18	**Equity account**										
19	Opening balance	0	38,490	56,940	65,590	67,850	71,910	71,910	71,910	71,910	71,910
20	Equity issued	38,490	18,450	8,650	2,260	4,060	0	0	0	0	0
21	Closing balance	38,490	56,940	65,590	67,850	71,910	71,910	71,910	71,910	71,910	71,910
23	**Debt account**										
24	Opening balance	0	19,245	28,465	32,780	33,910	35,937	26,953	17,969	8,985	8,985
25	Debt raised	19,245	9,220	4,315	1,130	2,027	0	0	0	0	0
26	Debt repaid	0	0	0	0	0	(8,984)	(8,984)	(8,984)	0	0
27	Closing balance	19,245	28,465	32,780	33,910	35,937	26,953	17,969	8,985	8,985	8,985
29	**Interest on debt account**										
30	Interest charge	481	1,193	1,531	1,667	1,746	1,572	1,123	674	449	449
32	**Interest on cverdraft**										
33	Interest charge	213	648	837	979	1,275	1,006	307	0	0	0
35	**Interest income on short term deposits**										
36	Interest income	0	0	0	0	0	0	313	781	1,006	1,171

To follow the transaction in the model, select the financing sheet in the completed version of the model (MAIN MENU → ACCOUNTING → FINANCING). Note that in row 13 the interest rate on debt has been assumed to be 5%. All figures are in thousands unless otherwise indicated. The calculation for the interest charge in year 8 is the average of the opening and closing cash balances (cells L24 and L27) multiplied by 5% (cell L13), which equals $674 (cell L30).

$$\text{Average loan balance} \times \text{interest rate} = \text{interest charge}$$

$$(\$17{,}969 + \$8{,}985) \div 2 \times 5\% = \$674$$

The accounting entries for this transaction are:

- debit: profit and loss account with interest charges $674
- credit: cash with the charge to the profit and loss of $674

It is assumed that interest is paid immediately and therefore the payments will be reflected in the profit and loss account (Chart 16.1), cash flow statement (Chart 16.3) and the balance sheet (Chart 16.2) through a reduction in cash.

The same approach is adopted in the model for the interest on overdrafts (see Chart 16.4, row 33 for the transaction). In year 6 the company has cleared its overdraft at the bank so there are no interest charges on overdrafts in year 8.

Interest income

In the case of interest income, the opening cash balance at the start of year 8 is $15,649, which can be found in the closing cash balance for the previous year in cell K17 of the balance sheet, and the closing balance is $23,423 (cell L17). The interest rate is assumed at 4% in row 15 of the financing sheet. The interest income for year 8 is therefore $19,536 (the average balance) multiplied by 4% which equals $781 (cell L36 of the financing sheet).

$$\text{Average cash balance} \times \text{interest rate} = \text{interest income}$$

$$(\$15{,}649 + \$23{,}423) \div 2 \times 4\% = \$781$$

The accounting entries for interest income are:

- debit: cash account with interest income $781
- credit: profit and loss account with interest income $781

Once again, no timing issues have been assumed. As before, the results will be reflected in the profit and loss account (Chart 16.1), the cash flow statement (Chart 16.3) and the balance sheet as an immediate increase in cash.

Principal repayments

In the forecast and the model it has been assumed that Newco repays some of the loan. It is assumed that $8,984 is repaid in years 6, 7 and 8. These entries can be seen in the financing sheet in cells J26, K26 and L26 and also in the cash flow statement in cells J35, K35 and L35.

The accounting entries for year 8 are:

- debit: debt in the balance sheet with the principal repaid $8,984
- credit: cash with the amount repaid to the bank $8,984

The debt balance falls from $35,937 in year 5 to $26,953 in year 6 (cell J34 in Chart 16.5 on the next page), $17,969 in year 7 and $8,985 in year 8 (cells J34, K34 and L34 respectively).

Chart 16.5 **Repayment of loans**

	A	B	C	D	J	K	L	M	N
1									
2		**Balance sheet**							
3		**Newco Corp**							
4		$ Thousands							
5									
6									
7		**Year**	H C	< >	**6**	**7**	**8**	**9**	**10**
31									
32		Equity		0	71,910	71,910	71,910	71,910	71,910
33		Retained profits		0	(33,957)	0	7,954	16,490	25,403
34		Debt		0	26,953	17,969	8,985	8,985	8,985
35									
36		**Total capital employed**		**0**	**64,906**	**89,879**	**88,849**	**97,385**	**106,298**
37									

Corporate taxation

The corporation tax calculations can be followed in the taxation sheet (see Chart 16.6). The assumptions relating to corporation tax can be found in rows 10, 11 and 12. The taxation rate and the tax creditor days are self-explanatory and have been assumed at 30% and 365 days respectively. The adjustments row allows adjustments to be made for items that appear in the profit and loss account but are disallowed for the purposes of calculating profits for taxation. The costs of staff or client entertainment, for example, might not be allowable for tax purposes. No such adjustments are assumed in this example. The starting point for calculating taxation is profit or loss before tax from the profit and loss account (row 15 of Chart 16.6).

Chart 16.6 **Taxation workings**

	B	C–D	E	F	G	H	I	J	K	L	M	N
1												
2	**Taxation**		**Your task**									
3	**Newco Corp**		Enter the tax rate, tax creditor days and any adjustments to profits liable to									
4	$ Thousands		corporation tax in the "Profit adjustments" row.									
5												
6												
7	**Year**	H C < >	**1**	**2**	**3**	**4**	**5**	**6**	**7**	**8**	**9**	**10**
8												
9	**Taxation assumptions**											
10	Tax rate		30%	30%	30%	30%	30%	30%	30%	30%	30%	30%
11	Tax creditor days		365	365	365	365	365	365	365	365	365	365
12	Profit adjustments											
13												
14	**Profit and loss taxation workings**											
15	Profits / (loss) before tax		(12,318)	(18,331)	(17,303)	(10,640)	2,618	22,017	35,826	45,451	48,778	50,932
16	Profits before losses		0	0	0	0	2,618	22,017	35,826	45,451	48,778	50,932
17	Losses carried forward		0	0	0	0	(2,618)	(22,017)	(33,957)	0	0	0
18	Other adjustments		0	0	0	0	0	0	0	0	0	0
19	Profits liable to corporation tax		0	0	0	0	0	0	1,869	45,451	48,778	50,932
20	Corporation tax		0	0	0	0	0	0	561	13,635	14,633	15,279
21												
22	**Corporation tax account**											
23	Opening balance		0	0	0	0	0	0	0	561	13,635	14,633
24	Tax charge in the period		0	0	0	0	0	0	561	13,635	14,633	15,279
25	Tax paid		0	0	0	0	0	0	0	(561)	(13,635)	(14,633)
26	Closing balance		0	0	0	0	0	0	561	13,635	14,633	15,279
27												
28	**Losses account**											
29	Opening losses		-	12,318	30,649	47,952	58,592	55,974	33,957	0	0	0
30	Increase in losses in the period		12,318	18,331	17,303	10,640	0	0	0	0	0	0
31	Losses utilised		0	0	0	0	(2,618)	(22,017)	(33,957)	0	0	0
32	Closing losses		12,318	30,649	47,952	58,592	55,974	33,957	0	0	0	0
33												

In years 1–4 the company generated losses (row 15 in Chart 16.6). In countries where tax losses can be carried forward to be offset against future profits, a company will only become liable for corporation tax once it has used up all its earlier losses. In the case of Newco, the losses have been fully utilised by year 7 (see row 17 and the losses account from row 28). In year 8, the profits liable to corporation tax are $45,451, as seen in row 19 of the taxation sheet, cell L19.

Corporation tax is computed by multiplying the profits liable to corporation tax by the tax rate, in this example 30%. The resulting corporation tax charge is $13,635 (cell L20).

Profits liable to corporation tax × tax rate = corporation tax charge

$45,451 × 30% = $13,635

The tax creditor day assumption of 365 days implies that tax is not actually paid until the following year (cell M25 in the taxation sheet), so a creditor is created in the balance sheet (cell L24). The tax actually paid in year 8, $561 (cell L25 of the taxation sheet), is the tax liability from the previous year.

The accounting entries for the corporation tax charge are:

- debit: profit and loss account with corporation tax $13,635
- credit: corporation tax creditors with tax liability $13,635

The accounting entries for the corporation tax paid are:

- debit: corporation tax creditor with tax paid based on the previous year $561
- credit: cash with tax paid $561

The results of these accounting entries can be seen in Charts 16.1–16.3 (pages 180–81), and you can trace them through the accounts as an exercise.

Taxation and valuations

To avoid double counting the tax shield on debt financing, a business model must be able to calculate tax paid as if the company was 100% equity financed. The reason for this approach is explained in Chapter 18. The model performs an identical, second taxation computation but the starting point is profit before interest. The taxation workings for valuation purposes can be found in the taxation sheet from row 35 onwards. As this calculation is for valuation purposes only, there are no accompanying accounting entries.

Profit after tax and dividends

Deducting tax from profits before tax gives profits after tax. As all costs, including interest payments to the providers of debt, have been included in calculating this figure, these profits are attributable entirely to the company's equity shareholders. Only equity shareholders can participate in the profits of the company once all its other liabilities have been met. Profits after tax represent the profits available for distribution as dividends to the company's shareholders.

Different countries have different accounting rules that constrain the ability of a company to pay dividends. One of the most common requirements is that it has sufficient distributable reserves. In the case of Newco, an inspection of the balance sheet reveals that the company has retained losses until year 6 (see row 33 of Chart 16.2). Only when these accumulated losses have been eliminated can the company declare a dividend. So despite generating profits at the after-tax level in years 5 and 6 (row 46 of Chart 16.1), Newco can only declare its first dividend in year 7 (cell K48 of Chart 16.1).

Companies can adopt different approaches to dividend policy. In the model, the dividends are based on a proportion of profits after tax in the year, in the example 75%, provided that all retained losses have been eliminated. This payout ratio is high by many company standards and is used here for illustration only. Later it will be seen that this high payout ratio may result in potential problems for the company in the longer term. The model has been simplified and assumes that dividends are paid immediately; in reality, a dividend is declared and a dividend creditor established before payment.

In year 8, dividends are based on 75% of profits after tax, $31,815, and the resulting dividend is $23,862. The calculation is simple because there are no retained losses from the previous year to deal with.

The accounting entries for the dividend are as follows:

- debit: profit and loss with dividend paid $23,862
- credit: cash with dividend paid $23,862

The accounting entries can be seen in Charts 16.1 and 16.3.

COMPLETING THE FINANCIAL STATEMENTS USING LEDGER ACCOUNTS

The business model automatically generates all the financial statements from the entered assumptions and applies the appropriate accounting. If the transactions had all been recorded using ledger or t-accounts, a trial balance would now have to be produced. First, each account would have to be balanced and all the debit and credit entries collected in the trial balance. All income and expenses items would be identified to create the profit and loss account. The remaining balances that relate to fixed assets, debtors and creditors and cash, for example, would be included in the balance sheet.

Completing the balance sheet

Cash balances

The cash movement for the period from the trial balance can be combined with the opening cash balance (zero in the example if you consider the first year of the forecast) to give the closing cash balance for inclusion in the balance sheet.

Retained profits

One of the final accounting entries is to calculate the retained profits or losses for the year in the profit and loss account. This is the amount of profit that remains after the declaration of dividends. The profits or losses retained in the business are either credited or debited to the accumulated retained profits and losses in the balance sheet, as these represent an increase or a decrease in shareholder funds.

If the double-entry book-keeping process has been adhered to, the balance sheet should balance. This is also a vital check when building a business model. In the model accompanying this book, an automatic check has been built in row 38 of the sheet entitled "Balance sheet". The check compares the net assets (row 30 in the balance sheet) with the total capital employed (row 36) to ensure they are equal. The result should be a row of zeros indicating that there is no difference between the two sets of figures.

Completing the cash flow statement

The cash flow statement is not derived directly from the trial balance but from the profit and loss account and the movement in working capital balances in the balance sheet as described above. The format of the cash flow statement provided at the start of this chapter can be used as the basis for preparation. All the information necessary to complete it can be obtained from the profit and loss and balance sheet.

17 Reviewing the financial statements

Ratio analysis involves the comparison of two or more figures in the financial statements to provide an indicator of the performance of the business. The calculation of business ratios is straightforward, but the value of them lies in their interpretation. The computed ratios must support the business plan "story" and must ring true in the context of the industry, sector and market in which the business operates. They are most useful when they can be compared with those of similar businesses that operate in the same market, competing for the same customers with similar products, and that have a similar business model and are at the same stage of development. For example, there is little point in analysing the working capital of Amazon, an online book retailer, and comparing the results with a traditional high-street bookseller. Furthermore, comparing a start-up with a business that has been operating successfully for over ten years will also be of limited value. Sometimes it is necessary to look back at a business's historic results and to examine its financial statements when it was at a similar stage of development. The fact that a ratio compares two figures from the same set of accounts means that issues related to the scale of the business are eliminated. Ratios can be calculated and compared for businesses of different sizes or for the same business at different points in time. To make the comparisons meaningful the ratios must also be calculated on the same basis. This chapter provides a set of definitions for some key ratios. The examples are based on the full financial results for Newco Corp which can be found in the Appendix.

ASSESSING PROFITABILITY

Profit margin calculations can be used to assess profitability, but profits can be altered dramatically by simply changing the accounting treatment of items such as depreciation and amortisation. The reliability and transparency of profits therefore diminishes as you move further down the profit and loss account or income statement. Even at the gross profit level, different businesses may use different accounting policies for the timing of the recognition of revenues and also for the value of the cost of sales attached to those revenues. The business plan should be drawn up in such a way that the accounting policies are clear and their implications fully understood.

Profit margins are all calculated on a similar basis. The measure of profit is divided by sales. The ratio expresses how efficiently the business turns sales into profit. All things being equal high margins are preferred. It is worth calculating a range of profit margins as they all provide additional insight into the performance of the business.

Gross profit margin

The gross profit margin is defined as follows:

$$\text{Gross profit margin} = \frac{\text{gross profit}}{\text{sales}} \times 100\%$$

A business must make sufficient gross margin to cover its operating costs if it is to make a profit at the operating level. Gross margins vary dramatically from industry to industry. In the software and publishing industries, for example, gross profit margins can be extremely high, possibly in excess of 90%. This is because there are high sunk costs involved in creating a new software package or magazine but, once produced, the actual cost of each incremental unit of sales (producing one more CD, for example) is extremely low. In other sectors, gross margins may be much lower because of the high cost of manufacture but the business may have a very low operating cost base.

A set of ratios has been calculated for Newco Corp. These can be examined by selecting MAIN MENU → FINANCIAL RESULTS → RATIOS. The ratio sheet is shown in Chart 17.1.

Chart 17.1 **Financial ratios**

	A B C D	E	F	G	H	I	J	K	L	M	N
1											
2	**Ratios**	**Information only**									
3	**Newco Corp**	No user inputs are required in this section.									
4											
5											
6											
7	**Year** H C < >	**1**	**2**	**3**	**4**	**5**	**6**	**7**	**8**	**9**	**10**
16	**Liquidity and the balance sheet**										
17	Current ratio	0.02	0.06	0.15	0.21	0.41	1.34	6.35	2.46	3.40	3.00
18	Quick ratio	0.01	0.03	0.08	0.11	0.20	0.60	3.80	1.44	1.84	2.00
19	Net book value of assets	60,312.5	69,687.5	62,500.0	63,437.5	67,812.5	59,687.5	50,562.5	50,437.5	42,750.0	38,750.0
20	Capital expenditure to depreciation	15.1	2.7	0.6	0.5	1.6	0.6	0.5	0.5	0.6	0.8
21	Asset turnover	0.0	0.1	0.3	0.8	1.3	1.7	1.7	2.0	1.9	1.7
22	Debtor days	15.0	19.3	21.8	21.5	22.4	24.1	26.0	27.7	29.4	30.0
23	Creditor days	22.2	43.5	17.1	35.6	26.5	20.2	20.7	28.4	28.7	23.1
24	Stock turnover days	36.5	51.0	60.7	72.5	70.2	85.1	97.8	120.1	151.1	189.8
25											
26	**Returns**										
27	Return on average capital employed (ROACE)	0.0%	0.0%	0.0%	0.0%	8.2%	32.7%	42.8%	41.3%	41.1%	40.2%
28	Return on total average assets (ROTAA)	0.0%	0.0%	0.0%	0.0%	11.9%	42.1%	41.5%	35.5%	36.3%	34.5%
29	Return on equity (ROE)	0.0%	0.0%	0.0%	0.0%	16.4%	58.0%	49.0%	39.8%	38.6%	36.6%
30	Dividend cover	0.0	0.0	0.0	0.0	0.0	0.0	27.0	1.3	1.3	1.3
31											
32	**Financial**										
33	Gearing	42.4%	52.0%	65.0%	78.6%	69.3%	41.5%	20.0%	10.1%	9.2%	8.5%
34	Debt/equity ratio	73.5%	108.3%	185.8%	366.3%	225.5%	71.0%	25.0%	11.3%	10.2%	9.2%
35	Debt/EBITDA	0.0	0.0	0.0	8.8	2.8	0.9	0.0	0.0	0.0	0.0
36	Interest cover (EBITDA/interest)	0.0	0.0	0.0	2.3	7.0	15.8	37.8	94.2	142.3	138.5
37											

For Newco, the gross profit margin in year 1 was 59.5% (from the profit and loss account, E17 ÷ E11 × 100 = 59.5%). Over the forecast period the margin falls to 53.6% in year 10, because reductions in the prices charged to customers fall faster than the purchase cost of zappers. However, by lowering the selling price to promote mass-market appeal for widgets at the expense of gross margins, the business is able to exploit economies of scale, which result in a significant improvement in margins at the operating level.

Operating profit margin

The operating profit margin is defined as follows:

$$\text{Operating profit margin} = \frac{\text{operating profit}}{\text{sales}} \times 100\%$$

The operating profit margin measures overall profitability after taking into account all operating costs: variable costs of sales and fixed or overhead costs. The business must be profitable at the operating level in order to cover the depreciation and amortisation charged for assets it employs as well as any financing charges.

Operating margins, which are often called EBITDA (earnings before interest, taxes, depreciation and amortisation) margins, are regularly used as the basis of interbusiness comparisons and for the purposes of valuation. Earnings is simply another word for profit. Valuations based on EBITDA are discussed in Chapter 18. Operating margins are a popular choice for comparisons as they are less susceptible to differences in accounting policies which can be most pronounced once depreciation and amortisation are taken into account. Operating profit or EBITDA is also the best measure of a company's ability to generate cash. Depreciation and amortisation are not cash-based accounting entries and these are not included in EBITDA.

Newco makes a loss during the first three years of operation because it is not achieving economies of scale. The company needs an office and an accounting department whether it sells one or 1m widgets. As the business grows, the costs of the office and accounting departments can be spread over a greater volume of sales, leading to economies of scale and improvements in operating margins.

Newco becomes profitable at the operating level in year 4. Operating margins grow until they reach a peak of 37.1% in year 6 (from the profit and loss account, J31 ÷ J11 × 100 = 37.1%). After this period margins start to erode as growth in the market slows and increased competition from Widgets Online forces Newco Corp to make further reductions in its selling price to customers.

Earnings before interest and tax margin

The earnings before interest (EBIT) and tax margin is defined as follows:

$$\text{EBIT margin} = \frac{\text{profit before interest and tax}}{\text{sales}} \times 100\%$$

The EBIT margin is calculated after deducting accounting charges (depreciation and amortisation) for the use of fixed assets, and so a positive EBIT margin indicates that the business is generating sufficient profit to cover the costs associated with its fixed assets. Comparisons of different businesses at the EBIT margin level are more challenging, however, as the accounting policies that determine the depreciation and amortisation charges are more subjective. Despite this increased subjectivity, the EBIT margin is useful for comparisons as it is calculated before interest charges and so ignores how the business has been financed. Two businesses with very different capital structures can be compared at the EBIT level.

Newco's EBIT margin becomes positive in year 5 and increases to just under 28% by the end of the forecast.

Profit before tax margin

The profit before tax (PBT) margin is a more holistic view of the business as it is calculated after interest and thus takes into account how the business has been financed. As the PBT margin is calculated before tax this helps with interbusiness comparisons as taxation is subject to choices over accounting policy. The PBT margin is defined as follows:

$$\text{PBT margin} = \frac{\text{profits before tax}}{\text{sales}} \times 100\%$$

The PBT margin indicates the profitability of the business once all costs have been included. Interbusiness comparisons are less straightforward at the PBT level because of differences in accounting policies.

Newco turns profitable at the PBT level a year after it turns EBITDA positive. Although the business is profitable at the PBT level in year 4, it is interesting to note that it is not until year 5 that it begins to generate cash. Towards the end of the forecast period the business reaches a steady state and PBT margins remain around the 26% level with a slight upward trend. You can perform a PBT margin calculation yourself to verify the result.

Earnings per share

Earning per share (EPS) can be defined simply as:

$$\text{EPS} = \frac{\text{profits after tax}}{\text{weighted average number of shares in issue}}$$

Earnings examine the profits that are available for distribution to shareholders and are a basis for valuation based on price/earnings (P/E) ratios, which are discussed in Chapter 18. Investors look closely at P/E ratios and the growth in EPS. It is from EPS that a business can pay dividends.

Newco has positive EPS in year 5 of $0.04 (from the profit and loss account, I46 ÷ ((I39 + I42) ÷ 2) from the financing sheet) and this grows dramatically over the next two years before it settles towards a steady state of around $0.5.

REVIEWING THE BALANCE SHEET

The balance sheet lists the assets and liabilities of the company and those reviewing it will want to ascertain whether the business has sufficient liquid assets to meet its liabilities. Poor cash management is one of the main causes of business failure. Liquid assets are assets that can be turned quickly into cash. A business can face liquidity problems if it is making inadequate sales; a business growing rapidly can also encounter liquidity problems and it may be at risk of overtrading. Overtrading occurs when increases in demand and activity result in increases in the number of customers owing money to the business and the stock necessary to meet demand. Increases in debtors and stock must be financed by higher levels of working capital. If the business is unable to raise sufficient funding to meet these higher levels of working capital, it is said to be overtrading.

Current ratio

The current ratio measures liquidity and is defined as:

$$\text{Current ratio} = \frac{\text{current assets}}{\text{current liabilities}}$$

Current assets – assets that can be readily turned into cash – can be taken from the balance sheet. An obvious example is debtors. Current liabilities are commitments that will become due within one year and must be met in terms of cash. The current ratio examines the ability of the business to meet its liabilities. Different definitions can be used for current assets and current liabilities provided they are used consistently. In the calculations in the model, cash, debtors and stock are included in current assets and creditors for stock purchased and capital expenditure on tangible and intangible assets are included in current liabilities. It is normal to express the current ratio and the quick ratio, described below, as a positive figure.

It is difficult to provide guidance on what the appropriate level for the current ratio should be in any one industry. Clearly, if the ratio is less than 1 it implies that the business may struggle to meet its immediate commitments. As a rough guide, anything above 2 would be regarded as robust and 1.5 would probably be acceptable, but the best benchmarks will come from other businesses within the sector.

In the case of Newco, the current ratio remains below 1 until year 6 when the value is 1.34 (balance sheet, J18 ÷ J26), after which it fluctuates as the business eliminates its overdraft and begins to build up cash balances. The low initial levels of the current ratio suggest that the business has liquidity problems, and an inspection of the cash flow statement reveals that it requires funding in each year until year 6. (See Chart 16.3 on page 181, row 31.)

Quick ratio

A stronger test of liquidity is provided by the quick ratio, which is defined as follows:

$$\text{Quick ratio} = \frac{\text{cash + short term securities + debtors}}{\text{current liabilities}}$$

The quick ratio recognises that some assets are closer to cash than others, so while cash, liquid short-term securities and debtors are included, stock (the least liquid of all current assets) is excluded from the numerator of the ratio. In the calculations in the model, debtors and cash are included in the numerator and current liabilities are as previously defined. In terms of benchmarks, once again industry norms should be looked at but a figure of 1 is usually regarded favourably, although the ratio can be lower and remain acceptable. Like the current ratio, the result must be placed in the context of the story told by the business plan and the stage of development of the business.

The quick ratio for Newco mirrors the story already depicted by the current ratio. In the second half of the plan, the current and quick ratios suggest a business that does not face any major liquidity constraints, which is in contrast to the first half of the forecast. For year 7, the quick ratio is 3.8 and is calculated from the balance sheet as follows: (K13 + K14 + K17) ÷ K26.

Asset base

The net book value (NBV) of assets should be looked at for the forecast period. In year 7, the figure is $50,563 (balance sheet, cell K11). Many initial business plans overlook the need to replace machinery that has reached the end of its useful economic life, so that, as a result of depreciation, the NBV of assets by the end of the plan is clearly insufficient to support the level of activity conducted by the business. The business plan should show adequate levels of reinvestment to maintain the asset base of the business. This becomes of major significance when valuing the business.

A graph of the NBV of the assets of the business helps you to see whether the asset base is maintained. An alternative is to calculate the ratio of capital expenditure to depreciation. For year 6 the result is 0.6 (J21 from the cash flow statement divided by J33 from the profit and loss account). To ensure that the asset base is being maintained, the ratio needs to be 1 or greater. The low level of this ratio and the declining level of the NBV of assets suggest that the business may not be investing sufficiently in the replacement of its fixed assets. Another common ratio is to compare the level of capital expenditure to sales: this ratio is commonly expressed as a percentage. It shows what proportion of sales revenue is reinvested to support future activity.

Asset turnover

This measure examines the capital intensity of the business. It looks at the level of assets required to support the sales of the business. A business which requires a lower asset base to deliver the same volume of sales will be, all things being equal, more attractive than a business with a higher asset base.

$$\text{Asset turnover} = \frac{\text{sales}}{\text{net operating assets}}$$

Net operating assets are defined as total fixed assets and net current assets. Newco has a steady-state asset turnover ratio of just under 2. For year 6, the result is 1.7 (J11 from the profit and loss account divided by J30 from the balance sheet).

Debtor days

Debtor days, as stated in Chapter 6, are the days it takes to collect sales revenue from debtors. They can be calculated from a set of financial statements as follows:

$$\text{Debtor days} = \frac{\text{average debtors during the period}}{\text{annual credit sales}} \times 365$$

For year 6:

$$24.1 = \frac{\text{sum (balance sheet I13, J13, I14, J14)} \div 2}{\text{profit and loss J11}} \times 365$$

In many cases, analysts use total annual sales in place of annual sales on credit, as the former is readily available from a set of published accounts whereas the latter rarely is. As an increase in debtors, all else remaining the same, implies a reduction in cash, any business will hope to keep debtor days to as low a level as possible to minimise its working capital requirements.

In the model, debtor days were input.

Creditor days

Creditor days for some cost items were inputs into the model, but the following formula can be used to calculate the result from the financial statements:

$$\text{Creditor days} = \frac{\text{average creditors during the period}}{\text{total cost of purchases}} \times 365$$

In the calculation in the model, capital expenditure is included among the cost of purchases.

For year 6:

$$20.2 = \frac{\text{balance sheet (sum of I20 to I23 and J20 to J23)} \div 2}{\text{profit and loss (J15 and J29) and cash flow (J21 and J22)}} \times 365$$

An increase in creditors, all else remaining the same, implies that more cash is being retained within the business and so is positive for cash flow. The business should seek to maintain good relations with its suppliers while attempting to increase the credit period they provide.

The creditor days calculation for Newco fluctuates as a result of the 180-day credit terms provided by the supplier of the widget patent. The average creditor days figure is around 20. The extension of creditor terms and reduction of debtor days would lead to a significant improvement in working capital.

Stock turnover

The definition of stock turnover is as follows:

$$\text{Stock turnover days} = \frac{\text{value of closing stock}}{\text{cost of sales}} \times 365$$

For year 6:

$$85.1 = \frac{\text{balance sheet J15 + J16}}{\text{profit and loss J15}} \times 365$$

An increase in stock, all else remaining the same, implies that less cash is being generated from sales and so represents a decrease in cash flow. Businesses should attempt to minimise their stock turnover days (in other words, they should maximise stock turnover) while ensuring that the business is capable of meeting demand.

In the case of Newco, stock turnover days rise rapidly throughout the forecast period, reaching a maximum of 190 days in 2012. Newco is carrying too much stock relative to its sales volumes and this is tying up cash within the business. Purchase assumptions for stocks should be examined to reduce the number of stock turnover days.

ASSESSING RETURNS

The ratios discussed so far have looked at the profit and loss account and the balance sheet in isolation. Business managers and investors will want to know how efficiently they are using the assets and capital of the business. If there were two companies, A and B, both with identical levels of profit, but A required twice as much capital to deliver the same level of profit as B, all things being equal we would prefer company B as it uses its capital more efficiently. Returns measure how efficiently the capital of the business is being used. To assess capital efficiency, figures from the profit and loss account and balance sheet must be combined to calculate a number of different rates of return. Appropriate benchmarks are returns from similar businesses and other investment opportunities that have a similar level of risk.

The following ratios may be computed in a number of different ways, but the calculation must be logically consistent such that the numerator (or the potential return from the investment) is consistent with the denominator (the capital base on which the return is calculated). Some measures focus on the operational efficiency of the business in relation to its operating asset base; others examine whether the business is making an efficient use of its total capital.

Return on average capital employed

Return on average capital employed (ROACE) measures how efficiently the business is using its operating assets. To separate how the business is funded from operational efficiency, profits are calculated before interest and after deducting taxes, as if the business were 100% equity financed. This allows for a more meaningful comparison with other businesses. The definition of ROACE is as follows:

$$\text{ROACE} = \frac{\text{profit before interest} - \text{taxes}}{\text{average net fixed assets} + \text{trade debtors} + \text{stocks} - \text{trade creditors}} \times 100$$

For year 6:

$$32.7\% = \frac{\text{profit and loss J36} - \text{taxation J45}}{\text{balance sheet (sum (I and J11,13,14,15,16,20,21,22,23))} \div 2} \times 100$$

If the business has generated a large cash surplus that it has not yet deployed or has high levels of debt, for example, this will not affect the results of this calculation.

The long-term ROACE for Newco is around 75%, which represents an exceptional financial performance for the company and suggests that it may be underinvesting in its fixed asset base. These high levels of return may not be sustainable if the company does not continue to reinvest. Newco has decided to pay out a high level of profits (75%) as dividends, and it may be better off retaining more profits within the company to reinvest in its asset base. However, if it were able to reduce debtors and stock balances and increase creditor days, it would be able to increase its ROACE.

Return on total average assets

Return on total average assets (ROTAA) examines how efficiently the business is using its entire capital base. The definition of ROTAA is as follows:

$$\text{ROTAA} = \frac{\text{profits before interest} - \text{taxes}}{\text{total average assets}} \times 100$$

For year 7:

$$54.0\% = \frac{\text{profit and loss K36} - \text{taxation K45}}{\text{balance sheet (J30} + \text{K30)} \div 2} \times 100$$

Once again, to make comparisons between businesses simpler, taxes are calculated as if the business were 100% equity financed. This ratio also highlights the importance of consistency between the numerator and denominator. Profits before interest represent the profits that are distributable to debt providers (through interest payments) and to shareholders (through dividends). As the numerator represents the flow of monies to both debt and equity holders, the denominator should include both debt and equity, which is a definition of total assets.

If a business has a large cash balance deposited at a bank on which it earns a low rate of interest, say 5%, this will depress the overall returns of the business if its operating assets generate, say, 40%. As the cash balance increases, the overall return on total capital employed will begin to fall. The business would be better off returning the cash to the shareholders if it does not have investment opportunities that yield high rates of return.

Return on equity

The ROTAA examined the returns on all forms of capital employed within the business. Shareholders will be interested in the returns that the business is achieving on just the shareholders' funds. The definition of return on equity (ROE) is as follows:

$$\text{Return on equity} = \frac{\text{profits after tax}}{\text{share capital and retained profit}} \times 100$$

For year 8:

$$39.8\% = \frac{\text{profit and loss L46}}{\text{balance sheet (L32} + \text{L33)}} \times 100$$

Shareholders' returns are paid through dividends, and dividends are paid once all other commitments have been met. As a result, the numerator is profits after tax and is after the payment of interest to debt holders. The denominator includes all capital belonging to the shareholders, not only equity share capital but also the profit and loss reserves.

Newco generates good levels of returns for its shareholders. However, a review of the financial statements raises the question of how long these returns can be achieved.

Dividend cover

As shareholders are interested in dividends they may wish to compute a dividend cover ratio. Dividend cover examines the amount of profit that is available from which dividends can be paid. Dividend cover is defined as:

$$\text{Dividend cover} = \frac{\text{profit after tax}}{\text{dividends}}$$

For year 8:

$$1.33 = \frac{\text{profit and loss L46}}{\text{profit and loss L48}}$$

The forecast shows that Newco has only modest levels of dividend cover because of its high payout ratio.

ASSESSING FINANCIAL RISK

Risk and return are discussed in more detail in the next chapter. However, a fundamental principle of corporate finance says that an investor will typically demand a higher rate of return the higher the risk associated with the investment. An important element of risk is financial risk.

Providers of debt, such as banks, are interested in a business's ability to service and repay any loans made to it. They will therefore be interested in the business's cash flows. They will also want to identify items of collateral over which they can place a charge if the business goes into liquidation. Debt providers will hope to be able to sell the collateral to redeem all or part of the monies lent.

Shareholders are interested in the financial risk of the business because the risk attached to their share capital will increase as the business takes on more debt. As it increases its debts, there is a greater risk that the business will find itself in financial difficulties. As shareholders are the last to receive any money in the event of collapse, increasing debt levels signify increases on the risk of their investment.

Financial gearing

Financial gearing or leverage examines what proportion of the business is financed by debt and provides a proxy for potential financial risk where higher levels of gearing are normally associated with higher levels of risk. The definition of financial gearing is as follows:

$$\text{Gearing} = \frac{\text{long-term debt}}{\text{long-term debt + share capital + reserves}} \times 100$$

For year 8:

$$10.1\% = \frac{\text{balance sheet L34}}{\text{balance sheet (L32 + L33 + L34)}} \times 100$$

The acceptable levels of gearing will depend on the sector and the stage of growth of the business. Benchmarks should be obtained from similar businesses. Chapter 19 discusses funding issues in more detail.

Newco experiences high levels of gearing in years 3–5, but from year 6 onwards gearing levels fall significantly.

Debt/equity ratio

Another way of looking at this is to calculate the debt to equity ratio. The definition of the debt/equity ratio is straightforward:

$$\text{Debt/equity ratio} = \frac{\text{long-term debt}}{\text{share capital + reserves}}$$

For year 8:

$$11.3\% = \frac{\text{balance sheet L34}}{\text{balance sheet (L32 + L33)}} \times 100$$

Newco's debt/equity ratio mirrors the pattern of its gearing.

Debt/EBITDA ratio

The debt to EBITDA ratio is another common measure of gearing:

$$\text{Debt} \div \text{EBITDA ratio} = \frac{\text{net debt}}{\text{EBITDA}}$$

This measure of gearing is similar to comparing the size of an individual's mortgage (a company's debt) on their home relative to their salary (a company's level of EBITDA). The greater the multiple the less well the individual will sleep at night. Historically, mortgage firms had been prepared to lend individuals between three and four times their salary. Similar multiples were also deemed appropriate for companies. These multiples increased over the years for both individuals and companies, reaching levels of up to seven, eight or even higher multiples of income or profits by the mid-2000s. The credit crunch of 2007 and 2008 was partly caused by the recognition that lending at these levels was too risky and the multiples have now returned to more normal levels. For Newco, by year 8 the company's cash balance exceeds that of the outstanding debt leaving a zero net debt position.

Interest cover

A high gearing ratio may be acceptable if the business is highly cash generative and can easily service its debts. Debt providers will often look at interest cover, which examines the business's ability to pay interest, in conjunction with gearing ratios. Interest cover is similar to comparing an individual's salary with how much they have to pay each month on their mortgage. The more times they can cover the mortgage the better the individual will sleep at night. Interest cover is defined as follows:

$$\text{Interest cover} = \frac{\text{operating profit}}{\text{interest}}$$

For year 8:

$$94.2 = \frac{\text{profit and loss L31}}{\text{profit and loss (L38 + L39)}}$$

Depreciation and amortisation are excluded from the calculation of profit as they do not reflect cash-related expenses in the accounting period and so do not constrain a business's ability to pay its interest charges. Some people extend the definition to include capital expenditure so as to include all operating cash flows.

Newco's high levels of interest cover from year 4 onwards should reassure any lenders that their loans are reasonably secure. Benchmarks from other businesses can be used, but another useful rule of thumb is to imagine the ratio represented your salary and mortgage payments and to consider how comfortable you would feel at these forecast levels.

LINKING RATIOS

Analytical ratios do not have to be used in isolation, and combinations of ratios can provide valuable insights into the drivers of value for a business. For example, the return on assets can be broken down into an asset turnover ratio and a profit margin.

$$\frac{\text{Profit before interest – tax}}{\text{total assets}} = \frac{\text{sales}}{\text{total assets}} \times \frac{\text{profit before interest – tax}}{\text{sales}}$$

This combination suggests that the returns of the business can be improved through increasing the rate at which its asset base generates sales and the profit margin it makes on those sales.

$$\frac{\text{Profit after tax}}{\text{equity}} = \frac{\text{profit after tax}}{\text{sales}} \times \frac{\text{sales}}{\text{assets}} \times \frac{\text{assets}}{\text{equity}}$$

Return on equity (profit after tax divided by equity) can be broken down in to a profit margin, an asset turnover ratio and a form of gearing ratio. If the business can increase any one of these ratios, all other things remaining the same, the return on equity of the business will increase.

REVIEWING THE FINAL YEAR CASH FLOW

The cash flow in the final year of any forecast has a significant impact on the valuation of the business through something called a terminal value calculation (see Chapter 18, page 218). This assumes that the business has reached a level of maturity and that it will continue to grow at a steady rate. For the terminal value calculation to be meaningful it must represent a steady state for the business, so the following checks should be carried out:

- The growth in revenues and operating profits in the final years of the plan should be slowing and showing a trend towards a steady rate of growth. Between 3% and 5% would not be abnormal, but the final result will depend on the business and its market. A good benchmark is to compare the rate of growth with the nominal growth rate of gross domestic product in the country in which the business operates. In maturity, in steady state, often we would expect to see the business growing in line with the economy as a whole.
- Operating profit margins should be consistent with the anticipated competitive nature of the market at the end of the forecast period. If it is believed that in ten years the market will be competitive, then the business should not be forecasting high levels of profitability, as competitive forces will force down margins.
- The asset base of the business should be sufficient to support the level of sales and operating profit generated in the final year, and the capital expenditure and depreciation figures for the final year should be roughly equal. This ensures that the asset base will be maintained.
- The returns generated by the business in the final year will indicate whether it has adequate assets. If the asset base is too low, the final year return calculations will yield results that are unachievable. The final year returns should also be consistent with the expected competitive nature of the market.
- The effective tax rate, calculated by dividing the tax charge in the profit and loss account by profits before tax, should be equal to the actual rate of tax. This ensures that the cash flow that enters the terminal value calculation includes the full, steady-state cash flow implications of corporation tax. In industries with long lead times on generating returns, the switch-point from not paying tax to paying tax can occur in the final year of the forecast. Dramatic changes in valuations can take place when sensitivities are run, as the final year cash flow switches from including tax payments to not including tax payments.

Many business plans adjust the final year cash flow to ensure that it is representative of the expected steady-state cash flows for the business. This might involve altering the final operating profit margin, increasing capital expenditure and calculating tax paid on the specified rate that will be in force at that time. It is important to appreciate how pervasive the final year cash flow can be and to ensure that it is representative of the business's steady state.

18 Evaluating strategic options

OBJECTIVES

Strategic planning is more of an art than a science. No amount of analysis will identify categorically which strategic option to select, but the analysis and techniques in this chapter can help the decision-making process. Ultimately, the choice will be based on experience and instinct.

QUALITATIVE EVALUATION OF STRATEGIC CHOICE

Elements in evaluating strategy

Five main qualitative areas should be examined when considering strategic options: consistency, validity, feasibility, business risk and flexibility. Each strategic option should be examined under each heading, and it can help to rate each criterion on a scale of 1–5. The analysis can also be extended to determine how effective the strategy is in the short, medium and long term. This simple technique may help to eliminate inappropriate strategies at an early stage.

Consistency

Strategic alternatives must be consistent with achieving the business's vision, mission and goals. Any option that is not can be eliminated. However, if all the options are not consistent, either the wrong options are being considered or the vision, mission and goals are not achievable.

Validity

The assumptions behind the strategic options must be valid. These assumptions may include the future business environment, the competition, customers and suppliers and how they will react to alternative strategies. A strategic option that involves lowering prices but does not recognise the possibility that competitors may lower their prices may not be valid.

Feasibility

A strategy may, in theory, be capable of delivering the business's vision, mission and goals, but in practice it must also be feasible. In other words, the business must have (or be capable of acquiring) the financing, resources, assets, experience, culture and skills to carry it out.

Business risk

Return on investment is related to risk, and all strategic options carry some form of risk.

They should also include ways of minimising the potential risk. The evaluation should aim to determine whether the residual risk of a strategic option is at a level commensurate with the anticipated return.

Flexibility

In today's rapidly changing business world, a strategy must have enough flexibility to work if circumstances change. If it can be broken down into a series of options that can be chosen, depending on circumstances, this is a considerable advantage.

PROJECT APPRAISAL

The evaluation of an individual project within a company as well as a valuation of the total company can be performed using the discounted cash flow technique discussed in this chapter. This section begins by discussing company valuations in general before examining discounted cash flow analysis on page 210. Internal rate of return calculations (page 220) can also be applied to both project and company valuations. Payback and discounted payback techniques (page 221) are better suited for individual project appraisal problems.

BUSINESS VALUATIONS

Providers of equity capital to a business want to see an increase in the value of their investment. The future value of the business's equity under each strategic option should be calculated. This is done is by assessing the trade-off between the risks of a particular strategy and the anticipated returns.

Limitations

A valuation relies upon the underlying forecast on which it is based and the assumptions used in the chosen valuation technique. Because the underlying forecasts and assumptions will contain flaws, it is better to present a range of values using different assumptions and techniques than a single point estimate. Providing a valuation range makes it clear that valuation is an inexact science. The wider the valuation range the more confident an investor can be that the true value lies within the given range. However, if the range is too wide it does not aid decision-making. A reasonable balance must be struck.

Enterprise and equity value

There is an important distinction between equity value and enterprise value. Valuations are based on cash flows, and what is included in the cash flows will determine whether an enterprise or an equity value is calculated.

Enterprise value

If the cash flows used are before the payment of interest charges, they represent the monies that will ultimately flow to the providers of debt (via interest and principal repayments) and the providers of equity (via dividends). These cash flows represent the flow of cash to all providers of capital to the enterprise. A value based on these cash flows is called the enterprise value (EV), which is also referred to as the firm value (the value of the entire business). The cash flows that are used to calculate the enterprise or firm value are called the free cash flow (see Chart 18.1).

Chart 18.1 **Free cash flow**

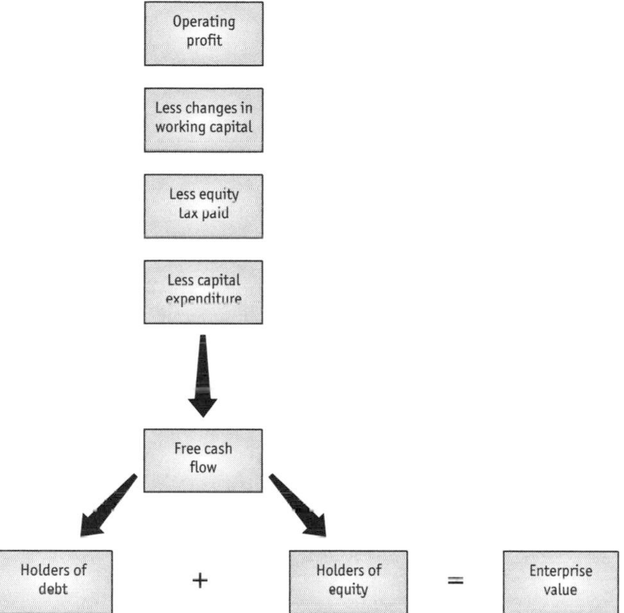

Free cash flow is calculated by deducting movements in working capital, the tax that would be paid were the business entirely financed by equity (why this is important is explained later) and capital expenditure from operating profit. This gives the free cash flow to both debt and equity holders. The value of all future free cash flow, as if it were received today and adjusted for the riskiness of the cash flows, is the enterprise or firm value of a business and represents the combined value of the business to both the debt and equity providers.

Equity value

Equity value is the risk adjusted value today of all future cash flows that flow only to the equity holders. These cash flows are called the free cash flow to equity (see Chart 18.2 on the next page).

Chart 18.2 **Free cash flow to equity**

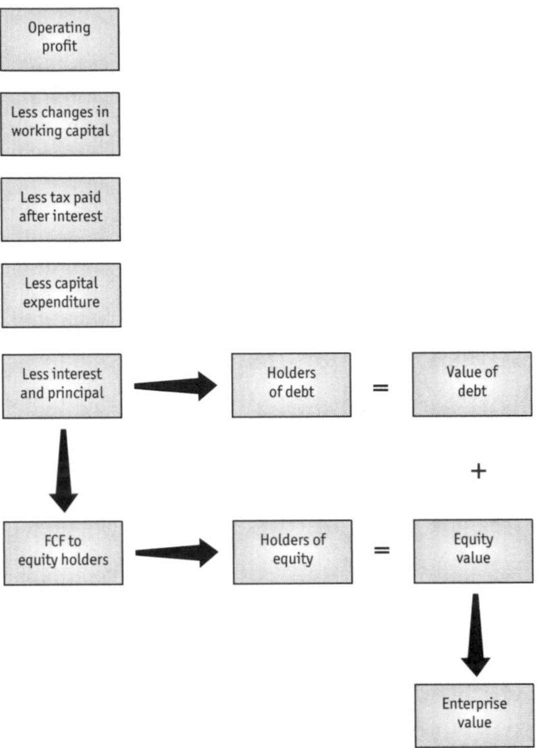

Free cash flow to equity is calculated by deducting movements in working capital, actual tax paid, capital expenditure, and interest and principal repayments from operating profit. The cash that remains is available exclusively for the equity holders and a valuation based upon these free cash flows is called the equity value.

Chart 18.2 also highlights the fact that interest and principal payments flow to the debt holders. The value today of all future interest and principal repayments is the value of the debt. The following important relationship can be derived from this chart:

Enterprise value – today's value of future interest and principal payments = equity value

Normally, it is assumed that today's value of future interest and principal payments are approximated by the value of debt in the balance sheet today. As a result, the equation can be rewritten as:

Enterprise value – net debt = equity value

Approaches to valuation

The value of an asset is what someone else would be prepared to pay for it. When presented with a purchase decision, such as a used car or a share in a business, buyers will want to ensure that they are paying a fair price. In the case of a used car, a purchaser might look at the prices similar cars are selling for in the local newspaper or ask friends who have recently purchased similar cars, what price they paid. The same approach should be adopted in business valuations. The equivalent of the local newspaper is the stockmarket and the price a friend paid is the value of recent comparable transactions. A business can be valued by comparing similar quoted companies and looking at recent corporate transactions.

There are two important points to consider when examining comparable business valuations:

- The ratios must be applied to the appropriate year. In many cases, the valuation will be based on a prospective price earnings (PE) or EV/EBITDA ratio, for example, where the ratio of the comparable quoted business is based on a forecast of its expected future earnings or profits. To ensure consistency, the ratio must be applied to the same year's forecast for the target business.
- The valuation must be put into some form of context, and the ratios must be applied with thought and deliberation. Typically, a high valuation ratio suggests that there is an expectation of rapid growth in the business's earnings. The growth prospects given in a business plan must be plausible compared with similar businesses.

The next section outlines different valuation techniques involving comparable businesses. The values used in the examples can be derived from the values of quoted companies on the stockmarket or from recent transactions: the approach is identical. As explained later, there can be problems using a comparable business approach, but when comparables are used the mean or median value for several businesses should be used in the calculation.

Valuation techniques involving comparable businesses

Price/earnings ratio

The first stage in valuing a business using price/earnings (PE) ratios is to identify a suitable comparable business. It should be similar in terms of its market, customers, products, business design and growth prospects. If a comparable business has been identified that is twice as large as the one to be valued, a PE ratio, a relative measure of value, can be used to value the smaller business.

Earnings per share (EPS), apart from the impact of accounting differences, should be a directly comparable, measurable indicator of performance. The share price of a business is also directly and objectively observable on the stockmarket. Combining the share price with the EPS gives a PE ratio, which provides a measure of value for a unit of earnings.

$$\text{Price/earnings ratio} = \frac{\text{price per share}}{\text{earnings per share}} = \text{value per unit of earnings}$$

Business A is to be valued using a comparable business, Business B, which currently trades at \$2.34 per share and has an EPS of \$0.083. The PE ratio for Business B is:

$$\$2.34 \div \$0.083 = 28$$

Business B is trading on a PE ratio of 28 times earnings. As the forecast EPS for Business A is \$0.062, the two figures can be used to generate a value for Business A.

$$\text{EPS} \times \text{PE ratio (Business B)} = \text{price per share}$$
$$\$0.062 \times 28 = \$1.736$$

Using the PE ratio of a comparable business (B), it is possible to arrive at a price per share for Business A. If there were 100m shares in issue, the value of Business A would be:

$$\$1.736 \times 100,000,000 = \$173,600,000$$

This represents an equity value, as EPS is based on profit after tax, and therefore the earnings, which are available solely for distribution to the equity holders.

Many analysts rely greatly on PE ratios for valuation purposes. However, in addition to the fact that this depends on being able to find suitable comparable companies and the problems there can be with earnings owing to different accounting policies, there are two other difficulties with using PE ratios. One is that there is an assumption that both companies have the same capital structure, that is, the same mix of debt and equity finance. The amount of debt a business carries has an impact on its valuation. The other is that unless the business has positive earnings, a PE-based approach is impossible. Chart 18.3 shows a profile of earnings for a start-up business.

Chart 18.3 **Valuation techniques for different stages of business development**

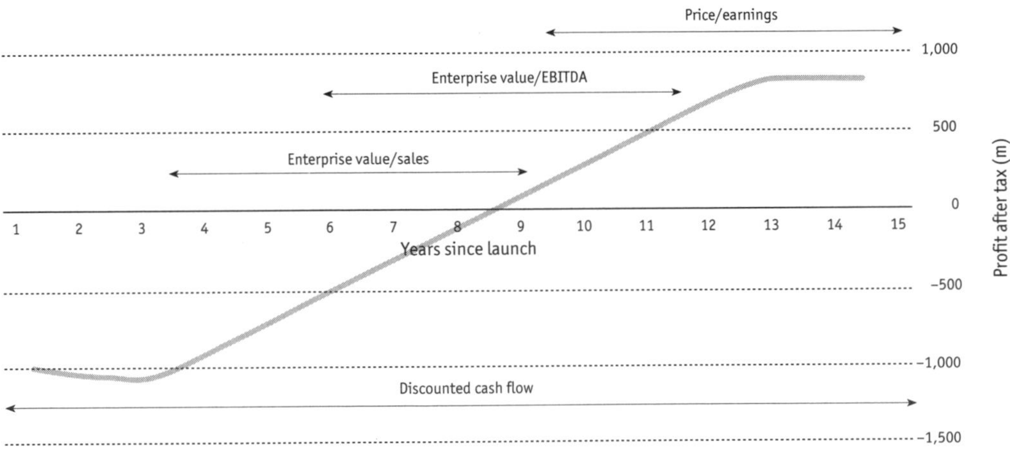

EPS is based on profits after tax, and the chart reveals that it is not until year 8 that the business makes a profit after tax.

EV/EBITDA ratio

Companies often make an operating profit or have positive earnings before interest, taxes, depreciation and amortisation (EBITDA) before they make a profit after tax, so a comparison with a similar business based on an EBITDA multiple can provide an alternative basis for valuation. The use of EBITDA multiples is identical to the application of PE ratios, but the end result is an enterprise value rather than an equity value. EBITDA is calculated before interest payments and so earnings are attributable to both debt and equity holders. The ratio used is called the enterprise value to EBITDA or EV/EBITDA ratio.

Another similar business, Business C, has an enterprise value of $330m and EBITDA of $23.6m, which gives an EV/EBITDA ratio of:

$$\text{EV} \div \text{EBITDA} = \frac{330}{23.6} = 14$$

The multiple can now be applied to Business A, which is forecast to have EBITDA of $13.8m:

$$\text{EV} = \text{EV multiple} \times \text{EBITDA (Business A)}$$
$$\text{EV} = 14 \times \$13{,}800{,}000 = \$193{,}200{,}000$$

Based on an EV/EBITDA multiple of 14, the enterprise value of Business A is $193.2m. It would be useful to compare this value with the equity value based on a PE valuation. The calculation is simple, as it is known that Business A has $50m of net debt in its balance sheet, and so:

$$\text{Enterprise value} - \text{net debt} = \text{equity value}$$
$$\$193{,}200{,}000 - \$50{,}000{,}000 = \$143{,}200{,}000$$

The equity value based on an EV/EBITDA multiple and using Business C is $143.2m, which is $30m lower than the valuation based on Business B using PE ratios. It can be said that the value of Business A lies between $143.2m and $173.6m. But it may lie outside this range, so other valuations should be made to increase confidence about the accuracy of the valuation range.

One advantage of using EV/EBITDA multiples is that EBITDA usually turns positive earlier, allowing valuations to be made using comparable companies earlier. The other advantage is that EBITDA is less prone to the influences of differences in accounting treatment as depreciation and amortisation have not yet been charged.

EV/sales ratio

For young businesses it may be necessary to rely upon an enterprise value to sales ratio. Sales will be positive from the moment the business starts trading, which means a valuation can be reached using comparable business data very early. The approach is exactly the same as applying an EV/EBITDA valuation.

This valuation approach is obviously less sophisticated than measures that also take into account the operating costs of the business (EV/EBITDA) and the charges for the use of assets and the costs of debt financing (PE ratios). However, it is better than nothing.

EV/customer ratio

During the dotcom boom there were many companies that did not have revenues, so analysts had to look for other bases for valuation. For example, internet portals such as Yahoo were often valued on the basis of the number of subscribers, as many had not yet discovered a method of generating sales revenue. An enterprise value to customer ratio was calculated for a similar business and then applied to the business for which a valuation was required. The approach is identical to ones described above involving enterprise values.

The subsequent bursting of the bubble and the collapse of many companies highlight the dangers of relying on such blunt valuation techniques. However, the approach has some merit when trying to assess the quality, in value terms, of a business's customer base. This approach is often used in the valuation of mobile telephony companies, for example.

Other ratios

There is an infinite array of potential valuation ratios that can be computed. Four more ratios are described Chart 18.4.

Chart 18.4 **More valuation metrics**

Ratio	*Calculation*	*Comments*
Price/cash	Price per share divided by the cash flow per share calculated after interest and principal payments	Provides an equity value and, as it focuses on cash, is less prone to the effects of different accounting policies
Price/asset value	Price per share divided by the net book value of the assets of the business	Provides an equity value for the business. Asset values can be highly subjective
Dividend yield	Dividends per share divided by the share price	A useful measure for mature companies with steady earnings
PEG	The PE ratio divided by the expected future compound annual growth-rate of earnings over the next five years	Examines whether the rating for a share is justified by its growth prospects. Typically, the lower the ratio the better

Comparable business valuations in the business planning model

The business planning model contains valuations based on a number of comparable business ratios for Newco Corp. The prospective business comparable ratios are based on year 2 and are shown in Chart 18.5, which is an extract from the valuation sheet (MAIN MENU → FINANCIAL RESULTS → VALUATION).

Chart 18.5 **Prospective business comparable ratios**

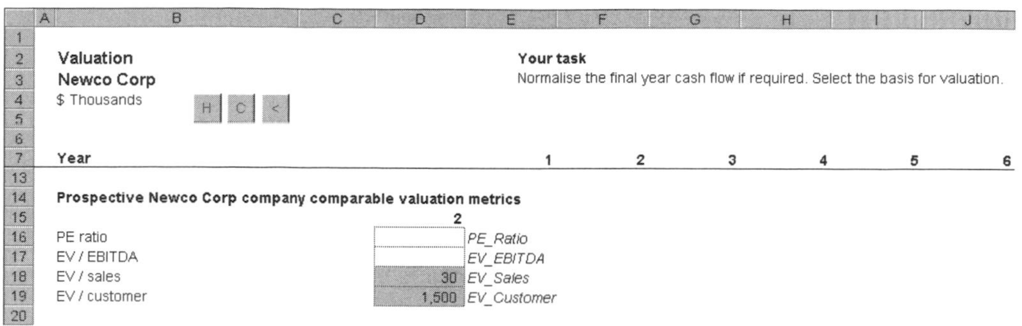

Valuation
Newco Corp
$ Thousands

Your task
Normalise the final year cash flow if required. Select the basis for valuation.

Year	1	2	3	4	5	6

Prospective Newco Corp company comparable valuation metrics

	2	
PE ratio		PE_Ratio
EV / EBITDA		EV_EBITDA
EV / sales	30	EV_Sales
EV / customer	1,500	EV_Customer

The year 2 forecast results for Newco from the model are as follows:

Profit after tax: profit and loss account cell F46 = ($18,331)
EBITDA: profit and loss account cell F31 = ($5,865)
Sales: profit and loss account cell F11 = $6,480
Closing customers: revenue sheet cell F12 = 150 customers

The valuation results are shown in Chart 18.6.

Chart 18.6 **Comparable business valuation results**

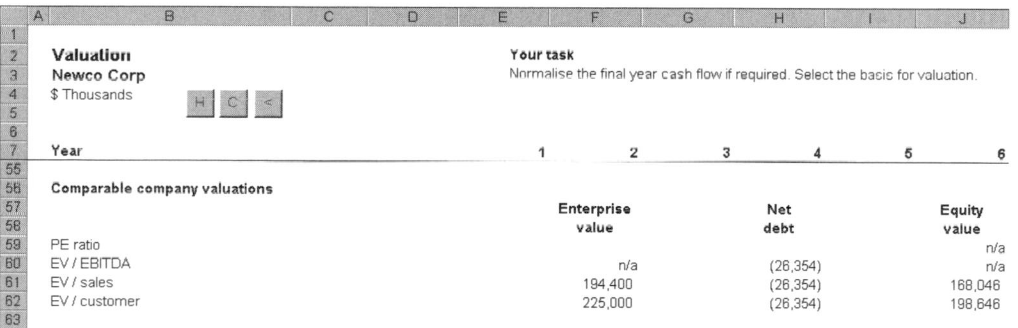

Valuation
Newco Corp
$ Thousands

Your task
Normalise the final year cash flow if required. Select the basis for valuation.

Year	1	2	3	4	5	6

Comparable company valuations

	Enterprise value	Net debt	Equity value
PE ratio			n/a
EV / EBITDA	n/a	(26,354)	n/a
EV / sales	194,400	(26,354)	168,046
EV / customer	225,000	(26,354)	198,646

As the business is loss making in year 2 at both operating and profit after tax levels, valuations are only possible based on EV/sales and EV/customer ratios. The resulting enterprise valuations are $194.4m and $225m and are calculated as follows based on an EV/sales ratio of 30 and an EV/customer ratio of 1,500:

Sales × EV/sales = enterprise value
6,480 × 30 = $194,400,000

Number of customers × EV/customer = enterprise value
150 × 1,500 = $225,000,000

For existing businesses, net debt is usually taken from the opening balance sheet, but in the case of Newco the opening balance is zero. A number of options can be used for calculating net debt. The maximum net debt achieved in the balance sheet over the forecast period is one option. An alternative is to assume an optional debt/equity ratio based on a similar existing business and apply that ratio to the enterprise value to derive the value of the debt and equity. In the example, net debt at the end of year 1 is used.

Net debt is calculated from the balance sheet based on long-term debt (cell E34), overdrafts (cell E25) netted against cash balances (cell E17). The figures are $19.245m, $7.109m and $0 respectively, giving total net debt of $26.354m. Deducting net debt from the enterprise value gives equity values of $168m based on the sales multiple and $199m based on the customer multiple.

DISCOUNTED CASH FLOW ANALYSIS

Principles of discounted cash flow

Discounted cash flow (DCF) analysis can be used at any stage of a business's life to generate a company valuation or can be applied to project cash flows to evaluate a specific project. There are two fundamental principles.

Principle 1

$1 today is worth more than $1 tomorrow.

DCF analysis is concerned with the value of future cash flows today. If offered the choice between $1 today and $1 in a year's time, investors would choose $1 today. $1 in a year's time is worth less than $1 today because $1 today could be invested and in a year's time would be worth more than $1. This is referred to as the time value of money concept. If, however, the choice was between $1 today or the chance of investing in Newco and expecting to receive $1.10 in a year's time investors would probably say: "Well, it depends."

Principle 2

A safe $1 is worth more than a risky $1.

Suppose the alternative to investing in Newco is to invest $1 in the Central Bank (CB), which pays interest at 10% per annum. Investors will choose to invest in the CB because it is almost certain to be able to pay the interest and return the $1 at the end of the year. In the case of Newco, there is a much higher risk that widgets are not bought in the quantities originally anticipated, that the machine necessary to manufacture them is more expensive than initially envisaged by the management, and that at the end of the year the company will not have the cash to return the $1, let alone pay the interest as well. Given the same level of return of 10%, investors would prefer the safer CB. A safe $1 is worth more than a risky $1. What would investors require to persuade them to invest $1 in Newco?

Risk and reward

Investors must be compensated for the time value of money and the additional risk associated with investing in Newco. They will expect a return at least equal to the rate they could achieve virtually free of risk at the CB. This is called the risk free rate of return. They will also require an additional return to compensate for the additional risk associated with Newco. This is called the risk premium. The combination of the risk free rate and the risk premium provides the minimum rate of return necessary to convince investors to invest in Newco. This is the discount rate that should be used to discount future cash flows back to the present day.

The principle of discounting

If $1 is invested in the CB and left there for a number of years the interest earned and the future cash values would develop as follows, assuming a 10% interest rate, based on the principles of compound interest. Compound interest implies that interest in T2 (T is a time period), for example, is calculated on the original $1 plus the interest earned in T1 ($0.10). In T2, therefore, interest is calculated on $1.10.

Chart 18.7 **Compound interest**

T0	*T1*	*T2*	*T3*
$1	$1 × (1 + 10%)	$1.10 × (1 + 10%)	$1.21 × (1 + 10%)
$1	$1.10	$1.21	$1.33

If T0 is the present day, then $1.10, $1.21 and $1.33 are all equal in present value terms to $1. It is clearly much easier to assess the value of future cash flows if they are all expressed in today's terms or as a present value.

Discounting is similar to interest calculations, only in reverse. If you wanted to know what $1.21 received in T2 was worth in present value terms, you would ask what amount would be required at T0 which if invested and subsequently earn 10% compound interest would give a figure of $1.21 two years later. To perform the calculation, divide $1.21 by (1+10%)^2. The ^2 or square is included because interest at 10% is earned over two years; this allows for the compound nature of interest. The answer is that the present value of $1.21 received in T2 is $1.

Chart 18.8 **Basic discounting**

T0	*T1*	*T2*	*T3*
$1	$1.10 ÷ (1 + 10%)	$1.21 ÷ (1 + 10%)^2	$1.33 ÷ (1 + 10%)^3
$1	$1	$1	$1

Applying the technique of discounting, what is the combined value at T0 of $1.05 received at the end of T1, $1.35 received at the end of T2 and $1.40 received at the end of T3?

Chart 18.9 **Simple investment decision**

T0	T1	T2	T3
	\$1.05 ÷ (1 + 10%)	\$1.35 ÷ (1 + 10%)^2	\$1.40 × (1 + 10%)^3
\$3.12	\$0.95	\$1.12	\$1.05

Discounting each cash flow back to T0 reveals that the combined present value of the future cash flows of \$1.05, \$1.35 and \$1.40 received at T1, T2 and T3 respectively is \$3.12 when discounted at a discount rate of 10%.

Suppose that, in order to be entitled to receive the stream of future cash flows described above, the investor must invest \$3 now at T0. It is assumed that the discount rate of 10% accurately reflects the investor's time value of money and required compensation for risk (risk premium). Should the investor invest?

The investment at T0 is already in today's terms or at present value. The present value of the future cash flows was calculated above at \$3.12, so the difference between the initial outlay and the present value of future cash flows is \$3.12 less \$3 which gives a net present value (NPV) of \$0.12.

Present value of future cash flows	\$3.12
Minus investment at T0	\$3.00
Net present value	\$0.12

The answer to the question is yes. The investor should invest because the value of the future cash flows in today's terms is greater than the amount the investor must invest today to be entitled to receive them.

This can be expressed formally. If the availability of capital is unconstrained (investors have sufficient capital to undertake all the investments they choose), it is possible to show, through financial theory, that accepting all projects with a positive NPV, when the future cash flows have been discounted by the appropriate discount rate, will increase shareholder value.

The discount rate

Before looking at DCF analysis in practice and applying the technique to Newco, the appropriate discount rate with which to discount the future cash flows must be determined.

In large organisations, there may be a set of discount rates laid down for use in any DCF analysis. If predetermined rates are not available, professional advice can be sought from, say, bankers or other advisers. If no such assistance is available or for those interested in the details, the following sections provide a comprehensive guide to calculating the weighted average cost of capital (WACC).

Capital structure and the WACC

The discount rate for debt and the discount rate for equity will differ because of the different risks associated with each type of funding. As debt holders are paid from profits before shareholders receive dividends, and they may have a charge over the assets of the business and rank above shareholders if the business goes into liquidation, their risk is lower. So their discount rate should be lower compared with that of equity holders, who carry the highest level of risk of any investor.

To discount the free cash flow to both debt and equity holders, the two separate discount rates need to be combined to produce a weighted average discount rate. The weights used in the calculation are provided by the total market value of the debt and equity funding in the business's balance sheet. The result is the weighted average cost of capital or WACC, which is the appropriate discount rate for discounting free cash flow to derive the business's enterprise value. It would be inappropriate, however, to use this discount rate to apply DCF analysis to the free cash flow to equity holders; in this case the cost of equity would be used. This highlights the importance of consistency.

A business may have many different classes of debt and equity, but the simple example below assumes that the business is funded by one class of debt and one class of equity:

- A is the proportion of the business financed by equity.
- E is the cost of equity in nominal terms.
- B is the proportion of the business financed by debt.
- R is the cost of debt in nominal terms.
- T is the tax rate.

The proportions A and B are based on the market value of the equity and the debt respectively. E is the cost of equity, which would be used to discount free cash flow to equity holders, and R is the cost of debt, which is the rate that would be used to discount interest and principal repayments to debt holders. The formula for the WACC can be written as:

$$WACC = (A \times E) + (B \times R \times (1 - T))$$

It is important to note that the cost of debt R is multiplied by (1 – T), 1 minus the tax rate. Interest charges on debt can be deducted from the profits on which corporation tax is calculated; this reduces the actual amount of tax paid by the business. A lower tax charge implies a higher level of free cash flow compared with an identical business entirely financed by equity. This cash flow benefit is called the tax shield on financing. The benefit of the tax shield on financing means that the effective cost of debt to the business is lower and hence the cost of debt is multiplied by 1 minus the tax rate. A numerical example is provided below: two identical companies, one 100% equity financed, the other with 50% of the business funded by debt and 50% by equity.

	Equity financed	*Equity and debt financed*
Profit before interest and tax	100	100
Interest	0	(20)
Profit before tax	100	80
Tax at 30%	(30)	(24)
Profit after tax	70	56

The equity and debt financed business will pay $6 less tax than the 100% equity financed business. This is equal to the interest charge multiplied by the tax rate: 20 × 30% = $6.

The WACC calculation, through the inclusion of (1 – T), automatically takes into account the value of the tax shield on financing. When free cash flow is calculated, it is essential to ensure that the tax shield is not double counted by erroneously calculating tax on profits which have been reduced by interest charges. In the free cash flow calculation, the actual tax paid is calculated as if the business were 100% equity financed. This can be achieved by:

- adding back the tax shield on financing to the free cash flow; this is calculated as the interest cost multiplied by the tax rate; or
- calculating the tax paid twice, once including interest charges and once without, the first for use in the profit and loss account and the second for use in the valuation. This dual approach was discussed in Chapter 16 (page 185).

In calculating the WACC, the costs of debt and equity are weighted according to the market value of debt and the market value of equity. In the case of debt, the value of the net debt in the balance sheet is normally used. In the case of equity, the market value of equity should be used. Unfortunately, this presents a problem.

To calculate the market value of equity, it may be necessary to perform a DCF analysis. To carry out a DCF analysis, a discount rate is required. To calculate a discount rate, it is necessary to calculate a WACC, and to calculate a WACC, the market value of equity is needed. The solution to this circularity problem is to assume that the business will adopt the optimal financing structure and that this structure provides the weightings for the WACC calculation. The optimal financing structure will be industry dependent, and the capital structures of other companies should be looked at in order to make the appropriate assumptions.

Most elements of the WACC formula, such as the cost of debt (the agreed rate of interest with the bank, for example), the tax rate and the proportions of debt and equity, are easy to obtain. Obtaining an assumption for the cost of equity can be more challenging.

The capital asset pricing model

The cost of equity can be estimated in a number of different ways, but the most common technique is to employ the capital asset pricing model (CAPM). The CAPM provides the following formula for calculating the cost of equity:

$$r_e = r_f + \beta_e \times (r_m - r_f)$$

Where:

r_e is the cost of equity
r_f is the risk free rate
r_m is the expected return on the market
β_e is the estimated beta of the business

The formula states that the cost of equity is equal to the risk free rate plus the risk premium, which is defined as the difference between the return that can be expected from the market and the risk free rate, multiplied by beta, an estimate of the risk of the project.

The risk free rate is usually assumed to be the rate on an appropriate government bond with a tenor that matches that of the future cash flows. In many cases, it will not be possible to match the duration of the forecast cash flows with a suitable bond yield curve and the closest approximation will often be used instead. The use of a bond of the country in which the investment is being made will capture the political and sovereign risk of investing in that country. However, for many projects with global investors a US dollar-denominated bond will be used.

The risk premium reflects the additional return required by investors for investing in projects with higher levels of risk compared with the risk free rate. The risk premium is calculated by deducting the risk free rate from the expected return on the market portfolio.

There are two types of risk that affect the performance of companies: unique or specific risk, which relates to the risks specific to one particular business and market; and systematic risk, which relates to the economy-wide risks that affect all companies. Individual business performance varies, and while some companies may be gaining value, others might be losing value. If an investor holds a diversified portfolio of shares, on average the over and under performance of the companies within the portfolio usually cancel out and the investor can eliminate specific risk through diversification. However, irrespective of how diversified a portfolio is, the investor can never fully eliminate market risk or systematic risk, as these affect all companies.

Beta is a relative measure of the systematic risk of the investment compared with the market. As investors are assumed to be able to diversify at minimal cost, the only risk that will be included in the cost of equity will be associated with market risk. Beta examines the impact of including the investment within a fully diversified market portfolio. A beta of 1 implies that the project has the same volatility as the market. A beta greater than 1 implies volatility greater than that of the market and the converse for a stock with a beta of less than 1. Stock with a beta of 1.5 will move 50% more than any movement of the market as a whole. Betas can be measured statistically by observing the historical performance of companies relative to the market. The importance of beta to the investment community means that betas for quoted companies are published regularly by brokerages and advisory services. A search on the internet can often uncover estimates of beta for most large publicly traded companies.

Combining the elements of the CAPM allows you to calculate a cost of equity for a particular investment that reflects the time value of money, the risk free rate and the additional return required to compensate for the additional risk of the investment. Examined below are practical issues in using CAPM to estimate the cost of equity for Newco.

CAPM in practice

It is assumed that the risk free rate on a US dollar government bond is 4% and that the expected return on the market is 9%. An estimate for beta from a quoted business similar to Newco is 1.2. Normally, betas from a range of companies would be obtained and the average calculated once the following procedure has been applied.

The betas obtained from the market will capture the risk associated with the nature of the business and its activities and the financial risk associated with its capital structure; for example, the more debt a business carries the greater is the risk for equity holders. To use these comparable business betas to estimate the cost of equity for Newco, they need to be "ungeared". This means eliminating the effects of financial risk so that only the risk associated with the investment remains. This is called the asset beta, which is equal to the following formula:

$$\beta_a = \frac{\beta_e}{[1 + (1 - T)\frac{D}{E}]}$$

Where:

β_a is the asset beta
T is the effective corporation tax rate
D is the value of debt
E is the value of equity

The comparable business with a beta of 1.2 has a debt/equity ratio of 0.67 and a taxation rate of 30%. The asset beta is therefore:

$$\beta_a = \frac{1.2}{[1 + (1 - 0.3) \times 0.67]} = 0.82$$

Before the cost of equity can be calculated, the asset beta must be geared up to reflect the optimal capital structure of Newco.

The above formula is rearranged to obtain:

$$\beta_e = \beta_a [1 + (1 - T) \times \frac{D}{E}]$$

The capital structure for Newco is 30% debt and 70% equity:

$$\beta_e = 0.82 \times (1 + (1 - 30\%) \times 30 \div 70) = 1.06 = 1.1$$

The cost of equity for Newco can now be calculated:

$$r_e = r_f + \beta_e \times (r_m - r_f)$$
$$r_e = 4\% + 1.1 \times (9\% - 4\%)$$
$$r_e = 9.5\% = \text{cost of equity}$$

Lastly, the WACC for Newco can be calculated:

$$\text{WACC} = (A \times E) + (B \times R \times (1 - T))$$
$$\text{WACC} = (70\% \times 9.5\%) + (30\% \times 5\% \times (1 - 30\%)) = 7.7\%$$

The steps necessary to calculate a WACC are as follows:

- Determine the optimal capital structure of the business.
- Assume a cost of debt for the business.
- Assume an effective tax rate for the business.
- Obtain a set of equity betas for comparable companies.
- "Ungear" the equity betas of the comparable companies and calculate an average asset beta.
- "Regear" the average asset beta using the assumed optimal capital structure of the business to gain an equity beta for the business.
- Obtain estimates for a risk free rate and the return on the market.
- Calculate the cost of equity using the CAPM formula.
- Calculate the WACC using the assumed optimal capital structure, the tax rate, the cost of debt and the previously calculated cost of equity.

Discounted cash flow analysis in practice

Business modelling approach

As well as the valuations based on the business comparable metrics described above, the business model includes a DCF analysis, which can be examined in the model or in Chart 18.10. The model calculates the free cash flow to debt and equity holders and uses the second tax paid calculation in the tax sheet (commencing at row 35) to avoid double counting the tax shield on financing. The model also calculates a series of discount factors (valuation sheet, row 29) based on a WACC of 7.7% (valuation sheet, cell D10) as calculated above.

Chart 18.10 **DCF analysis**

Valuation
Newco Corp
$ Thousands

Your task
Normalise the final year cash flow if required. Select the basis for valuation.

Year			**1**	**2**	**3**	**4**	**5**	**6**	**7**	**8**	**9**	**10**
Valuation assumptions												
Discount rate	7.7%	*Discount_Rate*										
Terminal value growth rate	2.0%	*Terminal_Value_Rate*										
EBITDA exit multiple	8	*EBITDA_Exit_Multiple*										
Free cash flow												
Operating cash flow			(7,095)	(6,365)	(3,699)	3,526	16,987	33,250	45,303	54,141	55,067	53,453
Capital expenditure			(51,986)	(21,918)	(5,822)	(5,000)	(19,178)	(8,658)	(8,000)	(8,000)	(8,000)	(8,000)
Intangibles expenditure			(5,068)	(4,932)	0	(5,068)	(4,932)	0	0	(5,068)	(4,932)	0
Cash taxes			0	0	0	0	0	0	0	(4,841)	(13,603)	(14,466)
Free cash flow			**(64,150)**	**(33,215)**	**(9,521)**	**(6,542)**	**(7,123)**	**24,592**	**37,303**	**36,232**	**28,533**	**30,986**
Discount factor												
Discount factor			1.04	1.12	1.20	1.30	1.40	1.50	1.62	1.74	1.88	2.02
NPV of free cash flow												
NPV of free cash flow			(61,814)	(29,717)	(7,909)	(5,046)	(5,101)	16,354	23,033	20,772	15,188	15,315
Total NPV of free cash flow			**(18,927)**									

In DCF analysis, it is customary to make the simplifying assumption that all cash flows are received at the same time and at the mid-point of the year. In the model, it is assumed that the value of the business, and therefore the calculation of the NPV of the future cash flows, is at the start of year 1 of the forecast. This implies that the cash flow for year 1 is received six months from the date of valuation and that all subsequent cash flows are received 12 months later than the preceding cash flow. As a result, the discount factor, which is calculated on a compound basis, reflects a period of six months only for the cash flows of year 1 (cell E29). The factor then grows by a full (1 + 7.7%) per year thereafter (row 29, column F onwards). The future cash flow is then simply divided by the discount factor to give the NPV of the cash flows (row 32). These are then summed to give a total NPV of the cash flows from the forecast of ten years in cell E34: ($18,927).

The negative result implies that initial cash outflows are greater on a discounted basis than the future cash inflows for the first ten years of the investment. So as the NPV is negative, an investor would not proceed with the investment. However, this assumes that the business simply ceases to exist at the end of year 10. In fact it will continue to operate after that date and, to give a fair valuation, a value for the future cash flows after year 10 should be included. The value of the cash flows after year 10 is called the terminal value.

The terminal value

Terminal value calculations assume that the business has reached a steady state and that cash flows will continue to grow at a stable rate. This is called the terminal value growth rate and is often assumed to be close to the long-term growth rate of GDP for the economy. The valuation of the business may be highly sensitive to the assumptions made about this growth rate. A range of growth rates should be used, and an investment decision that relies heavily on a terminal value should be treated with great caution.

There are a number of different approaches for calculating a terminal value. Two of the most common are the Gordon growth model and EBITDA exit multiples.

The Gordon growth model. A common basis for calculating a terminal value is to assume that the business is like a perpetuity, paying a cash flow indefinitely which grows each year by the terminal value growth rate. A common model for calculating the terminal value with growth is to use the Gordon growth model.

$$\frac{\text{Year 10 cash flow}}{(\text{Discount rate} - \text{growth rate})} \times (1 + \text{growth rate})$$

The result of this calculation must be discounted back to the start of the forecast period by the year 10 discount factor before it is combined with the net present value of the detailed cash flows. Chart 18.11 shows the workings for terminal values.

Chart 18.11 **Terminal value calculations**

	A	B	C	D	E	F	G	H	I	J	K
1											
2		**Valuation**			**Your task**						
3		**Newco Corp**			Normalise the final year cash flow if required. Select the basis for valuation.						
4		$ Thousands	H C <								
5											
6											
7		**Year**			**1**	**2**	**3**	**4**	**5**	**6**	**7**
35											
36		**Terminal value**									
37		**Method 1: Terminal value growth rate**					**Method 2: EBITDA exit multiple**				
38		Final year cash flow			30,986		Final year EBITDA				62,210
39		Final year cash grown 1 year by growth rate			31,606		Final year company value				497,679
40		Perpetuity calculation			554,494						
41		NPV of final cash flow to perpetuity			274,062						
42		Terminal value - method 1			274,062		Terminal value - method 2				245,980
43											

The model assumes a growth rate of 2% (cell D11 on the valuation sheet). The steps in the calculation can be followed in column E from row 38 downwards:

- The final year cash flow $30,986 (cell N26) is captured in cell E38.
- This is increased by the terminal value growth rate by multiplying $30,986 by (1 + 2%) to give $31,606.
- The perpetuity calculation is then performed in cell E40, which gives the NPV of the post-year 10 cash flows at year 10: $31,606 ÷ (7.7% – 2.0%) = $554,494.
- The NPV at year 10 must then be discounted back to the start of year 1 by dividing by the year 10 discount factor in cell N29: $554,494 ÷ 2.02 = $274,062 (to obtain the exact results more decimal places than shown here are required).
- The terminal value of $274,062 is presented in cell E42.

EBITDA exit multiples. An alternative to using a growth model calculation is to return to the use of business comparable multiples. In this method, the final year EBITDA figure is multiplied by a suitable EV/EBITDA multiple to give the enterprise value of the business at year 10. This figure must be then discounted back to the start of the detailed forecast period to be combined with the present value of the detailed cash flows. Once again, because of the importance of the terminal value, it is advisable to calculate a range of values based on different EBITDA exit multiples.

The business model uses a comparable EV/EBITDA exit multiple of 8 (cell D12 on the valuation sheet). The calculation can be followed in column K from row 37 downwards:

- Obtain the final year EBITDA figure of $62,210 from cell N31 of the profit and loss sheet and place in cell K38.
- Multiply the final year EBITDA by the exit multiple (cell K39): $62,210 × 8 = $497,679 (to obtain the exact results more decimal places than shown here are required).
- Divide $497,679 by the final year discount factor in cell N29: $497,679 ÷ 2.02 = $245,980.
- The terminal value using the EBITDA exit multiple approach is $245,980 (cell K42).

Enterprise and equity value for Newco

The final stage is to combine the NPV of the detailed cash flows with the two terminal values as shown in Chart 18.12 on the next page.

Chart 18.12 **Valuations for Newco Corp**

	A	B	C	D	E	F	G	H	I	J
1										
2		**Valuation**			**Your task**					
3		**Newco Corp**			Normalise the final year cash flow if required. Select the basis for valuation.					
4		$ Thousands	H C <							
5										
6										
7		**Year**			1	2	3	4	5	6
44										
45						**Terminal value**			**EBITDA**	
46		**DCF based company valuation**				**growth rate**			**exit multiple**	
47		Forecast cash flows				(18,927)			(18,927)	
48		Terminal value				274,062			245,980	
49		Enterprise value				255,135			227,054	
50										
51		Less: net debt				(26,354)			(26,354)	
52										
53		Equity value				228,780			200,699	
54										

The combination of the NPV of the detailed free cash flows and the terminal values gives an enterprise value of $255.1m based on the Gordon growth model (cell F49) and $227m based on an EBITDA exit multiple (cell I49). As in both cases Newco has a positive NPV at its WACC of 7.7% an investment should be made, as this will result in an increase in shareholder value. Investors should note, however, that the valuation is highly dependent upon the terminal value, which is sensitive to the assumptions concerning the final year cash flow and the terminal value assumptions used.

The calculation of the equity value for Newco is the final stage in the valuation process. The net debt taken from the balance sheet (debt, overdraft and cash balances) is deducted from the enterprise value to give the equity value. Net debt at the end of year 1 is $26,354. It is normal to take the opening debt figure, but with a start-up business there isn't one. The valuations of the equity based upon the Gordon growth model and EBITDA exit multiple are $228.8m (cell F53) for the former and $200.7m (cell I53) for the latter.

DCF in the presence of capital constraints

It was stated earlier that if there are no capital constraints, the business should accept any project that has a positive NPV when calculated at the appropriate discount rate. If capital is constrained, the business should invest in the project that provides the highest level of NPV per dollar invested. If there is a range of investments, the NPV of the project should be divided by the capital investment required. The investments should then be ranked with the highest NPV per dollar first, and the available capital should be allocated to them in descending order until it runs out.

OTHER ASSESSMENT CRITERIA

Internal rates of return

If a project involves investing $1 today and it grows to $1.10 in a year's time, the growth rate is 10%. If the growth rate is then used as the discount rate in a NPV calculation, $1.10 discounted by 10% for one year would give $1. If, in today's terms, $1 has been invested to earn $1, the NPV is zero. The NPV will always be zero if cash flows are discounted by their growth rate. It follows that if you experiment with different discount rates until you obtain a NPV equal to zero, the discount rate which gives a NPV equal to zero must also be the rate of growth of the cash flow. This discount rate is called the internal rate of return (IRR). The IRR is the discount rate which, when applied to a stream of cash flows, generates a NPV of zero. Most spreadsheet packages have an IRR function that will calculate the result. By calculating the IRR you have estimated the anticipated rate of growth for the project. Companies will set an IRR hurdle rate (a minimum required level of growth) and will then only accept projects that have an IRR or growth rate that exceeds this rate. The higher the IRR the greater is the strength of the future cash inflows and the more valuable is the project to the business. An IRR is quick and easy to calculate, but it has limitations. If the future cash flow stream follows the pattern of cash outflows followed by a series of inflows followed by a further set of cash outflows, there are then two solutions to the IRR calculation, which weakens its strength as an analytical tool. Furthermore, calculating an IRR implies nothing about the size of the project, so one worth a few thousand dollars could have the same IRR as one worth millions of dollars.

Payback and discounted payback

Another assessment criterion that is easy to apply is to calculate the payback period. For a project with a series of cash outflows followed by a series of cash inflows, the payback period refers to the length of time that will be required for sufficient cash to have been received to cover the initial cash outflows. The quicker the initial outlay is paid back, all things being equal, the better. For example, if in year 1 $100 is invested and at the end of years 2, 3, 4 and 5 the business receives $25, $35, $40 and $60 respectively, the payback period is three years as the business must wait three years to have recouped the initial $100. This simple approach ignores the time value of money and the risks associated with the cash flows as well as the value of cash flows received after the payback period.

A variation is to adopt the same approach but the future cash inflows are discounted by the WACC. This is called discounted payback analysis. The advantages of payback calculations are that they are conceptually easy to understand and a useful tool for companies that are cash constrained and rely on earlier cash flow forecasts that might be considered to be more certain. The disadvantages are that they imply nothing about the size of the project and do not provide a definitive decision rule.

Other approaches

The evaluation techniques discussed in this chapter will be more than adequate for nearly all business planning activity. There are other techniques that are more involved and go further beyond DCF analysis, and in some cases challenge the rationale of DCF-based techniques. These include:

- adjusted present value;
- economic value added;
- real option theory.

The references listed below[1] will be of interest to readers who wish to study this topic further.

References

1 For more information on these topics see Brealey, R.A. and Myers, S.C., *Principles of Corporate Finance*, 5th edition, McGraw-Hill, 1996; Bennett Stewart III, G., *The Quest for Value: A Guide for Senior Managers*, HarperCollins, 1990; Copeland, T. and Antikarow, V., *Real Options: A Practitioner's Guide*, Texere Publishing, 2001.

19 **Funding issues**

Funding can quickly become a complex topic and this chapter provides a broad overview of the main issues. It starts by explaining how to identify the funding requirement for a business or project and then examines different types of finance and who might provide it.

IDENTIFYING THE FUNDING REQUIREMENT

A business plan must identify the maximum or peak funding and for how long funding will be required before considering how best to finance it. The funding requirement can be presented graphically in a j-curve. The j-curve is based on the cumulative cash flows after all operational costs and capital expenditure cash flows have been accounted for.

The graph of cumulative cash flows before financing for start-up businesses and many other projects looks like the curve in Chart 19.1. A series of cash outflows causes the funding requirement to increase, reaching a peak at the bottom of the j-curve before diminishing and eventually becoming cumulative cash flow positive. The depth of the j-curve and the speed at which a business becomes cumulative cash flow positive will depend on the nature of the business. Small businesses will have a much shallower j-curve than the one depicted in Chart 19.1 which is more typical of a major infrastructure investment project.

Chart 19.1 **The j-curve for Newco Corp**

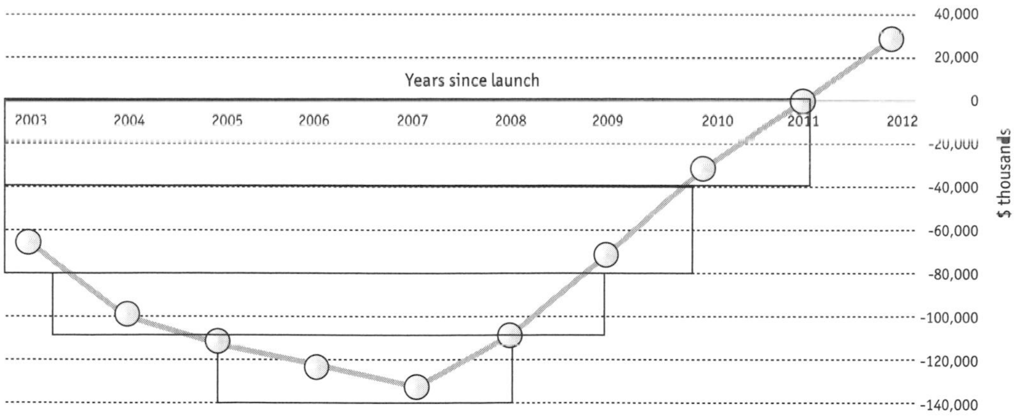

In the case of Newco Corp, the peak funding requirement is $131m and occurs in year 5. From year 6 onwards the business is cash flow positive, so the funding requirement steadily diminishes. If $131m were borrowed in full in year 1, there would be a large amount of unused finance at the start and end of the forecast period, during which time the business would have to pay interest charges on the full amount. The funding requirement should be broken down into funding strips so that the duration of any financing better matches the profile of the cash flows. A possible profile of financing for Newco may be as follows:

- $40m for 8.5 years
- $40m for 7.5 years
- $30m for 6 years
- $21m for 3 years

TYPES OF FINANCE

There are many different types of finance, but it is useful to make a simple distinction between equity and debt financing before examining each in more detail.

Debt finance

Debt finance can be obtained from a number of sources but is often provided by a bank. Debt finance requires a business to pay an agreed, regular interest charge, sometimes referred to as the servicing of debt, based on the amount of money borrowed and the duration of the loan. The business might also have to pay back the original amount borrowed, which is sometimes referred to as principal repayment. The interest charges have to be paid irrespective of the business's performance. If they are not, the lender may put the business into liquidation. Interest payments can be charged in the profit and loss account and so can reduce a business's tax liability. As lenders can recoup their money through the sale of assets in the event of liquidation, debt is considered less risky than equity, so there is a lower cost associated with it.

Equity finance

The shareholders of a business (who can range from private individuals to large institutions) provide equity finance. Equity also includes any retained profits of the business. Equity shares, unlike debt, represent ownership of a business and its assets and the right to a share of its profits, which is normally paid in the form of dividends. Unlike interest, dividends are paid after tax and are a less tax efficient form of financing compared with debt. Shareholders can participate in the profits of the business only when all other claims on the business, such as interest payments, have been met. In the event of liquidation, shareholders only have a claim on what is left after all other creditors have been satisfied. Thus the providers of equity take the highest risk of all finance providers.

Chart 19.2 shows the main distinctions between debt and equity and further classifications within each class of finance.

Chart 19.2 **Sources of finance**

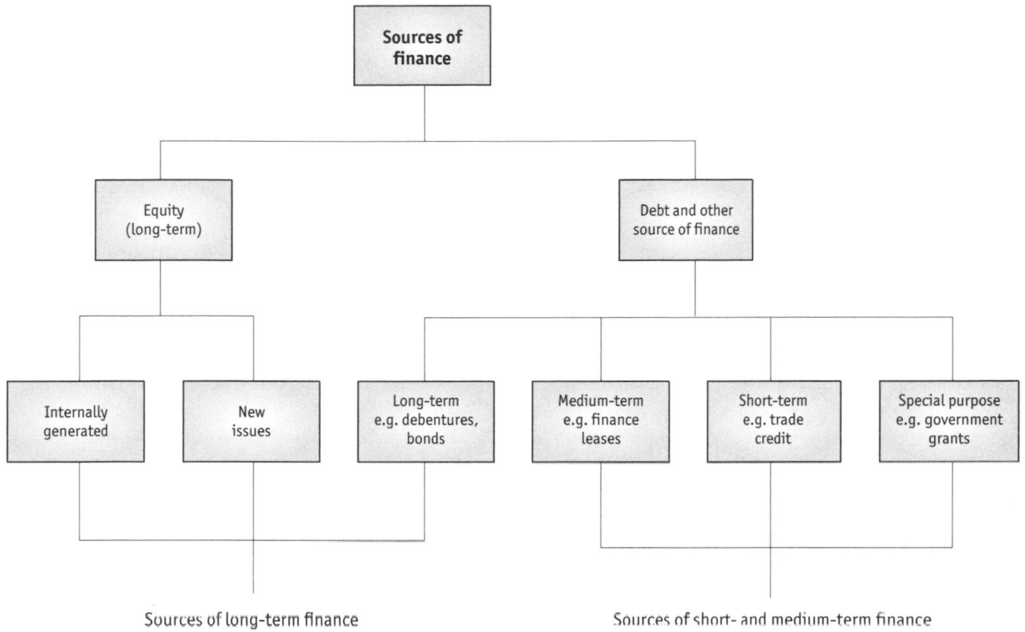

The definitions of short, medium and long term vary depending on the nature of the business. However, an approximate duration is:

- short term – up to 1 year;
- medium term – 1–10 years;
- long term – more than 10 years.

EQUITY

Different forms of equity

An equity share represents a share of a business's assets and also a share of any profits it generates. There are different classes of equity, each with different rights that relate to dividends, voting and the return of capital in the event of liquidation. The rights associated with a particular class of share are contained in a business's articles of association.

Ordinary shares

Ordinary shares, or common stock in the United States, are the last to be paid in terms of distributing profits and in the event of liquidation. They carry voting rights, and the owners of ordinary shares can gain value from their ownership through both a stream of dividends and a capital gain on the value of the shares themselves. The capital gain can be realised by selling the share in a stockmarket, through the business repurchasing its own shares or through the business being acquired by another business.

Preferred ordinary shares
Preferred shares rank above ordinary shares and attract an agreed rate of dividend. A business's articles of association will define the participation rights of preferred shares and may specify that preferred shares can further participate in profits over and above their original, agreed dividend rate. Preferred shares also have characteristics similar to debt and so are discussed in more detail later.

Non-voting shares
Non-voting shares rank in the same way as other classes of equity but they do not allow the holders of these shares to vote. Non-voting shares are typically issued in family businesses where family members do not wish to see a loss of control despite the need to raise additional capital. The absence of voting rights ensures that this class of share is not popular with institutional investors, so non-voting shares are not a common feature of the capital structure of many businesses.

DEBT

Short- and medium-term debt finance

Bank overdrafts
A bank overdraft gives a business the right to borrow up to a predetermined limit for an agreed period of time. Bank overdrafts represent a flexible approach to short- and medium-term financing as interest is paid only on the amount borrowed. Overdrafts are also immediately available and the costs of arranging this facility are low. However, some form of security is normally required through a charge over an asset. This charge allows the lender to sell the asset to recoup the monies lent in the event of liquidation. Bank overdrafts are usually an expensive form of debt financing, but the cost will vary with the credit rating of the business arranging the facility. Overdrafts are inherently short-term in nature as the lender can "call in" the overdraft at any time.

Term loans
A term loan is a more formal arrangement than an overdraft. It is an agreement to borrow a specific amount of money for a specific period of time at an agreed rate of interest. The loan is repayable over a fixed period and the repayment pattern can vary from lender to lender. Security for the loan is usually provided by a fixed charge over an asset (see below) and covenants (see below) may also be included. Although term loans offer more security to the borrower, inasmuch as they cannot be recalled, they are less flexible than an overdraft as a fixed repayment structure is imposed.

Finance and operating leases
When a business signs a finance lease, the ownership of the asset transfers to the business, which pays a regular amount covering both the cost of finance and the cost of the asset. The interest costs are often higher than other forms of finance, but finance leases may often be the only means of obtaining credit when no other alternatives are available.

Operating leases do not imply a transfer of ownership to the business but simply the right to use the asset. Although no finance charges are associated with the agreement, an operating lease does commit the business to a regular stream of payments, which must be met. The lease agreement can become complicated and may incorporate service agreements and cancellation options.

Factoring

Factoring takes place when a bank or other third party takes over some or all of the customer billing and debt collection activities of a business and offers finance of, normally, up to 80% of the value of the debts that it is collecting. The accounts payable services are usually charged on a fee basis, which normally represents 1–3% of the value of the debt. Furthermore, interest charges are incurred for the finance advanced to the business, and the interest rates are usually higher than those charged on overdrafts and loans. Factoring is sometimes regarded as a form of financing of last resort and so is shunned by some businesses, which may fear that creditors and shareholders will draw unfavourable conclusions about the financial strength of the business. In contrast, some firms outsource debt collection as a means of reducing operating costs to enhance financial performance.

Project finance

Project finance represents finance that is provided for a specific project and focuses on the risks and cash flows of that project, rather than the credit rating of the borrower. In the UK, it was developed in response to the discovery of North Sea oil, which required specific funding and was also associated with a well-defined future revenue stream. The providers of project finance lend against cash generating assets that are usually owned by a special-purpose business vehicle. The vehicle will have a separate legal identity and so the balance sheet of the sponsoring business will be insulated from the debt associated with the project. Project loans may be guaranteed by the sponsor business, which will become liable in the event of default, or they may be on a non-recourse basis, so that the lender is unable to approach the sponsor business if the future cash flows necessary to repay the debt do not materialise. The lender takes some form of security against the assets or cash flows. Project finance agreements may also specify additional financial support from the parties if required.

Project finance is a high-risk form of financing, but for some long-term infrastructure-based projects it may be the only source of finance available. The risks of project finance are compounded when the investment is to be made overseas, where political and foreign-exchange risks may increase the underlying risks associated with the project.

Long-term debt finance

Preference shares

Preference shares rank above equity in terms of participation in profits and the assets of a business in the event of liquidation. They therefore contain many of the features associated with debt when examined from a shareholder's perspective. However, preference shares rank below debt and so look like equity from a lender's perspective. The rights attaching to preference shares vary, but dividends on preference shares are usually paid before ordinary dividends and they also have a prior claim on the assets of the business. Preference shares can be non-cumulative, which implies that, if the business is unable to pay a dividend because of weak financial performance, for example, the dividend forgone is never paid. Non-cumulative preference shares do not usually have voting rights attached to them. In cases where unpaid dividends accumulate, cumulative preference shares usually have voting rights, but these are often restricted.

Convertible preference shares, which are similar to convertible loan stock, can also be issued. Preference shares, however, usually command a higher, specified rate than loan stock as they carry higher levels of risk. In contrast to loan stock, where the interest charges can be deducted from profits before computing a business's corporation tax liability, preference shares are paid from post-tax profits and are therefore regarded as being less efficient from a taxation perspective.

Debentures

Debentures are fixed interest, long-term loans that are normally secured on a business's assets. Either a fixed or a floating charge (see below) and occasionally both provides the security for the debentures. The provisions relating to a debenture are laid down in a trust deed, and a trustee is appointed to act on behalf of the debenture holders.

Unsecured loan stock

As the name suggests, unsecured loan stock does not have a charge over a business's assets and therefore commands a higher coupon or interest rate compared with secured debentures because of the increased level of risk. However, the deed relating to the unsecured loans may limit the business's ability to raise further debt unless the holder of the unsecured stock is offered equal or better rights than the new debt that is raised. The interest rates associated with the loan will vary with the credit rating of the business as well as the normal considerations, such as the duration of the loan and the underlying risk associated with the business.

Convertible unsecured loan stock

Convertible unsecured loan stock provides the holder with an option to convert the unsecured loan stock into ordinary shares, within a given time period at a specified price. If the option is not exercised, however, the normal redemption path for the stock is followed. The compensating inclusion of the option allows a business to offer a lower coupon rate on the loan. The reduced servicing costs during the early life of the business and the protection from changes in interest rates and inflation are the two main motivations for offering convertible loan stock. A variation on convertible loan stock is to issue loans with warrants. The loan stock remains in its original form, but the holders of loan stock have the option to purchase equity for cash rather than in exchange for debt.

Other features of debt instruments

Fixed and floating rates

Lenders, such as banks, often require security for their loans. They obtain this security by placing a charge on the assets of the business. Charges can be either fixed or floating. Fixed charges require a specific asset to be set aside as security for the loan whereas floating charges relate to a group of assets; the charge does not materialise on a particular asset until the business is in default.

Redeemable and irredeemable

A supplier of redeemable loan stock will be able to demand repayment of the principal amount of the monies lent at a predetermined time in the future. In contrast, irredeemable loan stock continues to exist indefinitely. A secondary market is necessary to allow holders of loan stock to trade both irredeemable and redeemable stock.

Coupon rates

Coupon rates determine the interest that is paid on a debt instrument. They are often expressed in terms of the par or value at which the loan stock is issued. The rates may be fixed or may float in line with the benchmark debt instrument of the country. The choice between fixed and floating rates will depend on a business's expectations of interest rates, the need for certainty and the stability of future cash flows. However, the existence of the swap market, where companies can exchange fixed and floating-rate debt instruments, allows businesses to move in and out of floating and fixed rates as the market changes. The variability in rates can also be managed through caps (maximum levels to which the rate can rise) and floors (minimum levels) or collars (a combination of maximum and minimum levels).

Deep discounting

Deeply discounted loans have a low coupon rate at issue and are issued at prices considerably below par or the face value of the loan. The low initial servicing charges are attractive to businesses and lenders have the advantage of potential capital gains because of the deep discount, but lenders are locked in for longer.

Call provisions

Call provisions might be included in the loan agreement to allow borrowers to redeem loans early in order to restructure their balance sheets to take advantage of changes in interest rates or the tax status of the business. Lenders sometimes resist call provisions as they increase the uncertainty associated with the loans.

Restrictive covenants

Lenders often include restrictive covenants in their loan agreements in order to provide additional security for their loans and to limit a business's ability to take a course of action that could damage the security of the loan. Some typical restrictive covenants are shown in Chart 19.3 on the next page.

Chart 19.3 **Restrictive covenants**

Covenant type	*Commentary*
Negative pledge clauses	Restrict the issuance of further debt that could undermine the security of existing creditors
Poison puts	Require a business to repay loans if a large quantity of shares are sold to an outside investor
Cross-default clauses	Imply that all loans are deemed to be in default if any loan is found to be in default
Dividend policy	Limitations can be imposed to prevent an excessive distribution of profits and cash that might hamper a business's ability to service its debts
Asset backing	Requires a business to maintain minimum amounts of working capital or net assets to ensure sufficient liquidity to maintain the servicing of debts

Repayment arrangements

There are many variations on the repayment arrangements that businesses negotiate with the providers of debt finance. Some of the more typical arrangements are shown in Chart 19.4.

Chart 19.4 **Repayment arrangements**

Repayment arrangement	*Commentary*
Bullet	The principal amount of the loan is paid in one lump sum at the end of the term of the loan
Balloon	Repayments are low at the beginning of the loan term and increase in size towards the end
Mortgage	Regular fixed payments are made which, over the lifetime of the loan term, service the interest on the debt and fully repay the principal
Grace periods	Periods when a business is given a debt-servicing holiday

FINANCING DECISIONS

There are four principal financing decisions that must be addressed in a business plan:

- The optimal capital structure (the ratio of debt to equity). The capital structure will be closely related to the stage of a business's development, industry norms and the availability of different types of finance. As interest charges can reduce the tax paid by the business, they are an efficient form of finance. Some level of debt finance will probably be desirable for most businesses, as the tax shield on financing can raise the value of the business by lowering the weighted average cost of capital. The financial theory surrounding the optimal capital structure is complex and is discussed in a separate section.
- The proportion of profits, if the business is profit-making, that should be retained to finance future projects and the proportion that should be paid out as dividends.
- The appropriate debt instruments, if debt has been chosen as part of the capital structure. The business must also identify its short-, medium- and long-term borrowing requirements.
- The potential sources of the different types of debt and equity. For some businesses, the availability of finance may determine the answers to the three previous questions.

Capital structure and the business life cycle

At each stage of the business life cycle different forms of financing may be required. During the start-up phase, a business has limited assets, and the assets that it does have are likely to be intangible. The business also has no proven track record and there may be considerable uncertainty over the future demand for its product. During this start-up phase it may have to rely predominantly on equity.

As the business grows it will develop a track record. It will have purchased assets that can act as security for a loan and will hopefully be generating cash that can be used to service debts. The growth and maturity phases of the business cycle are potentially a good time to be raising debt.

Considerations for selecting debt or equity financing

The quality of a business's assets is a major consideration in the selection of debt rather than equity. An asset-rich business with extensive physical assets provides plenty of security for lenders, and with reduced risk, the cost of debt falls. Businesses with high-quality assets generally prefer higher levels of debt financing. In contrast, services businesses, whose assets are mainly their employees, typically have much lower levels of debt financing because of the poor quality of the assets from the lenders' perspective.

A further consideration for asset-rich businesses is that businesses which have invested heavily in physical assets may have a high level of operational gearing. High operational gearing implies that a business's fixed costs are much higher in relation to its variable costs. Fixed costs must be paid irrespective of the level of sales, whereas variable costs vary directly with the level of sales. A highly operationally geared business may wish to consider avoiding compounding its operational gearing by taking on high levels of debt and thus adding financial gearing. The combination of operational and financial gearing increases the risk of potentially defaulting on any loans during a period of slow sales.

Other considerations are as follows:

- Debt financing can be useful in the case of funding overseas projects, as it can be used to hedge the risks on movements in foreign exchange.
- The adoption of high levels of debt may result in lenders imposing restrictive covenants that can damage a business's future flexibility.
- Issuing further equity can raise concerns about the future control of a business.
- Equity finance can be costly to raise, and a business's ability to do this will depend on the state of the capital markets and their appetite for new issues. Most businesses prefer to raise additional debt rather than issue further equity because of the higher costs of the latter, but in some cases issuing further equity may be the only alternative.

Chart 19.5 on the next page summarises the principal considerations concerning the debt versus equity decision.

Chart 19.5 **Debt versus equity**

Prefer debt	*Prefer equity*
Lower weighted average cost of capital	Existing financial gearing levels are high
Low current levels of financial gearing	Start-up business with no track record
Track record of performance	Initial losses and cash flow deficits forecast
Strong projected future cash flows	Interest rates expected to rise
Expectation of low or falling interest rates	Mostly intangible assets
Quality asset base for security of loans	Business risk high
Finance to support foreign projects	Business does not pay corporation tax
Low levels of operational gearing	Wish to avoid restrictive covenants
Low levels of business risk	High levels of operational gearing
Business in the growth or maturity phase	Markets have strong appetite for the issue
Wish to avoid earnings per share dilution	
Potential tax shield from interest payments	
Desire to retain control of the business	
Lower arrangement costs	

Timing and duration of debt financing

If a business selects debt as its main source of finance, it should take into account the maturity dates of existing loans as it should avoid all the loans maturing at the same time. The other important consideration is the duration of the loans. Typically, interest rates are lower for short-term loans, as the risk of default is lower. However, when interest rates are expected to fall, the term structure of interest rates can reverse, such that short-term loans become more expensive than long-term loans. Short-term loans also provide greater flexibility: when the cash is not required they can be paid off and so save the business unnecessary interest charges. The disadvantage of short-term loans is that there are higher transaction costs associated with rearranging loans. However, the general rule is that long-term assets should be funded by long-term funds and short-term assets should be funded by short-term funds, on the basis that the cash flows from the asset should match the maturity of the debt.

The optimal capital structure

The advantages of including debt in a business's capital structure are that the cost is low because of the lower levels of risk and that corporate tax relief can be claimed on the interest charges. The disadvantage is that debt interest and principal payments must be paid or the business may face liquidation, with the potential loss of all equity capital for the shareholders. The numerical example in Chart 19.6 illustrates how including debt within the capital structure can significantly enhance a business's financial performance.

Chart 19.6 **The financial impact of debt financing**

	Earnings before interest and tax $5m		*Earnings before interest and tax $10m*	
	All equity	*50% debt 50% equity*	*All equity*	*50% debt 50% equity*
Earnings before interest and tax	-5.0	-5.0	10.0	10.0
Interest	0	−1.0	0	−1.0
Earnings before tax	-5.0	-6.0	10.0	9.0
Tax	0	0	2.0	1.8
Earnings after tax	-5.0	-6.0	8.0	7.2
Shares	20	10	20	10
Earnings per share	-0.25	-0.6	0.4	0.72

Chart 19.7 shows that in the early stages of the business, when it is loss-making at the earnings before interest and tax (EBIT) level, the best financial performance is achieved through a capital structure based on equity. As the business begins to generate increasing levels of profit there is an advantage in debt financing

Chart 19.7 **Financial performance and gearing**

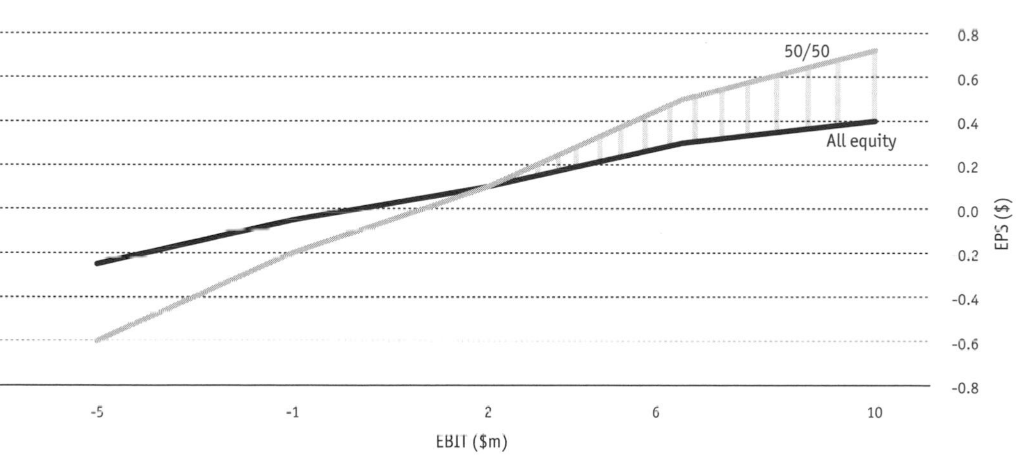

The tax shield on financing implies that financial performance can be improved by increasing levels of debt. Franco Modigliani and Merton Miller, two economists, demonstrated that in perfect capital markets, in the presence of taxation, a business should take on as much debt as possible, as high levels of debt enhance earnings and therefore the value of the business. However, critics argued that the increased risk of bankruptcy associated with high levels of debt, as well as the restrictions that bankers may place on the actions of a business, would eventually damage the value of the business. As debt levels increase the financial risk to equity holders increases, which raises the cost of equity. There is a trade off, and the optimal gearing ratio that balances the financial benefits against the increased financial risk must be identified. It will be the ratio that minimises the weighted average cost of capital (WACC). Chart 19.8 shows that the WACC initially falls as gearing increases, but after a certain point the cost of both equity and debt begins to rise as financial risks increase. The optimal gearing ratio is the lowest point of the WACC curve.

Chart 19.8 **The WACC and the optimal level of gearing**

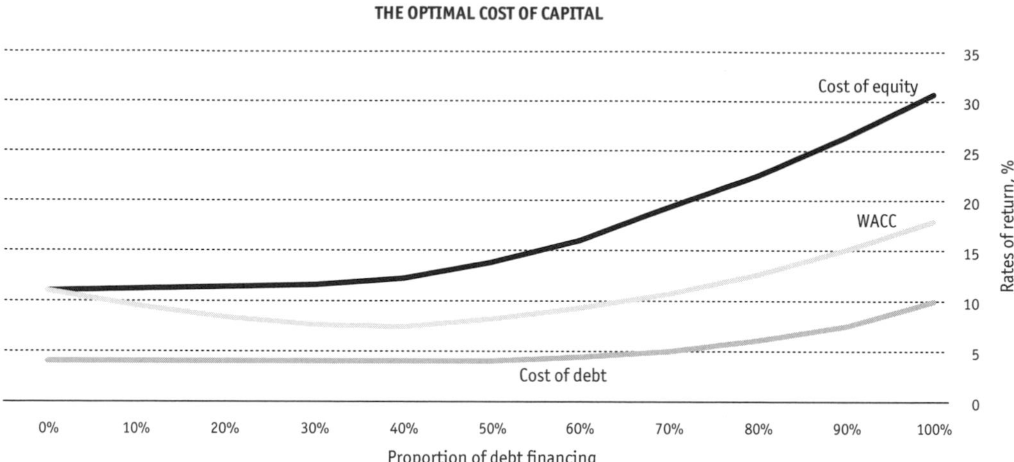

In Chart 19.8, the optimal gearing ratio is associated with the lowest point on the WACC curve, which occurs when the business is 35% financed by debt. This represents the business's optimal gearing.

SOURCES OF EQUITY

Friends and family

For small businesses, the entrepreneurs with the business ideas will usually invest their own funds in the business. Friends and family will often provide additional financing. These sources of equity are cheap and easy to obtain.

Venture capital

Many smaller businesses may look to venture capitalists to provide equity funding. Venture capitalists offer various types of capital including equity and debt finance and are often subsidiaries of major banks. Venture capital funding can usually be broken down into seed, start-up and early-stage capital, where finance is provided to research and develop an idea or to set up a manufacturing operation and distribution system, for example. Late-stage venture capital funding may also be available for businesses seeking to expand or develop a new project and may be used to expand their sales and marketing operations.

Venture capitalists invest varying amounts of money, but typical investments are over $400,000. As the investments are usually in start-ups and new projects, they involve a high risk and some are unlikely to succeed. Because of these high risks, the providers of capital to venture capitalists require a high rate of return: 20% a year is not untypical. As many projects are likely to fail, the venture capitalist will be looking for an expected return much higher than this target rate of 20%. A typical expected return on an investment might be around 45% a year compounded. If the projected rate of return is less than 40% there is usually little interest, and if the returns are over 60% fund managers are likely to view the project with considerable scepticism. Venture capitalists also want to realise their investment and so will be looking for an exit route, usually after 3–5 years. Typical exit routes include going public, the business's purchase of its own shares or the acquisition of the business.

Retained earnings and dividends

For many existing businesses, retained earnings are a major source of finance. This is not surprising as retained earnings have no issue costs and do not require extensive justification in front of the shareholders. Retained earnings do affect a business's ability to pay dividends, but using financial theory it is possible to show that, under certain conditions, dividend policy is irrelevant to the value of the business. Empirical evidence, however, suggests that dividend policy does affect business valuations and so a business plan must ensure that fundraising based on retained earnings is consistent with the business's dividend policy. Large unutilised cash balances, however, will depress the business's return on equity, if projects cannot be found that equal or exceed its current returns. If suitable projects cannot be identified, the cash should be returned to shareholders.

Stockmarkets

Routes to market

There are various ways of raising money on the stockmarket and some of them are listed below:

- An offer for sale to the general public.
- Public placing, where shares are privately placed with private and institutional clients.
- Introduction, when shares are held on another market or are already widely held by the public.
- Private placing, when a limited offering of shares is made to a specific, identified group of individuals, provided a company's articles of association permit this.

The best route to the stockmarket will depend upon the size of the business, the issue costs, the spread of existing ownership and the business's expected future performance. When a business decides to go public it will employ advisers, including accountants, stockbrokers, merchant bankers and lawyers, and must meet minimum requirements that will vary with each stockmarket.

Advantages

There are a number of advantages in becoming a listed, publicly quoted business:

- The shareholders will enjoy increased liquidity, as their shares can now be readily sold on the stock exchange.
- The various routes to market provide access to additional sources of finance such as institutional investors, who prefer listed securities.

- The listed shares can become valuable assets when a business is considering a takeover or merger.
- Being quoted enhances a business's reputation and improves its credit rating, which can be useful when it next needs to raise finance.

Disadvantages

Although a listing is valuable, the costs of becoming a quoted business are high and the process requires considerable management time. As a result, listing is usually an option considered by larger businesses. Once a business becomes quoted it will come under considerably more scrutiny. Additional reporting and disclosure will be required, and there will be increased requirements and costs associated with corporate governance. There will also be the risk of takeover by other businesses and restrictions on the dealings of directors in the shares of their own business.

Secondary issues

Businesses can also raise additional funds through a rights issue. This occurs when a business offers new shares to existing shareholders in accordance with their existing shareholdings. It is a cheaper form of raising additional equity capital.

Other sources of equity capital

Equity capital can be obtained from many sources. Examples of typical equity providers are:

- business partners;
- suppliers and distributors;
- institutional investors;
- investment businesses;
- private equity businesses;
- takeovers.

SOURCES OF DEBT

The sources of debt finance are similar to those of equity finance. Commercial banks and the bond markets are examples of sources of debt finance. There is also the possibility of gaining some form of government loan or grant, which may be awarded at a local, national or international level, including by organisations such as the European Commission.

FINANCING ISSUES AND THE BUSINESS PLAN

Financing is one of the most common reasons for preparing a business plan. The following two sections highlight the information that should be included in the business plan that will be presented to bankers and potential providers of equity to secure finance for the business.

Business plans presented to bankers

The following information should be included in a business plan presented to bankers and other potential sources of debt finance:

- Purpose of the borrowings.
- Amount and timing of funds required.
- Other sources of finance that, together with the debt sought, ensure that the business is fully funded until it starts climbing out of the j-curve.
- Details of the security to be offered, including valuations of assets and any personal guarantees.
- Schedules for repayment of the loan and interest payments which should be supported by realistic profit and cash flow projections.
- Computation of benchmarks such as debt/equity ratios and interest cover.
- Sensitivities, including the impact of changes in interest rates and key assumptions to which the business plan is sensitive.

Business plans presented to providers of equity

Much of the information contained in a business plan presented to providers of equity finance will be similar to that for debt providers; it is often only the emphasis that alters. The important elements to address in a business plan for equity investors are as follows:

- Structure of the proposed equity deal and the resulting ownership structure of the business.
- Amount of equity being offered and the price.
- What the funds will be used for.
- Commitments from the management team in terms of their own investment in the business, as other equity investors will feel more confident if the managers of the business are risking their own capital.
- Exit strategy and potential exit dates.
- Any fees associated with arranging and executing the deal.
- Any restrictions placed on the business by shareholders.
- The expected role of shareholders in terms of decision-making and whether they will have a seat on the board.

20 Risk analysis

Innovation and business development are inherently risky. This chapter identifies different types of risk as well as describing strategies to manage and minimise the impact of risk on a business.

THE NATURE OF RISK

The dimensions of risk

Risk varies from business to business, but the dimensions of risk are similar across all businesses. The level of risk associated with a particular business or project will depend upon the following:

- The value of resources devoted to the project.
- The proportion of total business resources represented by those resources.
- The length of time for which the resources will be devoted to the project.
- The inherent risk of the project.
- The cost of exiting the project.
- The recoverable costs were the project to fail.

Visibility of risks

Many potential risks can be identified during the business planning process and strategies can be developed to mitigate them. There will also be unforeseen risks that a business must be able to deal with as and when they arise. A business's ability to manage unforeseen risks will largely depend on the calibre and experience of management and the nature of the event. An important aspect of business planning is that, as a result of having developed a comprehensive business plan, when unforeseen events occur, managers have the time and the resources available to tackle them.

Types of risk

Business risks can be categorised as:

- operational
- industry
- financial
- political

Operational

Operational risks are internal to the business and relate to its ability to achieve its chosen strategy. They include the following:

- Key staff resign or are poached by a competitor.
- Unforeseen problems occur in the production process.
- Machinery breaks down or is incompatible with the raw materials.
- Stocks become damaged.
- Fire, theft and floods.
- Information technology problems occur.
- The product is so successful that the business cannot meet demand.
- The actions of a rogue employee result in large liabilities for the business.

Industry

Industry risks are caused by external developments in the industry and may develop as a result of actions by the business itself. They include the following:

- A new firm enters the market.
- A key supplier closes and prevents the supply of crucial raw materials.
- Demand for the product falls or fails to materialise.
- A competitor aggressively cuts prices.
- A new technology is developed making existing products obsolete.
- Two competitors merge providing them with a major cost advantage.

Financial

Potential financial risks include the following:

- A stockmarket collapse prevents a crucial fundraising equity issue or a merger with a competitor.
- Interest rates increase dramatically, raising the cost of servicing the business's debts.
- There is a significant devaluation, which increases the costs of raw materials purchased from abroad.
- High demand for the product leads to overtrading and a lack of available working capital to fund the business's activities.

Political

Political risks include not only governmental risks but also those resulting from the actions of trade unions, lobbyists and activists. They include the following:

- Sanctions imposed on a country prevent access to customers or raw materials.
- Taxation rates are changed or taxation policy is altered.
- Grants, loans and subsidies are altered.
- Trade unions organise industrial action, preventing production from continuing.
- Pressure from lobbyists requires a change in the business practices of the business.
- The business suffers organised vandalism by radical protesters.

RISK ASSESSMENT

Identifying risks

The first task of risk assessment is to try to identify as many potential risks for a business as possible. Many of the existing outputs from the business planning process can be used in this exercise. The results of the SWOT (strengths, weaknesses, opportunities, threats) analysis, in particular the weaknesses and the threats, will provide an initial overview of the risks facing the business. The results of conducting PEST (political, economic, social, technological) analysis may well highlight political and financial risks. Lastly, a brainstorming exercise, examining each of the four risk categories, should be performed.

Quantifying the risks

The business planning model can be used to examine the financial impact of risk. A useful technique is to run a sensitivity analysis across the key inputs in the model that best relate to the identified risks. Examples of typical inputs are as follows:

- The quantity demanded of the product.
- The selling price of the product.
- Distribution costs.
- Sales and marketing costs.
- The cost of raw materials.
- Interest rates.
- Taxation rates.
- Exchange rates.

Take a key output from the model, such as the enterprise value, and record the proportionate change in enterprise value for a 10% change in each of the key inputs. You can then rank inputs in descending order of impact on the business to identify the potentially most damaging.

Monte Carlo simulation techniques

Various techniques, including Monte Carlo simulations, can be used to perform extensive, automated testing of a business model. In simple terms, the technique involves entering a randomly generated set of inputs into the model to obtain a set of possible outputs. Probabilities are attached to each of the outputs to allow you to estimate the probability that an outcome from the business, such as net present value, lies in a particular range. Chart 20.1 shows a normal distribution for a company's enterprise value generated by such techniques, with probabilities on the y-axis and enterprise value on the x-axis. The upper 95% confidence interval implies that there is a 95% probability that the enterprise value of the business lies to the left of that line.

Chart 20.1 **Probability distribution for enterprise valuation from Monte Carlo simulation**

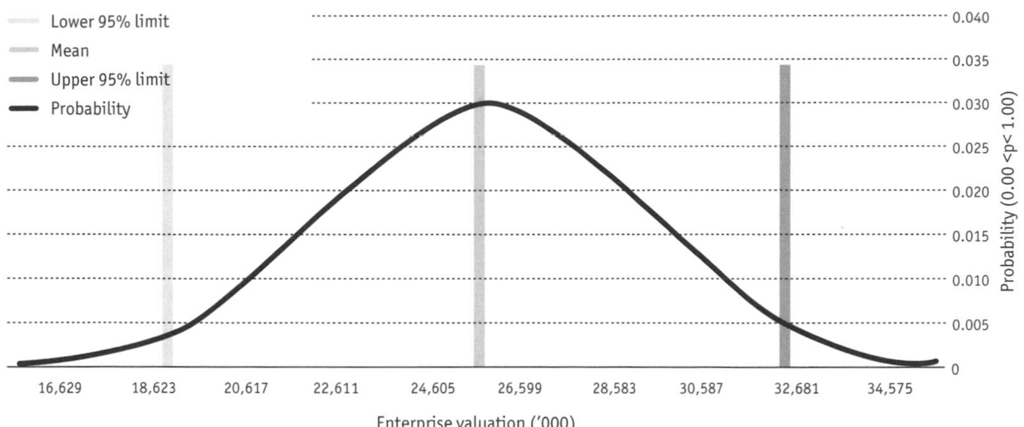

A detailed explanation of the process is beyond the scope of this book. However, *The Economist Guide to Business Modelling* explains how to perform similar forms of analysis in Excel.

Simulation techniques can often be the only option in the case of some business modelling problems, and despite their limitations, they do provide an indication of the magnitude of the potential risks facing the business. Although useful, these forms of automated sensitivity testing can never substitute for a considered, analytically based review of the risks facing a business.

Worst case

To test how robust the business plan is, it should be examined in the context of a worst case. The top five most damaging potential risks to the business should be used to develop a worst case scenario, and the strategy and tactics of the business should be examined against that scenario. The business model should also be used to examine the worst case, and the financial results should be studied closely to ensure that any banking covenants or borrowing limits would not be exceeded.

STRATEGIES FOR MANAGING RISK

The tactics and strategies for managing and mitigating the identified business risks will be specific to the business, its industry and its position within that industry. The strategies for mitigating potential risks, however, must be based on influencing one of the dimensions of risk. In the case of Newco Corp, for example, the business could choose to rent all plant and machinery rather than investing in its own equipment. This would reduce the amount of resources initially invested in the business. Another strategy is to form a partnership or joint venture with a supplier or distributor to share some of the financial and operational risks of the project. Of course, entering into such arrangements can be risky, and this must also be considered. The length of time the business will be exposed to risk should also be managed.

For some projects, it may be possible to lease office space, and rather than employing a large number of full-time staff, contract staff could be used while demand in the market is tested. The operational costs of this risk-mitigating strategy may be higher, but this may be acceptable if it reduces the period during which the business is exposed to high levels of risk; it may also reduce the costs of exiting. Short-term contracts with suppliers can be negotiated initially as a further extension of the same strategy.

Some types of operational risk, such as fire, theft and floods, can be insured against. Insurance can also be used to counter the risk of legal claims that the business may have to make, or to defend itself against claims made by third parties. Many businesses, such as banks, for which maintaining day-to-day operational effectiveness is paramount, have disaster recovery plans in the event of catastrophic business failure. Lastly, attempting to negotiate foreign contracts in a stable international currency such as the euro or the dollar can reduce some elements of financial risk. When contracts must be signed in a local currency, a business can rely on some financial risk management techniques, such as hedging, to minimise the risks of adverse movements in foreign exchange.

CONTINUING RISK ASSESSMENT

The environment in which the business operates continually changes. Regular risk assessment reviews should be undertaken to identify any new areas of risk that have developed in the market.

21 Presenting the business plan and obtaining approval

OBJECTIVES

Before drawing up a business plan you should have identified the potential audience. Chapter 2 covers what should be contained in a business's plan and explains the structure of the business plan document. This goes a long way towards ensuring success. However, it is important to present the business plan in a way that avoids and overcomes objections and instils confidence in decision-makers. The objective is to get the support of all stakeholders, who may include colleagues and senior managers, and investors and lenders.

PREPARATORY WORK

Throughout the preparation of the business plan, relevant team members and decision-makers should be involved and, if possible, asked for inputs. This extends a sense of ownership of the business plan to the people who will take part in the decision to approve the plan. The early sharing of key assumptions and outputs invites comments and objections that can be dealt with before the final plan is presented. Bear in mind that in an organisation there are many vested interests and personal agendas. Some people may feel threatened by a business plan because funding may be taken away from their projects. A co-operative approach is more likely to overcome objections and allows good use to be made of the experience and knowledge of a range of people.

Imparting a sense of ownership among colleagues will also help successfully to implement the plan. People will be more motivated and ready to "go the extra mile" to ensure that the plan is turned into a success if they feel that they have been part of it from its inception.

In cases where the main objective is to get funding from banks or venture capital funds, it will not be possible to involve them in the preparation of the business plan. However, it helps to establish a relationship with those from whom financing will be sought and to give them a rough outline of what the aim of the plan is and (realistically) when it will be ready.

Early contact with investors will provide useful feedback; for example, an aversion to investing in particular industries or that the amount of finance being sought is too small or too large. It also allows investors to make room in their diaries to meet you once the business plan is complete. At an early meeting it is also possible to gauge investors' expectations in terms of format and level of detail, so that when the actual business plan is presented it does not appear "out of the blue" and you have ensured that these expectations are met. Investors will then feel more receptive and are likely to look at the plan more seriously.

EXECUTIVE SUMMARY AND PRESENTATION SLIDES

It is important to communicate your message effectively. Different decision-makers require different levels of detail. A succinct two-page executive summary may be all a board of directors will look at. Depending on the audience, this would normally include the following:

- A short introduction, normally taken from the vision and mission.
- The objectives of the business.
- Why you intend to do it, that is, the rationale for the rest of the business.
- The current state of the business.
- Strategy and sources of competitive advantage.
- What you intend to do, that is, aspects of the marketing mix.
- Target market segments.
- Demand and market share forecast.
- How you intend to do it, that is, outline of operations, required resources.
- Summary balance sheet and profit and loss account (income statement) figures.
- Key ratios.
- Required funding.
- The valuation.
- Implementation time line.

Some people prefer to look at PowerPoint slides rather than reading through documents. This means the executive summary should also be available in the form of a PowerPoint presentation. In any event, you will have to prepare slides for a face-to-face presentation.

Chart 21.1 **The investment opportunity story board**

The investment opportunity is located in country with a population of x and per head GDP of y. The market is worth $x with x major competitors serving the market. The investment fits with our overall corporate strategy.

We would compete on the basis of [unique selling point or positioning] and obtain a market share of x% generating $x of revenue by year x. Our cost of sales will be $x, leaving a gross margin of $x or x% of revenue.

The main opex items are a, b, c with total opex amounting to $x, giving an EBITDA of $x or x% of revenue in year x. Capex consists mainly of a, b, c and amounts to $x for the first three years and x% of revenue in the longer term.

The business will require a funding of $x before turning cash flow positive in quarter x of year y. Payback is achieved in year x. The NPV of the opportunity is $x and the IRR is x%, assuming an exit after five years based on 8 x EBITDA.

The main risks associated with the investment are a, b, c. These risks can be mitigated by x, y, z.

The presentation slides of the main body of the presentation should follow the narrative of an investment opportunity story board (see Chart 21.1) in around 20–30 slides. The story board provides a one-page summary of the investment opportunity. There should also be detailed appendices. Sections and relevant appendices must be clearly labelled to make navigation within the presentation easy. This means if someone in the audience is particularly interested in an issue, you can immediately go into the relevant appendix and then resume the presentation at the higher level. Appendices should be available for any major point. Frequently, the audience is interested in the results from any market survey and more detailed financial projections.

You should tailor your presentation to address the concerns of different members of the audience:

- Lenders need to know that interest will be paid and that eventually their loan will be repaid. Thus they will be more interested in cash flow than profits. They will also focus on the risk of not being fully funded because this represents the greatest insolvency risk.
- Bondholders have an interest in ratings. Ratings are also driven by solvency and interest cover ratios.
- Shareholders are interested in return on investment and increases in shareholder value.
- Staff and trade unions need information on job creation, training, health and safety, and job security. This is particularly important where board approval is sought and the board includes representatives of the workforce.

The presentation should have the right mixture of words and charts. It is recommended that any time series, such as the quarterly sales forecast or cumulative cash flow, are shown as charts. The chart type should include the values, so that viewers can read key figures off the chart without having to trace the top of a bar to the vertical axis scale. Avoid complex charts that require a lengthy explanation. If necessary, express the point in two separate charts.

PRESENTING THE PLAN

Investors do not just look at documents; they must also have confidence in the ability of the people who will run the business. Assuming that these people will also present the plan, a professional, smooth presentation is an essential element of gaining approval for a business plan.

Begin the presentation by introducing everyone, mentioning relevant experience and qualifications. Decision-makers must get to know you and start to believe in you. However well researched and supported your business plan is, personal credibility and the ability to execute the plan are what investors are looking for.

Even when the presentation has been circulated in advance, do not assume that anyone has actually looked at it. Almost invariably there will be questions during the presentation. Rehearse the presentation and be sure to have key data in your head. You must be able to answer questions such as sales growth or time to break even without referring to a document. Try to find out who will be at the meeting. This may allow you to tailor the presentation to particular people and anticipate their questions.

If a question is not straightforward or requires a detailed answer, try to find out why it is being asked. Understanding the motive for a question will allow you to give the answer the person is looking for, rather than getting lost in detail. If you sense a potential stumbling block, you can gloss over it and modify your business plan to remove it. This does not mean that you misrepresent facts. Sometimes a question is not really a question but a request to modify certain aspects of the business plan. By listening to your audience and showing flexibility you increase the chances of success.

At the end of the presentation, agree what the next steps are and make dates in your diary for follow-up meetings. This makes it easier to chase decision-makers for responses. Before you leave the room ensure that you have everyone's contact details and that they have yours. Also leave sufficient copies of the business plan and the presentation with the audience and offer to e-mail copies of both.

GAINING APPROVAL

It is unlikely that the business plan will be approved after the first presentation. Despite having taken the utmost care in covering all angles, there will be questions based on the written business plan. Bear in mind that decision-makers are duty bound to exercise due diligence. The easier you can make their task, the more support you will gain. Do not just answer questions with an avalanche of detail, but provide what is asked for and what is relevant.

Depending on the size and complexity of the business plan and whether it is an internal or external plan, approval may take several months. During this time you must stay in touch with the decision-makers and be ready to modify your business plan. Use this time to refine the plan, gather additional information and update the plan if events materially affect it.

In cases where finance is sought from investors, the business plan acquires legal status. You must ensure that there is nothing misleading in the document and that the appropriate form of words for "forward-looking statements" is used. You must have appropriate references and certificates, especially where documentary evidence of overseas activity or agreements is required. This may take a long time to obtain and could delay approval.

Beware of any covenants or performance bonds that investors may want to impose. For example, some loan covenants require the business to produce a certain EBITDA within so many quarters. If the target is not reached this will trigger interest rate increases. Such covenants are extremely restrictive and may exacerbate a situation that is already bad. They could spark a cash flow crisis and lead to business failure unless new funds are injected.

Do not make substantial commitments before all decision-makers and investors are fully on board. Only start spending money after everyone has signed and, if several investors fund the business, all funds have been received and are in the bank. Once cash has been paid it cannot be taken back.

22 Implementing the business plan

OBJECTIVES

The business plan contains the strategy, a high-level operational plan and financial forecasts. When moving to the implementation stage, an implementation plan has to be drawn up. This consists of a more detailed operational plan, an organisation plan (including job descriptions) and operational budgets. The detailed operational plan includes an organisation chart and job descriptions as well as procedures and manuals. Detailed operational budgets are required to control execution against plan. This involves the setting of budgetary objectives and monitoring progress towards achieving the strategic objectives.

Chart 22.1 **From business plan to implementation plan**

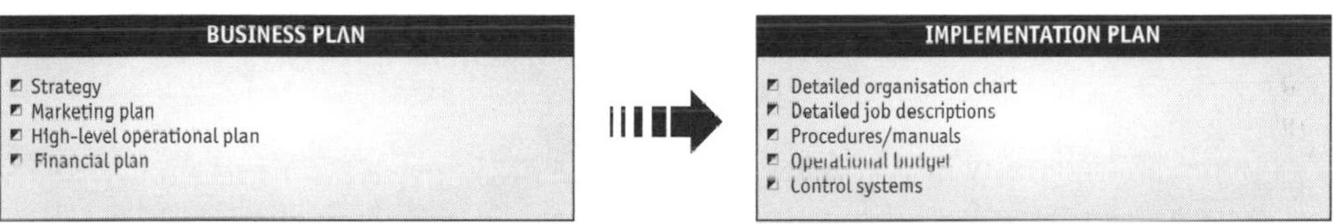

THE IMPLEMENTATION PLAN

The business plan contains a high-level operational plan, which includes an organisation chart and a headcount. This is required to allocate resources and calculate employment and related costs, which often account for a large proportion of operational expenditure.

The detailed organisation chart in the implementation plan should include job descriptions and identify budget holders. The reporting lines are defined and the people responsible for delivering against budgetary targets and strategic objectives are identified. Job descriptions tell people what they are responsible for and what tasks they must execute. The procedures tell people how things are to be done.

Manuals and quality management

Procedures are communicated in the form of manuals, and these should be prepared for every department. Procedures are important not only because they guide people on how to do things, but also because of their role in ensuring consistent quality. Indeed, ISO 9000 Quality Management Certification (see box on next page) is largely about having written procedures and following them, including the documentation of execution. This means that if a quality problem occurs, it can be tracked to the cause and rectified.

Writing procedures and producing manuals are therefore not just bureaucratic exercises, but actually get a business a long way towards ISO 9000 certification. Depending on the industry and customers, ISO 9000 certification may be a requirement to win business. It is advisable to involve an accredited certification firm early on. This helps to ensure that the

ISO 9000 Quality Management Systems Standard

This International Standard describes fundamentals of quality management systems, which form the subject of the ISO 9000 family, and defines related terms.

This International Standard is applicable to the following:

- organisations seeking advantage through the implementation of a quality management system;
- organisations seeking confidence from their suppliers that their product requirements will be satisfied;
- users of the products;
- those concerned with a mutual understanding of the terminology used in quality management (eg, suppliers, customers, regulators);
- those internal or external to the organisation who assess the quality management system or audit it for conformity with the requirements of ISO 9001 (eg, auditors, regulators, certification/registration bodies);
- those internal or external to the organisation who give advice or training on the quality management system appropriate to that organisation;
- developers of related standards.

Source: International Organisation for Standardisation, www.iso.ch

manuals are written with the right level of detail and in a suitable format.

Operational budgets

The financial plan in the business plan will probably be in quarters or even years and at a suitably high level. When moving to implementation, it becomes necessary to establish an operational budget, for example in the form of a spreadsheet model. This budget model is a more detailed business planning model. The term budget is to be understood in terms of both expenditure budgets, which include operational and capital expenditure, and revenue budgets. If the budget is met, profit margins will be delivered. The budget model serves several purposes:

- It provides managers with specific objectives.
- It is a tool to exercise financial control, notably planning of cash flow.
- It is used to measure progress against plan.

The budget model should be set up to reflect departmental budgetary responsibility. Ideally, there is a clear link between the organisation chart and the budget model. For example, if the budget model is created in Excel, there could be one worksheet for each budget holder. This approach means departmental managers have specific financial objectives. It also pins the responsibility for delivery against targets on budget holders.

Cash management is an important aspect of any business. The timing of payments and receipts has to be narrowed down to a monthly level. This enables you to ensure that adequate working capital is available. Therefore the budget should be on a monthly basis.

The budget model should be capable of tracking actuals against budget. For a continuing business, there would be at least one year's worth of historic data, so that month-by-month prior year comparisons can be made. This implies that the budget model must cover a forecast period of two years. This also ensures that there will always be a full

12-month future planning period, regardless of the month of the financial year. Monthly figures should be aggregated into a rolling annual total and year-to-date figure. The rolling annual total allows managers to make a constant comparison with past performance. The year-to-date figure shows how close the business is to achieving the annual target and fulfilling strategic objectives.

COMMUNICATING THE PLAN AND MOTIVATING STAFF

The strategy and business plan have to be communicated to managers and staff in a way that makes them take ownership of the plan. Senior managers will present the strategy to departmental managers, who will cascade it down through the organisation, providing the detailed operational directions to ensure its successful implementation.

Managers require detailed information to carry out their tasks and direct staff. They will not just be involved in the budgeting exercise but also in drawing up procedures. To avoid departmental myopia, managers must have a view of the overall organisation. Access to the plan and information systems is an essential part of this.

The business plan is also an important element in motivating employees. Knowing where and how they contribute to the success of an organisation motivates employees. Those who have a good understanding of the business plan will also be able to provide qualified feedback if they see an opportunity to improve procedures. Managers and staff should not just understand their area of work, but also have sight of and subscribe to the mission, vision and objectives of the business. This enables them to communicate these purposefully to fellow staff, customers, suppliers and the wider community.

Appendix

THE COMPLETE MODEL

The input sheets for different sections of the model are shown on the following pages. The names are those used on the tabs at the bottom of the Excel worksheets.

The model can be downloaded from www.guidetobusinessplanning.com. Two versions are available. The Complete Model represents the end result of working through the examples in this book. The Blank Model is designed to help you understand and apply the accounting techniques discussed in Chapters 15–17.

Model set-up

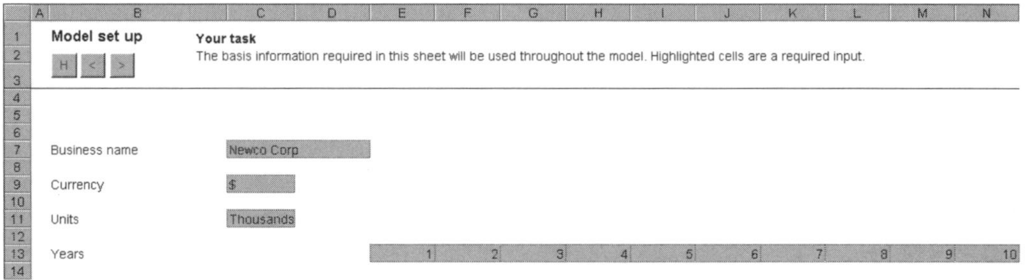

	A	B	C	D	E	F	G	H	I	J	K	L	M	N
1														
2		**Revenue**			**Your task**									
3		**Newco Corp**			Enter the assumptions as indicated below to create a revenue									
4		Units as specified			forecast.									
5														
6														
7		**Year**	H C	< >	**1**	**2**	**3**	**4**	**5**	**6**	**7**	**8**	**9**	**10**
8														
9		**Revenue line 1**												
10		Revenue description			widgets									
11		Opening customers - 000s			-									
12		Closing customers - 000s			50	150	330	890	1,900	3,330	4,880	5,960	6,350	6,480
13		Sales of widgets per customer			2.0	1.8	1.7	1.6	1.5	1.4	1.3	1.3	1.3	1.3
14		Selling price widgets $			37	36	35	34	32	30	28	25	23	22
15														
16		Average customers			25	100	240	610	1,395	2,615	4,105	5,420	6,155	6,415
17		Total revenue 1			1,850	6,480	14,280	33,134	66,960	109,830	149,422	176,150	184,035	183,469
18														
19														
20		**Revenue line 2**												
21		Revenue description												
22		Opening customers - 000s												
23		Closing customers - 000s												
24		Sales of widgets per customer												
25		Selling price $												
26														
27		Average customers			-	-	-	-	-	-	-	-	-	-
28		Total revenue 2			-	-	-	-	-	-	-	-	-	-

Home / Model set up / Operational forecasts / **Revenue** / Cost of sales / Operating costs / Accounting / Depreciation / Amortisatio

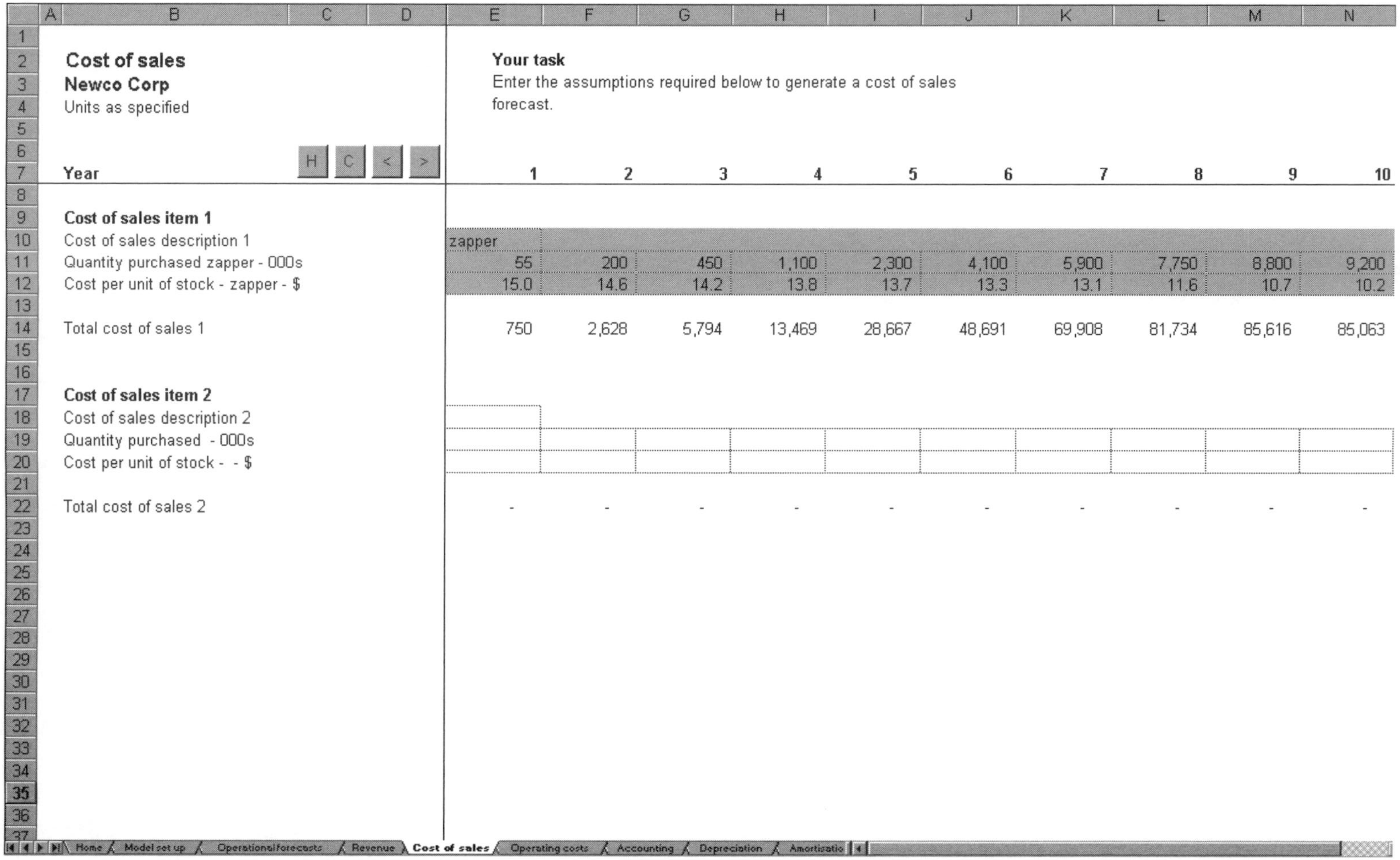

Cost of sales
Newco Corp
Units as specified

Your task
Enter the assumptions required below to generate a cost of sales forecast.

H C < >

Year	1	2	3	4	5	6	7	8	9	10
Cost of sales item 1										
Cost of sales description 1	zapper									
Quantity purchased zapper - 000s	55	200	450	1,100	2,300	4,100	5,900	7,750	8,800	9,200
Cost per unit of stock - zapper - $	15.0	14.6	14.2	13.8	13.7	13.3	13.1	11.6	10.7	10.2
Total cost of sales 1	750	2,628	5,794	13,469	28,667	48,691	69,908	81,734	85,616	85,063
Cost of sales item 2										
Cost of sales description 2										
Quantity purchased - 000s										
Cost per unit of stock - - $										
Total cost of sales 2	-	-	-	-	-	-	-	-	-	-

Home / Model set up / Operational forecasts / Revenue / Cost of sales / Operating costs / Accounting / Depreciation / Amortisatio

	A/B	C	D	E	F	G	H	I	J	K	L	M	N
1													
2	**Operating costs**			**Your task**									
3	**Newco Corp**			This section examines staff costs, other operating costs and bad debt.									
4	$ Thousands			Enter the assumptions as indicated below.									
5													
6		H C < >											
7	**Year**			1	2	3	4	5	6	7	8	9	10
8													
9	**Staff cost assumptions**												
10	Headcount			22	28	30	35	40	61	125	175	199	205
11	Opening salary			35									
12	Salary growth			3%									
13	Additional salary costs			30%	30%	30%	30%	30%	30%	30%	30%	30%	30%
14													
15	**Staff numbers**												
16	Opening staff			-									
17	Closing number of staff			22	28	30	35	40	61	125	175	199	205
18	Average number of staff			11	25	29	33	38	51	93	150	187	202
19													
20	**Salary costs**												
21	Salary levels			35	36	37	38	39	41	42	43	44	46
22	Total salary costs			385	901	1,077	1,243	1,477	2,049	3,887	6,457	8,291	9,225
23	Additional employment costs			116	270	323	373	443	615	1,166	1,937	2,487	2,767
24	Total staff costs			501	1,172	1,400	1,616	1,920	2,664	5,053	8,394	10,778	11,992
25													
26													
27	**Operating costs - 000s**												
28	Rent			2,100	2,200	2,320	2,520	3,090	3,190	3,280	3,360	3,480	3,590
29	Light and heat			210	221	235	255	310	320	330	340	350	360
30	Advertising			1,500	1,800	2,400	3,200	3,930	4,370	4,520	4,630	4,740	4,800
31	Legal and professional			600	800	1,000	1,100	1,200	1,260	1,330	1,390	1,460	1,530
32	Telephone, fax and IT			550	700	750	875	920	1,220	1,500	1,750	1,990	2,050
33	Stationery			300	310	320	335	450	600	900	1,200	1,300	1,350
34	Leasing of equipment			2,300	2,040	2,080	2,400	2,600	2,700	2,800	2,850	2,900	2,970
35	Travel and subsistence			220	280	300	350	600	800	1,250	1,750	1,990	2,050
36													
37													
38	**Bad debt**												
39	Bad debt rate zapper			3%	3%	3%	3%	3%	3%	3%	3%	3%	3%
40	Bad debt rate												
41													
42	Bad debt zapper			56	194	428	996	2,009	3,295	4,483	5,285	5,521	5,504
43	Bad debt			0	0	0	0	0	0	0	0	0	0
44	Total bad debt			56	194	428	996	2,009	3,295	4,483	5,285	5,521	5,504

Home / Model set up / Operational forecasts / Revenue / Cost of sales / **Operating costs** / Accounting / Depreciation / Amortisatio

Depreciation
Newco Corp
$ Thousands

Your task
Enter the assumptions relating to capital expenditure and depreciation.

Year		1	2	3	4	5	6	7	8	9	10
Assumptions											
Capital expenditure		55,000	20,000	5,000	5,000	20,000	8,000	8,000	8,000	8,000	8,000
Depreciation period		8									
Depreciation of opening gross capex											
Gross capex to date											
Accumulated depreciation to date											
Tangible fixed asset account											
Opening balance		0	55,000	75,000	80,000	85,000	105,000	113,000	121,000	129,000	137,000
Capital expenditure		55,000	20,000	5,000	5,000	20,000	8,000	8,000	8,000	8,000	8,000
Closing balance		**55,000**	**75,000**	**80,000**	**85,000**	**105,000**	**113,000**	**121,000**	**129,000**	**137,000**	**145,000**
Depreciation account											
Opening balance		0	3,438	11,563	21,250	31,563	43,438	57,063	71,688	87,313	100,500
Depreciation charge		3,438	8,125	9,688	10,313	11,875	13,625	14,625	15,625	13,188	9,500
Closing balance		**3,438**	**11,563**	**21,250**	**31,563**	**43,438**	**57,063**	**71,688**	**87,313**	**100,500**	**110,000**
Tangible net book value		**51,563**	**63,438**	**58,750**	**53,438**	**61,563**	**55,938**	**49,313**	**41,688**	**36,500**	**35,000**
Depreciation workings											
Opening fixed assets	0	0	0	0	0	0	0	0	0	0	0
1	55,000	3,438	6,875	6,875	6,875	6,875	6,875	6,875	6,875	3,438	
2	20,000		1,250	2,500	2,500	2,500	2,500	2,500	2,500	2,500	1,250
3	5,000			313	625	625	625	625	625	625	625
4	5,000				313	625	625	625	625	625	625
5	20,000					1,250	2,500	2,500	2,500	2,500	2,500
6	8,000						500	1,000	1,000	1,000	1,000
7	8,000							500	1,000	1,000	1,000
8	8,000								500	1,000	1,000
9	8,000									500	1,000
10	8,000										500
		3,438	8,125	9,688	10,313	11,875	13,625	14,625	15,625	13,188	9,500

Home | Model set up | Operational forecasts | Revenue | Cost of sales | Operating costs | Accounting | **Depreciation** | Amortisatio

Amortisation
Newco Corp
$ Thousands

Your task
Enter the assumptions relating to expenditure on intangible assets and their amortisation.

Year		1	2	3	4	5	6	7	8	9	10
Assumptions											
Intangible expenditure		10,000			10,000				10,000		
Amortisation period		4									
Amortisation of opening intangible spend											
Gross intangible expenditure to date											
Accumulated amortisation											
Intangible fixed asset account											
Opening balance		0	10,000	10,000	10,000	20,000	20,000	20,000	20,000	30,000	30,000
Capital expenditure		10,000	0	0	10,000	0	0	0	10,000	0	0
Closing balance		**10,000**	**10,000**	**10,000**	**20,000**	**20,000**	**20,000**	**20,000**	**30,000**	**30,000**	**30,000**
Amortisation account											
Opening balance		0	1,250	3,750	6,250	10,000	13,750	16,250	18,750	21,250	23,750
Amortisation charge		1,250	2,500	2,500	3,750	3,750	2,500	2,500	2,500	2,500	2,500
Closing balance		**1,250**	**3,750**	**6,250**	**10,000**	**13,750**	**16,250**	**18,750**	**21,250**	**23,750**	**26,250**
Intangible net book value		**8,750**	**6,250**	**3,750**	**10,000**	**6,250**	**3,750**	**1,250**	**8,750**	**6,250**	**3,750**
Amortisation workings											
Opening intangible assets	0	0	0	0	0	0	0	0	0	0	0
1	10,000	1,250	2,500	2,500	2,500	1,250					
2	0		0	0	0	0	0				
3	0			0	0	0	0	0			
4	10,000				1,250	2,500	2,500	2,500	1,250		
5	0					0	0	0	0	0	
6	0						0	0	0	0	0
7	0							0	0	0	0
8	10,000								1,250	2,500	2,500
9	0									0	0
10	0										0
		1,250	2,500	2,500	3,750	3,750	2,500	2,500	2,500	2,500	2,500

Model set up / Operational forecasts / Revenue / Cost of sales / Operating costs / Accounting / Depreciation / **Amortisation** / W

Working capital
Newco Corp
$ Thousands

Your task
Enter assumptions relating to debtor and creditor days.

Year	1	2	3	4	5	6	7	8	9	10
Debtors account widgets										
Debtor days widgets	30	30	30	30	30	30	30	30	30	30
Opening balance	0	152	533	1,174	2,727	5,504	9,027	12,281	14,478	15,126
Sales in the period	1,850	6,480	14,280	33,184	66,960	109,830	149,422	176,150	184,035	183,469
Cash received	(1,698)	(6,099)	(13,639)	(31,630)	(64,184)	(106,306)	(146,168)	(173,953)	(183,386)	(183,515)
Closing balance	152	533	1,174	2,727	5,504	9,027	12,281	14,478	15,126	15,080
Stock account zapper										
Opening stock	0	75	367	963	2,675	5,517	11,356	18,738	26,904	35,448
Stock purchased	825	2,920	6,390	15,180	31,510	54,530	77,290	89,900	94,160	93,840
Cost of goods sold	(750)	(2,628)	(5,794)	(13,469)	(28,667)	(48,691)	(69,908)	(81,734)	(85,616)	(85,063)
Closing stock	75	367	963	2,675	5,517	11,356	18,738	26,904	35,448	44,225
Creditors account zapper										
Creditor days zapper	30	30	30	30	30	30	30	30	30	30
Opening balance	0	68	240	525	1,248	2,590	4,482	6,353	7,389	7,739
Costs in the period	825	2,920	6,390	15,180	31,510	54,530	77,290	89,900	94,160	93,840
Cash paid	(757)	(2,748)	(6,105)	(14,458)	(30,168)	(52,638)	(75,419)	(88,864)	(93,810)	(93,866)
Closing balance	68	240	525	1,248	2,590	4,482	6,353	7,389	7,739	7,713
Capital expenditure creditors account										
Capex creditor days	20	20	20	20	20	20	20	20	20	20
Opening balance	0	3,014	1,096	274	274	1,096	438	438	438	438
Costs in the period	55,000	20,000	5,000	5,000	20,000	8,000	8,000	8,000	8,000	8,000
Cash paid	(51,986)	(21,918)	(5,822)	(5,000)	(19,178)	(8,658)	(8,000)	(8,000)	(8,000)	(8,000)
Closing balance	3,014	1,096	274	274	1,096	438	438	438	438	438
Intangible expenditure creditors account										
Intangible creditor days	180	180	180	180	180	180	180	180	180	180
Opening balance	0	4,932	0	0	4,932	0	0	0	4,932	0
Costs in the period	10,000	0	0	10,000	0	0	0	10,000	0	0
Cash paid	(5,068)	(4,932)	0	(5,068)	(4,932)	0	0	(5,068)	(4,932)	0
Closing balance	4,932	0	0	4,932	0	0	0	4,932	0	0

Operationalforecasts / Revenue / Cost of sales / Operating costs / Accounting / Depreciation / Amortisation / **Working capital**

Financing
Newco Corp
$ Thousands

Your task
Enter assumptions relating to the financing of the business.

Year	1	2	3	4	5	6	7	8	9	10
Financing sssumptions										
Equity issued	38,490	18,450	8,650	2,260	4,060					
Debt raised	19,245	9,220	4,315	1,130	2,027					
Debt repaid						8,984	8,984	8,984		
Interest rate on debt	5%	5%	5%	5%	5%	5%	5%	5%	5%	5%
Interest rate on overdraft	6%	6%	6%	6%	6%	6%	6%	6%	6%	6%
Interest on cash deposits	4%	4%	4%	4%	4%	4%	4%	4%	4%	4%
Dividend proportion	75%	75%	75%	75%	75%	75%	75%	75%	75%	75%
Equity account										
Opening balance	0	38,490	56,940	65,590	67,850	71,910	71,910	71,910	71,910	71,910
Equity issued	38,490	18,450	8,650	2,260	4,060	0	0	0	0	0
Closing balance	38,490	56,940	65,590	67,850	71,910	71,910	71,910	71,910	71,910	71,910
Debt account										
Opening balance	0	19,245	28,465	32,780	33,910	35,937	26,953	17,969	8,985	8,985
Debt raised	19,245	9,220	4,315	1,130	2,027	0	0	0	0	0
Debt repaid	0	0	0	0	0	(8,984)	(8,984)	(8,984)	0	0
Closing balance	19,245	28,465	32,780	33,910	35,937	26,953	17,969	8,985	8,985	8,985
Interest on debt account										
Interest charge	481	1,193	1,531	1,637	1,746	1,572	1,123	674	449	449
Interest on cverdraft										
Interest charge	213	648	837	979	1,275	1,006	307	0	0	0
Interest income on short term deposits										
Interest income	0	0	0	0	0	0	313	781	1,006	1,171
Shares in issue										
Opening shares in issue	-	38,490	56,940	65,590	67,850	71,910	71,910	71,910	71,910	71,910
Shares issued during the year	38,490	18,450	8,650	2,260	4,060	-	-	-	-	-
Shares repurchased during the year										
Closing shares in issue	38,490	56,940	65,590	67,850	71,910	71,910	71,910	71,910	71,910	71,910
Average shares in the year	19,245	47,715	61,265	66,720	69,880	71,910	71,910	71,910	71,910	71,910

Working capital / Financing / Taxation / Financial results / Profit and loss / Balance sheet / Cashflow / Ratios / Valuation

Taxation
Newco Corp
$ Thousands

Your task
Enter the tax rate, tax creditor days and any adjustments to profits liable to corporation tax in the "Profit Adjustments" row.

Year	1	2	3	4	5	6	7	8	9	10
Taxation assumptions										
Tax rate	30%	30%	30%	30%	30%	30%	30%	30%	30%	30%
Tax creditor days	365	365	365	365	365	365	365	365	365	365
Profit adjustments										
Profit and loss taxation workings										
Profits/(loss) before tax	(12,318)	(18,331)	(17,303)	(10,640)	2,618	22,017	35,826	45,451	48,778	50,932
Profits before losses	0	0	0	0	2,618	22,017	35,826	45,451	48,778	50,932
Losses carried forward	0	0	0	0	(2,618)	(22,017)	(33,957)	0	0	0
Other adjustments	0	0	0	0	0	0	0	0	0	0
Profits liable to corporation tax	0	0	0	0	0	0	1,869	45,451	48,778	50,932
Corporation tax	0	0	0	0	0	0	561	13,635	14,633	15,279
Corporation tax account										
Opening balance	0	0	0	0	0	0	0	561	13,635	14,633
Tax charge in the period	0	0	0	0	0	0	561	13,635	14,633	15,279
Tax paid	0	0	0	0	0	0	0	(561)	(13,635)	(14,633)
Closing balance	0	0	0	0	0	0	561	13,635	14,633	15,279
Losses account										
Opening losses	-	12,318	30,649	47,952	58,592	55,974	33,957	0	0	0
Increase in losses in the period	12,318	18,331	17,303	10,640	0	0	0	0	0	0
Losses utilised	0	0	0	0	(2,618)	(22,017)	(33,957)	0	0	0
Closing losses	12,318	30,649	47,952	58,592	55,974	33,957	0	0	0	0
Valuation taxation workings										
Profit before interest and tax	(11,624)	(16,490)	(14,934)	(7,994)	5,639	24,595	36,944	45,343	48,222	50,210
Profits before losses	0	0	0	0	5,639	24,595	36,944	45,343	48,222	50,210
Losses carried forward	0	0	0	0	(5,639)	(24,595)	(20,808)	0	0	0
Other adjustments	0	0	0	0	0	0	0	0	0	0
Profits liable to corporation tax	0	0	0	0	0	0	16,136	45,343	48,222	50,210
Corporation tax	0	0	0	0	0	0	4,841	13,603	14,466	15,063
Corporation tax account										
Opening balance	0	0	0	0	0	0	0	4,841	13,603	14,466
Tax charge in the period	0	0	0	0	0	0	4,841	13,603	14,466	15,063
Tax paid	0	0	0	0	0	0	0	(4,841)	(13,603)	(14,466)
Closing balance	0	0	0	0	0	0	4,841	13,603	14,466	15,063
Losses account										
Opening losses	-	11,624	28,114	43,048	51,042	45,403	20,808	0	0	0
Increase in losses in the period	11,624	16,490	14,934	7,994	0	0	0	0	0	0
Losses utilised	0	0	0	0	(5,639)	(24,595)	(20,808)	0	0	0
Closing losses	11,624	28,114	43,048	51,042	45,403	20,808	0	0	0	0

Working capital / Financing / **Taxation** / Financial results / Profit and loss / Balance sheet / Cash flow / Ratios / Valuation

	Profit and loss										
	Newco Corp	**Information only**									
	$ Thousands	No inputs are required in this section.									
	Year	1	2	3	4	5	6	7	8	9	10
	widgets	1,850	6,480	14,280	33,184	66,960	109,830	149,422	176,150	184,035	183,469
	Total revenue	**1,850**	**6,480**	**14,280**	**33,184**	**66,960**	**109,830**	**149,422**	**176,150**	**184,035**	**183,469**
	zapper	(750)	(2,628)	(5,794)	(13,469)	(28,667)	(48,691)	(69,908)	(81,734)	(85,616)	(85,063)
	Total cost of sales	**(750)**	**(2,628)**	**(5,794)**	**(13,469)**	**(28,667)**	**(48,691)**	**(69,908)**	**(81,734)**	**(85,616)**	**(85,063)**
	Gross profit	**1,100**	**3,852**	**8,486**	**19,715**	**38,293**	**61,139**	**79,514**	**94,416**	**98,418**	**98,406**
	Bad debt	(56)	(194)	(428)	(996)	(2,009)	(3,295)	(4,483)	(5,285)	(5,521)	(5,504)
	Staff dosts	(501)	(1,172)	(1,400)	(1,616)	(1,920)	(2,664)	(5,053)	(8,394)	(10,778)	(11,992)
	Rent	(2,100)	(2,200)	(2,320)	(2,520)	(3,090)	(3,190)	(3,280)	(3,360)	(3,480)	(3,590)
	Light and heat	(210)	(221)	(235)	(255)	(310)	(320)	(330)	(340)	(350)	(360)
	Advertising	(1,500)	(1,800)	(2,400)	(3,200)	(3,930)	(4,370)	(4,520)	(4,630)	(4,740)	(4,800)
	Legal and professional	(600)	(800)	(1,000)	(1,100)	(1,200)	(1,260)	(1,330)	(1,390)	(1,460)	(1,530)
	Telephone, fax and IT	(550)	(700)	(750)	(875)	(920)	(1,220)	(1,500)	(1,750)	(1,990)	(2,050)
	Stationery	(300)	(310)	(320)	(335)	(450)	(600)	(900)	(1,200)	(1,300)	(1,350)
	Leasing of equipment	(2,000)	(2,040)	(2,080)	(2,400)	(2,600)	(2,700)	(2,800)	(2,850)	(2,900)	(2,970)
	Travel and subsistence	(220)	(280)	(300)	(350)	(600)	(800)	(1,250)	(1,750)	(1,990)	(2,050)
	Total operating costs	**(8,036)**	**(9,717)**	**(11,233)**	**(13,646)**	**(17,029)**	**(20,419)**	**(25,445)**	**(30,948)**	**(34,509)**	**(36,196)**
	Operating profit	**(6,936)**	**(5,865)**	**(2,747)**	**6,069**	**21,264**	**40,720**	**54,069**	**63,468**	**63,909**	**62,210**
	Depreciation	(3,438)	(8,125)	(9,688)	(10,313)	(11,875)	(13,625)	(14,625)	(15,625)	(13,188)	(9,500)
	Amortisation	(1,250)	(2,500)	(2,500)	(3,750)	(3,750)	(2,500)	(2,500)	(2,500)	(2,500)	(2,500)
	Profits before interest and tax	**(11,624)**	**(16,430)**	**(14,934)**	**(7,994)**	**5,639**	**24,595**	**36,944**	**45,343**	**48,222**	**50,210**
	Interest paid on debt	(481)	(1,193)	(1,531)	(1,667)	(1,746)	(1,572)	(1,123)	(674)	(449)	(449)
	Interest paid on overdrafts	(213)	(648)	(837)	(979)	(1,275)	(1,006)	(307)	0	0	0
	Interest received on cash deposits	0	0	0	0	0	0	313	781	1,006	1,171
	Profit before tax	**(12,318)**	**(18,331)**	**(17,303)**	**(10,640)**	**2,618**	**22,017**	**35,826**	**45,451**	**48,778**	**50,932**
	Taxation	0	0	0	0	0	0	(561)	(13,635)	(14,633)	(15,279)
	Profit after tax	**(12,318)**	**(18,331)**	**(17,303)**	**(10,640)**	**2,618**	**22,017**	**35,265**	**31,815**	**34,145**	**35,652**
	Dividends declared	0	0	0	0	0	0	(1,308)	(23,862)	(25,609)	(26,739)
	Retained profit for the year	**(12,318)**	**(18,331)**	**(17,303)**	**(10,640)**	**2,618**	**22,017**	**33,957**	**7,954**	**8,536**	**8,913**

Working capital / Financing / Taxation / Financial results / **Profit and loss** / Balance sheet / Cashflow / Ratios / Valuation

Balance sheet
Newco Corp
$ Thousands

Information only
No inputs are required in this section.

Year		1	2	3	4	5	6	7	8	9	10
Tangible fixed assets	0	51,563	63,438	58,750	53,438	61,563	55,938	49,313	41,688	36,500	35,000
Intangible fixed assets	0	8,750	6,250	3,750	10,000	6,250	3,750	1,250	8,750	6,250	3,750
Total fixed assets	0	60,313	69,688	62,500	63,438	67,813	59,688	50,563	50,438	42,750	38,750
Debtors widgets	0	152	533	1,174	2,727	5,504	9,027	12,281	14,478	15,126	15,080
Debtors	0	0	0	0	0	0	0	0	0	0	0
Stock zapper	0	75	367	963	2,675	5,517	11,356	18,738	26,904	35,448	44,225
Stock	0	0	0	0	0	0	0	0	0	0	0
Cash at bank	0	0	0	0	0	0	0	15,649	23,423	26,872	31,674
Total current assets	0	227	900	2,137	5,402	11,021	20,383	46,668	64,805	77,446	90,979
Creditors zapper	0	(68)	(240)	(525)	(1,248)	(2,590)	(4,482)	(6,353)	(7,389)	(7,739)	(7,713)
Creditors	0	0	0	0	0	0	0	0	0	0	0
Capital expenditure creditor	0	(3,014)	(1,096)	(274)	(274)	(1,096)	(438)	(438)	(438)	(438)	(438)
Intangible expenditure creditor	0	(4,932)	0	0	(4,932)	0	0	0	(4,932)	0	0
Taxation creditor	0	0	0	0	0	0	0	(561)	(13,635)	(14,633)	(15,279)
Overdraft	0	(7,109)	(14,495)	(13,420)	(19,218)	(23,275)	(10,244)	0	0	0	0
Total current liabilities	0	(15,122)	(15,831)	(14,219)	(25,671)	(26,961)	(15,165)	(7,352)	(26,394)	(22,811)	(23,431)
Net current assets	0	(14,895)	(14,931)	(12,082)	(20,269)	(15,940)	5,219	39,317	38,411	54,635	67,548
Total assets less current liabilities	**0**	**45,417**	**54,756**	**50,418**	**43,168**	**51,873**	**64,906**	**89,879**	**88,849**	**97,385**	**106,298**
Equity	0	38,490	56,940	65,590	67,850	71,910	71,910	71,910	71,910	71,910	71,910
Retained profits	0	(12,318)	(30,649)	(47,952)	(58,592)	(55,974)	(33,957)	0	7,954	16,490	25,403
Debt	0	19,245	28,465	32,780	33,910	35,937	26,953	17,969	8,985	8,985	8,985
Total capital employed	**0**	**45,417**	**54,756**	**50,418**	**43,168**	**51,873**	**64,906**	**89,879**	**88,849**	**97,385**	**106,298**
Check	0	0	0	0	0	0	0	0	0	0	0

Working capital / Financing / Taxation / Financial results / Profit and loss / **Balance sheet** / Cashflow / Ratios / Valuation

Cash flow statement
Newco Corp
$ Thousands

Information only
No inputs are required in this section.

Year	1	2	3	4	5	6	7	8	9	10
Operating profit / (loss)	(6,936)	(5,665)	(2,747)	6,069	21,264	40,720	54,069	63,468	63,909	62,210
Debtors widgets	(152)	(381)	(641)	(1,554)	(2,776)	(3,524)	(3,254)	(2,197)	(648)	46
Debtors	0	0	0	0	0	0	0	0	0	0
Stock zapper	(75)	(292)	(596)	(1,711)	(2,843)	(5,839)	(7,382)	(8,166)	(8,544)	(8,777)
Stock	0	0	0	0	0	0	0	0	0	0
Creditors zapper	68	172	285	722	1,342	1,892	1,871	1,036	350	(26)
Creditors	0	0	0	0	0	0	0	0	0	0
Movement in working capital	(159)	(500)	(952)	(2,542)	(4,277)	(7,470)	(8,765)	(9,327)	(8,842)	(8,757)
Cash flow from operating activities	(7,095)	(6,365)	(3,699)	3,526	16,987	33,250	45,303	54,141	55,067	53,453
Tangible capital expenditure	(51,966)	(21,918)	(5,822)	(5,000)	(18,178)	(8,658)	(8,000)	(8,000)	(8,000)	(8,000)
Intangible capital expenditure	(5,068)	(4,932)	0	(5,068)	(4,932)	0	0	(5,068)	(4,932)	0
Tax paid	0	0	0	0	0	0	0	(561)	(13,635)	(14,633)
Cash flow before financial cashflows	(64,150)	(33,215)	(9,521)	(6,542)	(7,123)	24,592	37,303	40,512	28,501	30,819
Interest paid on debt	(481)	(1,133)	(1,531)	(1,667)	(1,746)	(1,572)	(1,123)	(674)	(449)	(449)
Interest paid on overdrafts	(213)	(648)	(837)	(979)	(1,275)	(1,006)	(307)	0	0	0
Interest received on cash deposits	0	0	0	0	0	0	313	781	1,006	1,171
Cash flow before financing	(64,844)	(35,056)	(11,890)	(9,189)	(10,144)	22,015	36,186	40,620	29,057	31,541
Equity issued	33,490	18,450	8,650	2,260	4,060	0	0	0	0	0
Debt issued	13,245	9,220	4,315	1,130	2,027	0	0	0	0	0
Debt repaid	0	0	0	0	0	(8,984)	(8,984)	(8,984)	0	0
Cash flow for the period before dividends	(7,109)	(7,386)	1,075	(5,799)	(4,057)	13,031	27,202	31,636	29,057	31,541
Dividends paid	0	0	0	0	0	0	(1,308)	(23,862)	(25,609)	(26,739)
Cash flow for the period	(7,109)	(7,386)	1,075	(5,799)	(4,057)	13,031	25,893	7,774	3,449	4,802
Cash account										
Opening cash balance	0	(7,109)	(14,495)	(13,420)	(19,218)	(23,275)	(10,244)	15,649	23,423	26,872
Cash movement in the year	(7,109)	(7,386)	1,075	(5,799)	(4,057)	13,031	25,893	7,774	3,449	4,802
Closing cash balance	(7,109)	(14,495)	(13,420)	(19,218)	(23,275)	(10,244)	15,649	23,423	26,872	31,674

Working capital / Financing / Taxation / Financial results / Profit and loss / Balance sheet / Cash flow / Ratios / Valuation

Ratios
Newco Corp

Information only
No user inputs are required in this section.

Year	1	2	3	4	5	6	7	8	9	10
Profitability										
Gross profit margin	59.5%	59.4%	59.4%	59.4%	57.2%	55.7%	53.2%	53.6%	53.5%	53.6%
Operating profit margin (EBITDA margin)	-374.9%	-90.5%	-19.2%	18.3%	31.8%	37.1%	36.2%	36.0%	34.7%	33.9%
Earnings before interest & tax margin (EBIT margin)	-628.3%	-254.5%	-104.6%	-24.1%	8.4%	22.4%	24.7%	25.7%	26.2%	27.4%
Profit before tax margin (PBT margin)	-665.8%	-282.9%	-121.2%	-32.1%	3.9%	20.0%	24.0%	25.8%	26.5%	27.8%
Earnings per share (EPS)	(0.64)	(0.38)	(0.28)	(0.16)	0.04	0.31	0.49	0.44	0.47	0.50
Liquidity and the balance dheet										
Current ratio	0.02	0.06	0.15	0.21	0.41	1.34	6.35	2.46	3.40	3.88
Quick ratio	0.01	0.03	0.08	0.11	0.20	0.60	3.80	1.44	1.84	2.00
Net book value of assets	60,312.5	69,687.5	62,500.0	63,437.5	67,812.5	59,687.5	50,562.5	50,437.5	42,750.0	38,750.0
Capital expenditure to depreciation	15.1	2.7	0.6	0.5	1.6	0.6	0.5	0.5	0.6	0.8
Asset turnover	0.0	0.1	0.3	0.8	1.3	1.7	1.7	2.0	1.9	1.7
Debtor days	15.0	19.3	21.8	21.5	22.4	24.1	26.0	27.7	29.4	30.0
Creditor days	22.2	43.5	17.1	35.6	26.5	20.2	20.7	28.4	28.7	23.1
Stock turnover days	36.5	51.0	60.7	72.5	70.2	85.1	97.8	120.1	151.1	189.8
Returns										
Return on average capital employed (ROACE)	0.0%	0.0%	0.0%	0.0%	8.2%	32.7%	42.8%	41.3%	41.1%	40.2%
Return on total average assets (ROTAA)	0.0%	0.0%	0.0%	0.0%	11.9%	42.1%	41.5%	35.5%	36.3%	34.5%
Return on equity (ROE)	0.0%	0.0%	0.0%	0.0%	16.4%	58.0%	49.0%	39.8%	38.6%	36.6%
Dividend cover	0.0	0.0	0.0	0.0	0.0	0.0	27.0	1.3	1.3	1.3
Financial										
Gearing	42.4%	52.0%	65.0%	78.6%	69.3%	41.5%	20.0%	10.1%	9.2%	8.5%
Debt/equity ratio	73.5%	108.3%	185.8%	366.3%	225.5%	71.0%	25.0%	11.3%	10.2%	9.2%
Debt/EBITDA	0.0	0.0	0.0	8.8	2.8	0.9	0.0	0.0	0.0	0.0
Interest cover (EBITDA/interest)	0.0	0.0	0.0	2.3	7.0	15.8	37.8	94.2	142.3	138.5

Financing / Taxation / Financial Results / Profit and Loss / Balance Sheet / Cash Flow / **Ratios** / Valuation

Valuation
Newco Corp
$ Thousands

H C <

Your task
Normalise the final year cash flow if required. Select the basis for valuation.

Year		1	2	3	4	5	6	7	8	9	10
Valuation assumptions											
Discount rate	7.7%										
Terminal value growth rate	2.0%										
EBITDA exit multiple	3										
Prospective Newco Corp company comparable valuation metrics	2										
PE ratio											
EV / EBITDA											
EV / sales	30										
EV / customer	1,500										
Free cash flow											
Operating cash flow		(7,095)	(6,365)	(3,699)	3,526	16,987	33,250	45,303	54,141	55,067	53,453
Capital expenditure		(51,986)	(21,918)	(5,822)	(5,000)	(19,178)	(8,658)	(8,000)	(8,000)	(8,000)	(8,000)
Intangibles expenditure		(5,068)	(4,932)	0	(5,068)	(4,932)	0	0	(5,068)	(4,932)	0
Cash taxes		0	0	0	0	0	0	0	(4,841)	(13,603)	(14,466)
Free cash flow		**(64,150)**	**(33,215)**	**(9,521)**	**(6,542)**	**(7,123)**	**24,592**	**37,303**	**36,232**	**28,533**	**30,986**
Discount factor											
Discount factor		1.04	1.12	1.20	1.30	1.40	1.50	1.62	1.74	1.88	2.02
NPV of free cash flow											
NPV of free cash flow		(51,814)	(29,717)	(7,909)	(5,046)	(5,101)	16,354	23,033	20,772	15,188	15,315
Total NPV of free cash flow		**(18,927)**									

Terminal value

Method 1: Terminal value growth rate		**Method 2: EBITDA exit multiple**	
Final year cash flow	30,986	Final year EBITDA	52,210
Final year cash grown 1 year by growth rate	31,606	Final year company value	497,679
Perpetuity calculation	554,494		
NPV of final cash flow to perpetuity	274,062		
Terminal value - method 1	274,062	Terminal value - method 2	245,980

DCF based company valuation	**Terminal value growth rate**	**EBITDA exit multiple**
Forecast cash flows	(18,927)	(18,927)
Terminal value	274,062	245,980
Enterprise value	255,135	227,054
Less: net debt	(26,354)	(26,354)
Equity value	228,780	200,699

Comparable company valuations	**Enterprise value**	**Net debt**	**Equity value**
PE ratio			n/a
EV / EBITDA	n/a	(26,354)	n/a
EV / sales	134,400	(26,354)	168,046
EV / customer	225,000	(26,354)	198,646

Working capital / Financing / Taxation / Financial results / Profit and loss / Balance sheet / Cash flow / Ratios / **Valuation**

Index

Figures in *italics* indicate charts; those in **bold** indicate the Appendix.

A

G